GATEWAY TO ASIA: SINKIANG

Gateway to Asia:

SINKIANG

Frontier of the Chinese Far West

by

MARTIN R. NORINS

INTRODUCTION BY OWEN LATTIMORE

Illustrated with Maps and Photographs

Issued in co-operation with the International Secretariat, Institute of Pacific Relations, New York

THE JOHN DAY COMPANY

New York

MR2.18
S5N6

33097

IMPORTANT

Government wartime restrictions on materials have made it essential that the
amount of paper used in each book be reduced to a minimum. This volume is
printed on lighter paper than would have
been used before material limitations became necessary, and the number of words
on each page has been substantially increased. The smaller bulk in no way indicates that the text has been shortened.

To the family

CONTENTS

MAPS

A section of illustrations from photographs will be found following page 32.

INTRODUCTION

Sinkiang's Place In the Future of China

By OWEN LATTIMORE

THERE CAN BE few large regions in the world that combine, in the way that Sinkiang does, isolation and a rich literature of travel and of natural and social sciences. Though Sinkiang has never been open to the casual tourist, it has been the setting of some of the major geographical, geological, botanical, archeological and historical investigation and writing of the nineteenth and twentieth centuries. The names of those who have contributed to the literature include, from the middle ages, William of Rubruck, Carpini, and Marco Polo; the British from Atkinson to Shaw, and Forsyth, and later Ney Elias, Younghusband, Stein and Skrine; the Russians, with perhaps the greatest list of all, including Prjevalskii, the Grum-Grjimailo brothers, Kozlov, Obruchev, and a host of others; the French with Grenard and Pelliot; the Germans with Grünwedel, von le Coq and many writers on linguistics; the Austrian Merzbacher; the Dutch historian De Groot; the Italian De Filippi; Sven Hedin and many younger Swedes and Danes like Bergman and Haslund; and Americans like Schuyler and Huntington. Indeed, it is easier to write a long list than a short one, because the material relating to Sinkiang has led to so much comment, research and speculation in so many countries.

It is noticeable, however, that in the literature of Sinkiang the most important contributions of the Chinese are to be found in the chronicles of the past. Were it not for the Chinese genius for compiling history, our knowledge of the peoples and tribes and politics of Sinkiang for more than two thousand years would be much more shadowy. In the nineteenth century, however, Chinese concern with Sinkiang became more and more perfunctory, and the Chinese literature less important and poorer in quality. Even when dealing with the distribution, characteristics, and political grouping of the peoples of Sinkiang, Chinese writers began to show a weak tendency to forego direct observation and rely instead on quotation.

9

This fading out of the Chinese interest in Sinkiang reflected a major change in China's fortunes. During the nineteenth century Western imperialism began to press heavily on China from the seacoast, and consequently Chinese thought drew away from the landward frontiers. It is true that Tsarist Russia threatened to penetrate and even to annex Mongolia and Sinkiang, while the British exercised more real control in Tibet than did the Chinese; but these were the least Chinese territories of China, most of whose people differed in their way of life from the Chinese, and few of whom even spoke Chinese. Naturally, in a long period of great danger to the Chinese nation as a whole, attention was concentrated on the areas of densest Chinese population near the coast, and on political relations with those countries which had the kind of power that expressed itself in the "gunboat policy" of the nineteenth century.

In our own time we can see why the Chinese, without turning away from their long maritime coast and the future developments in trade and politics with which they will have to deal along that coast, are also turning back to their long inland frontiers and enquiring into the future opportunities and problems of the deep hinterland. The Sino-Swedish Scientific Expedition, which carried on Sven Hedin's later exploration work in Sinkiang, included several Chinese scientists who published not only scientific papers but accounts of their travels, with comments on contemporary affairs in Central Asia. In the same period a Chinese diplomat, Aitchen K. Wu, published a lively personal account of the political intrigue and civil war out of which there finally developed the recent progressive tendencies of Sheng Shih-ts'ai. An English version of his book has been published under the title of *Turkistan Tumult*.

In the same period there flourished a considerable periodical literature, including such journals as the *Northwest Monthly* and many articles in other journals, like *New Asia* and the scholarly *Yü Kung*, or *The Chinese Historical Geography*. The early years of this literature have seen the publication of much that is of only secondary value; but there is a clear tendency for the literature to increase in importance, and the time will come when Western political scientists and economists who wish to deal authoritatively with the questions of Central Asia will have to depend more and more on Chinese materials.

Mr. Norins' work marks the beginning of this trend. He has not been able to travel in Sinkiang, but by study of contemporary Chinese source materials he has been able to expand the observations of Western travelers and to produce an interesting and important book. The trend will go on. There is a clear prophecy of this in the fact that in his use of Chinese sources Mr. Norins finds evidence of lively differences of views and interpretations. China's rediscovery of Chinese Central Asia will be accompanied by controversy, and the different policies advanced in controversy will have an international as well as a domestic significance.

Within the area occupied by Sinkiang there probably lies the geographical center of gravity between the Atlantic, Arctic, Pacific and Indian Oceans. There was a time, toward the end of the last century, when Kipling was writing about the "grey menace" of Tsarist Russia, and when Russian and British explorers, apprehensively watching each other and sometimes actually putting each other under arrest, were trying to discover and list all the passes across the Pamirs, the Karakoram and the Himalayas. What they were looking for was an "artillery pass"—a way by which wheeled vehicles could link up the zones of British and Russian imperialist expansion in Inner Asia. During this period Sinkiang, like Afghanistan, was in danger of being ground between the upper Russian millstone and the lower British millstone. The serious way in which the rival seekers of the White Man's Burden sent envoys, gifts, and windy despatches to Yakub Beg, a dancing-boy turned brigand, who had overthrown the Manchu-Chinese power at Kashgar, makes grotesque and sometimes bloody reading.

This period ended in an anti-climax. It was discovered that there was no "artillery pass." It would be too expensive either for the British to encroach on territory coveted by the Russians, or for the Russians to push their Central Asian conquests actually to within snatching distance of the "brightest jewel in the British crown." It then became convenient to recall the sovereignty of Afghanistan and China. With appropriate solemnity, frontiers were delimited in such a way that a narrow corridor was created across the Pamirs, the western end of it held by the Afghans and the eastern end by the Chinese. In this way the British and Russians were insulated from each other, and enabled to fall back on bearing the White Man's Burden at the expense of more accessible "natives."

Since then, there have been two rather commonly held opinions, or rather preconceptions, about Sinkiang: that its proper function is to be a buffer between China and Russia, or that it is destined to be absorbed by Russia and amalgamated with Soviet Turkestan. Neither concept is adequate. As the center of gravity of the largest land-mass in the world, and as a territory ruled by a minority and inhabited by subject races greatly exceeding in number the ruling minority, the fate of Sinkiang will affect, and be affected by, everything that happens in India, Afghanistan and Iran, as well as China and Soviet Asia.

The geography of this complex relationship is interesting. Sinkiang is at once a place of isolation and a vast area of passage; a blank space between different kinds of world, and a world in itself of prolix variety. The changing phases of history bring different aspects into emphasis.

Some two thousand years ago the Chinese were brought into contact with Sinkiang by geographical peculiarities which made Sinkiang two kinds of frontier. The side of Sinkiang lying nearest to what is now called "China proper" was a barrier. The Chinese, as an agricultural people, spread up to this barrier. They were not only a farming people, but a people whose farming was already identified with habitual techniques and a social structure which did not easily adapt itself to changes. The Chinese gravitated toward areas which could be intensively cultivated and closely settled. Transportation of farm products over long distances was difficult and uneconomic, except where rivers and canals could be used.

Consequently trade tended to circulate in small unit-areas; a typical unit being a walled city, drawing grain from the countryside and supplying goods made by artisans to the countryside. The wealthy areas of China, in which the highest culture flourished, were those in which the radius of trade between a city and its unit area did not exceed from twenty to thirty miles—a day's journey by cart, or a day's journey by a man carrying burdens. Areas in which the radius of trade exceeded two days' journey were noticeably poorer and less "civilized." Areas with an even larger radius of trade were decidedly underpopulated, poor, and backward. Sinkiang, as a frontier, represented the line of diminishing returns at which the Chinese way of living tended to peter out, because of poor rainfall, the inability to live closely together and till small fields by intensive methods, and the impossibility of sustaining cities, except at excessive distances apart.

A permanent, linear frontier would have resulted had it not been for the fact that the very land which was marginal and only doubtfully attractive for Chinese agriculture was decidedly profitable for pastoral nomads. Just as the Chinese order of life produced close settlement in villages and cities, the nomad order of life expressed itself in widely scattered encampments. The two social structures met, but did not interlock. Throughout centuries of history, they never fused. The radical difference between the two structures encouraged trade, it is true; but it also bred war.

The most marginal outlying Chinese settlements were, by the prevailing standard of China, unprofitable both for taxation and for trade. Grain was the essential standard of both trade and taxation. The dry margins of the steppe produced little grain per acre, and the distance to grain-consuming cities was so great that the profit on a cartload was more than eaten up by the animals which drew the cart.

For the pastoral nomads, the marginal areas held quite different values. Land which was poor in terms of grain crops might well be rich in terms of grazing for sheep, cattle and horses. If, therefore, the trend of the time was toward war, the nomads would try to drive the Chinese out of the marginal area. If, on the other hand, the general balance of the factors at work made for peace rather than war, the trade of these areas tended to be oriented toward the nomads instead of toward China. Throughout Asia, the nomads of the pastoral areas have always disliked to grow grain, but liked to acquire it, either by trade or as a tribute levied from settled regions. Grain which it was unprofitable to transport "inward" to areas in China which grew plenty of grain for themselves could be transported profitably "outward" to regions which grew no grain at all. This, however, resulted in divorcing the border Chinese from the main body of the Chinese people. Either their own economic interest in trade with the nomads inclined them to seek the political protection of nomad chiefs; or the combined political and economic interests of tribal chiefs urged them to assert rights of taxation and levy over the border villages.

Out of this kind of relationship there grew an ebb and flow which prevented the formation of a permanent linear frontier. Either the nomads, enriched by the tribute of border villages, tried to press deeper into China, demanding increased tribute, or the Chinese, trying to make safe the territory which they did want, made expeditions into territory which they did not want, but were forced to try to control, in order to prevent the power of the nomads from becoming too great. The Roman Empire had similar problems, and the British Empire has also been plagued by them, especially on the Northwest Frontier of India.

Sinkiang's history was governed for a score of centuries by phenomena of this order. What is now Northern Sinkiang (Jungaria) is a steppe land, in which the herds of nomads have grazed since the formation of the Chinese frontier, and through which have passed some of the very greatest nomadic migrations. Southern Sinkiang (Chinese Turkestan) is a land of deserts, too poor for continuous grazing, and of rich, but small and widely separated agricultural oases. Control of these oases was often important in determining the balance of power between China and nomads. The intensive agriculture of the oases was akin to that of China, but the intervening deserts made it impossible for the Chinese to spread up evenly to the oases and absorb them. They could only be held as Chinese outposts; the object of the Chinese being, in some periods, to turn the flank of the nomads and in other periods to protect the flank of China by denying to nomads the tribute of the oases.

In the last century most Chinese and most Westerners lost sight of these regions and forgot the significance of their history. Firearms had destroyed the advantage which nomads, in the day of the bow and arrow, had held over agricultural peoples. China was no longer threatened by nomad invasions through the line of the Great Wall. The Manchus, the last of these invaders, held with difficulty in the nineteenth century the empire which they had seized in the seventeenth century. China's most vulnerable side was now the long seacoast, along which the Western powers had established the Treaty Ports.

In this period the old ebb and flow of the history of Sinkiang, and of all Central Asia and Mongolia, settled into relative stagnation, disturbed chiefly by the spread and growth of Tsarist Russia. Sinkiang became a kind of Chinese India, of many peoples, languages, and religions, and of mixed agricultural and pastoral economy. The most numerous people were the Turki—now officially known, by the revival of a medieval tribal name, as the Uighurs—but they had no political unity because they were scattered in widely separated oases. Nor were the nomads politically united, because some were Moslems, speaking different forms of the Turkish language, while others were Mongol-speaking Lama-Buddhists. Even the Chinese, numbering only about ten per cent of the total population, were weakened by the division between Moslems and non-Moslems.

We are now in a new period. Even if we restrict our view to Sinkiang alone, it can be seen that the stagnation has ended. If we widen our view, it is easy to see that although the coast of China is not losing its importance, the long inland frontier is certainly gaining in importance. We can also see, from the events related by Mr. Norins, that the revival of the importance of the inland frontier has been stimulated by Japan's aggression driving inward from the coast. The contemporary phase of Sinkiang's history dates from 1932, when the whole structure of China had been shocked and weakened by Japan's invasion of Manchuria in 1931.

The Japanese factor cannot be overemphasized in assessing recent developments in Sinkiang. It is undoubtedly the key factor in explaining Russian policy. In 1932 the Japanese installed a bogus government of "Manchukuo" in China's Northeastern Provinces. In 1933 they overran the province of Jehol—a hundred thousand square miles of territory—and subjected it to "Manchukuo." This opened to them a corridor leading westward through Inner Mongolia. From 1933 to the unleashing of the general Japanese attack on China in 1937, a series of efforts was made to create a puppet Mongol system in Inner Mongolia subservient to Japanese military ambitions, and to get into touch with the powerful Moslem minorities in Northwest China. If these measures had succeeded, the Japanese would have been able to cut China off entirely from Russia, in which case the Russians would never have been able to send through the important supplies which did so much to keep China going, especially in the critical years from 1939 to 1941, when American supplies to China were at a minimum and American sales to Japan were booming.

Looking back over the past ten years, it can now be seen with what boldness of action and sureness of political touch the Russians countered Japan's attempted penetration. The first step was to give military support to the faction in Sinkiang's civil wars which was both militarily the most competent and politically the most legitimate successor to the previously established provincial government. Sheng Shih-ts'ai, the head of this faction, came originally from Manchuria. Accordingly, one form of help given him was to allow Chinese troops, who had retreated into Siberia and had there been interned after fighting the Japanese in Manchuria, to be "repatriated" to Sinkiang. This gave Sheng Shih-ts'ai a nucleus of troops who would be loyal to him personally, and who would at the same time reinforce his loyalty to China, since their ambition was not to remain in Sinkiang, but to return eventually to their own homes in the Northeast.

This was not the only aid. Soviet tanks and planes were also sent into Sinkiang, and even troops, who were called "Altai Volunteers." These "volunteers" appear to have been a mixture of trained Soviet troops with Russians, domiciled in Sinkiang, who years before had fought against or fled from the Soviet Revolution. Concerning these Russians of widely different experience there is a remark, recorded by Sven Hedin in "The Flight of 'Big Horse,'" which deserves wide quotation. Hedin asked one of the "White" Russians what he thought of being in service with the Red Russians. "When we asked how it was possible for Reds and Whites to work together, a powerfully built, fair-haired fellow replied: 'Why, when we've got a common object we get on all right.' "

The ultimate significance of Soviet activity in Sinkiang has only recently been revealed. For years the Russians maintained an armored motorized unit on Sinkiang soil. Its post was at or near Hami (Qomul) near the eastern frontier, guarding the approach from Kansu. What was the purpose of this detachment? Was it to defend Sinkiang from intervention by the National Government? Or was it an advance guard of Soviet penetration?

By withdrawing the force, the Russians have in my opinion made its purpose clear. Motorized exploring expeditions like those of Roy Chapman Andrews, Sven Hedin and the Citroën Expedition had opened up new possibilities. The motorized Japanese occupation of the rugged terrain of Jehol in ten days had proved that the Japanese knew how to exploit these possibilities. A Chinese truck company, using the experience of the Hedin explorations, had worked out a fast route westward through Inner Mongolia to Sinkiang.

Militarily, the threat of this route was less to Sinkiang than to the provinces of Kansu and Ningsia. A successful dash westward might enable the Japanese to swing south into these provinces, divide them from Sinkiang, cut the Sinkiang supply route, lodge a mobile force in the rear of Chiang Kai-shek's armies, and make a strong appeal to the Moslems of the Northwest to earn preferential treatment by dissociating themselves from other Chinese and accepting Japan's hegemony. A threat of motorized action like this could only be countered by the ability to meet motorized movement with motorized movement. The Chinese did not have the equipment. The Russians did; but they could only act in time from a forward base.

This, to my mind, was the major reason for stationing a Soviet force at Hami. It is very likely that there was more than one reason which influenced the Russians to withdraw from this position in 1943; but the greatest significance of the move, in my opinion, is that it proved that the Russians considered the Japanese no longer capable of a bold forward strategy in Northwest China.

A political course of action beyond one's own frontiers does not necessarily involve military measures; but military action on foreign soil always entails political consequences. Having enabled a Chinese, non-Moslem faction, representing a population minority of ten per cent, in a predominantly Moslem province, to take over control of Sinkiang, the Russians had to follow through with some kind of policy that would work. Looking back on the situation as it was then, and on the sequence of events narrated by Mr. Norins, it is evident that there were three alternatives:

1. The Russians could follow a policy that would invite and facilitate the intervention of China's Central Government and give it control over the province. This would not have been a realistic policy at the time. It would have required weakening the provincial government, without any assurance that the Central Government would be strengthened. In the early thirties the Central Government was employing all of its best troops far away, south of the Yangtze, against the Communists. It could not have penetrated to Sinkiang without using many of these troops, and they would have had to pass through the territories of powerful Moslem war lords in Northwest China who were not yet ready to allow Chiang Kai-shek to extend real control over their affairs. (They were ready to allow this only when the Chinese Communists moved to the Northwest, and the Government troops, following and blockading them, established civil and political control.)

2. The Russians could themselves have annexed and absorbed Sinkiang. Evidently they did not want to do so. Since we do not know in detail why they did not want to, we can only guess at the reasons. One guess, or series of guesses, would take the following into account: The Russians were feverishly industrializing their own territories, because they had plenty of raw materials but not nearly enough industry. Sinkiang would have given them only greater surpluses of what they already had in surplus, while making even greater a problem of industrialization which had not yet been mastered. Politically, moreover, the Russians were more anxious to consolidate their own territory than to seize new possessions, it being their proclaimed belief that they were in danger of attack.

18

3. There remained the policy which was actually followed; help for the provincial government; furtherance of trade and economic development; aid in education and medicine. This policy had interesting consequences. Although the provincial government had been given enough military aid to end civil war, the Chinese minority was in no position to rule indefinitely by force. The Chinese in Sinkiang could be compared with the British in India only if we imagine the British in India without a Suez Canal short cut for bulk trade, unable to receive reinforcements from England, and unable to manufacture arms locally. This was the background of the reforms of Sheng Shih-ts'ai, enumerated by Mr. Norins. The continuance of Chinese rule had to be made welcome; and to be made welcome it had to be identified with peace, careers opened to the native peoples, education to enable them to aspire to those careers, and economic prosperity.

A new period has succeeded the period of successful Chinese-Russian collaboration in Sinkiang. My guess, that the Russians no longer fear a swift Japanese thrust to the heart of Asia, may or may not be right; but it seems to be borne out by the broad trend of Russian policy. The power of the National Government is now well established in Northwest China. Whatever danger there may once have been that Moslem adventurers might flirt with the Japanese is now past. Not only Moslem leaders but all the Moslem communities have shown that they are Chinese patriots, devoted to the cause of absolute victory over the Japanese invaders.

Consequently the time has come for direct and normal relations between the National Government and the provincial government of Sinkiang. With their resumption, it was proper for the Russians to step out of the picture entirely. With the energy not uncommon in their foreign policy, they have not merely stepped out: they have jumped out. This will undoubtedly mean a certain amount of dislocation in the economic life of Sinkiang, but it has the advantage of making policies, decisions, and responsibilities perfectly clear. The native peoples cannot doubt and wonder how much to attribute to the Chinese and how much to the Russians. If things go well, the credit will go to the Chinese provincial and National authorities; if there are mistakes, they will also be Chinese. The only "Machiavellian" motive that can be imputed to the Russians is this: if things go badly, the people will remember "how much better it was in the days when the Russians were so active."

Until the record of Chinese performance in Sinkiang begins to unfold, there can be little profit in discussing the details of alternative policies. It is better to restrict discussion to a broad statement of problems. The primary problem is this: the Sinkiang frontier can no longer be described as either a linear or an areal problem in the old sense. While the old problems of minorities and how to handle them remain, all major policies must henceforth be policies for China as a whole. In the concluding stages of the war and the initial stages of the peace, China will not be able to experiment with double standards of policy.

As an illustration, consider the great problem of land ownership in China. Sinkiang is not the only Chinese territory with room for more population. The question is not only one of empty land, but of the utilization of land. The "overpopulated" areas of China are those in which traditional methods of cultivation are traditionally allied with a system of landlords who take most of the profits of good years, and tenants who suffer most of the consequences of bad years. There are vast areas of China which could be usefully settled; but not under this system—only under a system of free proprietors, with diversification of agriculture by the development of mixed farming, dairying, fruit-growing, and the encouragement of scattered light industries as well as centralized heavy industries.

Unless this is taken into account, the migration of large numbers of poor peasants to Sinkiang, with no capital, would merely result in spreading landlordism, usury, and rural bankruptcy. This would be no solution for China, and in Sinkiang it would inevitably lead to friction between Chinese and non-Chinese. The problem may be summed up by saying that for the heart of China and the fringes of China the alternative equations are now the same: either progressive politics and progressive economic measures, going hand in hand, or economic stagnation and political reaction, going hand in hand.

There remain some words to be said about the place and function of Sinkiang in the winning of the war. There is an essential distinction between the use that might have been made of the Sinkiang supply route before Pearl Harbor and the use that could be made of it from now to the end of the war. Before Pearl Harbor, and from Pearl Harbor to the battle of Midway in 1942, when American naval power began to reassert itself, Japanese blockade of the coast of China was tightening, with no naval pressure against Japan to offset it. During this period the Sinkiang supply route was more important, though less publicized, than the Burma Road. It could have been made much more important, if there had been a concerted agreement between America, Britain and Russia to increase aid to China by getting more material into Siberia and organizing and improving traffic from Siberia through Sinkiang.

That period is closed, but Mr. Norins fails to appreciate, in his final chapters, the reasons for which it has closed. America has now organized and deployed an immense naval, military, and air potential in the Pacific. One way of describing this is to say that the American war effort in the Pacific is now geared to a strategy in which aid *for* China far outweighs aid *to* China. Great as America's manpower and war production are, they are not so great that we could organize a vast air, ship, rail and truck effort to get material into Siberia and through Siberia into China, in addition to our mobilization and deployment in the Pacific. Sinkiang was the shortest way through to China only for a limited period, because of the neutrality of America and Britain in the Pacific. It has now become, logistically, the longest way round.

It is true that logistic problems would again be radically changed if Russia were at war with Japan; but in that case the logical thing to do would be to support the Russian effort in the area nearest to Japan, rather than to detour men and materials around the Central Asian Robin Hood's barn of Sinkiang. This in no way detracts from the future importance of Sinkiang in the continental development of the heart of Asia; but full realization of the long-term importance of Sinkiang should not be allowed to throw out of focus our perception of the phases through which the war has already passed and the phases which have still to develop.

FOREWORD

SINKIANG, China's northwesternmost province, lies deep inland on the Central Asian frontier of Russia and China. The region offers colonists something of the rugged pioneer attractions which California presented to the United States in the days of '49. But Sinkiang means even more in 1944. Prompt use of the transportation facilities of the province by the United Nations can help to bring about Japan's defeat in the Pacific war.

Due to the seclusion enforced concerning Sinkiang in recent years few outsiders know what has actually been taking place there. Not only has it been difficult for foreigners to obtain permission to enter, but even reliable second-hand information has been rare. From the opening of air service between China and the Soviet Union in 1939 until very recently only a few foreigners like Sir Stafford Cripps of Britain and Mr. Wendell L. Willkie of the United States have been permitted to pass through Sinkiang. Even they have gone through merely in transit. Secrecy has been less stressed where Chinese and Russians have been concerned, yet it has operated to keep out even certain Chinese from other provinces.

That this has happened is largely due to unique political developments. Although Sinkiang is officially a Chinese province, the authority of the Chinese National Government over the region in the not too distant past has in certain cases been almost unavailing, and many exaggerated reports have hinted that Sinkiang had come under Soviet Russian political domination. In this book I attempt to appraise these developments impartially.

It is unwise for problems of Sinkiang to be glossed over any longer, even despite a mistaken supposition that by bringing them before the United Nations public one might give aid to the enemy. The enemy is better aware of conditions in Sinkiang than are most Americans, and hopes to exploit those conditions. There should be adequate knowledge not only of Sinkiang's physical and historical background, but of at least some of the more important questions which have arisen in recent years and of the opportunities and dangers brought by the war.

This book is admittedly not a complete study—of that, circumstances and the times would not permit; but it may at least serve to bring to general attention certain material about present-day Sinkiang to which I have had access but which has not been easily available in the United States. This material quite obviously reflects opposing points of view which it is sometimes difficult to assess. And though I have attempted to be exceedingly scrupulous in the use of sources, figures in regard to the Chinese Far West are largely estimates and undoubtedly subject to error. For this, and other shortcomings of the study, I beg the reader's indulgence.

It is impossible to express gratitude properly to all those to whom I am indebted for help in the writing of this book. I feel compelled to mention here, however, the names of certain persons to whom I owe special thanks: Mr. Robert J. Kerner, Department of History, University of California, through his graduate seminars inducted me into the field of serious study concerning Sinkiang. Mr. Peter Boodberg, Department of Oriental Languages, University of California, gave me my first training in the Chinese language. Mr. Chang Wei-hua of Cheeloo University, Mr. S. H. Hsieh, Sun Yung-fu, and a host of other friends in Chengtu and elsewhere in China, were understanding, friendly, and helpful while I was a guest in their country from 1939 to 1941. Mr. Mortimer Graves, Executive Secretary of the American Council of Learned Societies, has been sympathetically helpful, particularly since my return from China in August, 1941. Mr. William L. Holland, Research Secretary of the Institute of Pacific Relations, has kindly helped me with some preliminary editorial work. Mr. Owen Lattimore, whose writings in themselves have obligated me as well as any other student of Chinese inland Asia, has generously given me of his personal time and friendly suggestions on numerous occasions. I am also especially obligated to Mr. Lattimore for his kindness in having consented to write the introduction to the present book. Of course, responsibility for the facts, conclusions, and translation as here presented, rests solely with me.

In the text, for distance measurements I have usually converted kilometer references to miles and the less well-known Chinese weights and measures to their approximate English language equivalents. So far as the place-name problem is concerned each separate instance has presented its own difficulty and, since there have been many such instances, the results of my effort necessarily have been limited. As much as has been practicable, I have been guided in my selection of preferred place names by what I have thought to be (1) common English language usage and (2) the modern Chinese names. In many cases common English language usage has been based, not without intent, on what is actually transliteration or translation from a "native," or sometimes the Russian, language. The principles by which I have been guided in my transliteration of place names from Chinese into English, are summarized on the introductory page of the appended glossaries. For the lay reader who may experience difficulty in pronouncing the name "Sinkiang," I recommend the usage offered in *Webster's Collegiate Dictionary* (fourth edition of the Merriam Series, G. & C. Merriam Co., 1934, p. 1164)—"sĭn′ kyäng′" (sin-kyahng′). It is also good practice to use the pronunciation "Hsin-chiang′" (Shin-jyang′), which closely approximates the sound of the name as it is spoken in the Chinese national language.

MARTIN R. NORINS.

Los Angeles,
April 25, 1944.

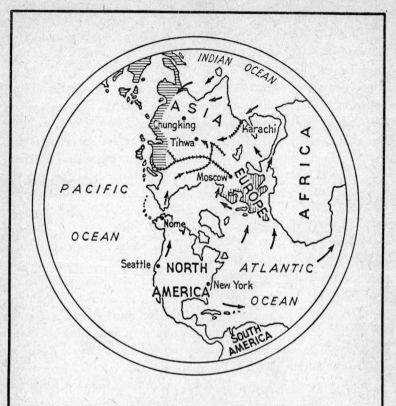

MAIN UNITED NATIONS
TRANSPORT ROUTES
TO EURASIA AND SINKIANG

Transport routes to Eurasia with special emphasis upon
those going from: (1) New York to Moscow, Tihwa (Sinkiang),
and Chungking; (2) New York to Karachi, Tihwa (Sinkiang), and
Chungking; and (3) Seattle to Nome, Tihwa (Sinkiang) and Chungking.

　　　≡≡≡　Japanese War Periphery

　　　|||||||||　German-Italian War Periphery

　　　++++++++　Railroads

Martin R. Norins, January, 1944

HAGSTROM CO., N.Y.

I

THE SINO-RUSSIAN REAR

MOST AMERICANS have begun to appreciate, though probably not yet adequately, the importance of China and Soviet Russia as *war fronts*. But that still vague appreciation is largely bound up with the concept of *American war fronts*—and almost not at all with the question of how much of China and Russia is war front and how much is not in the eyes of Chinese and Russians themselves. This clouded outlook can be considerably clarified if one will but envisage the fighting of China and Russia as protecting and stemming from one geographical entity, a "Sino-Russian Rear" with Sinkiang near its core. Then the *Chinese war front* in the Orient and the *Russian war front* in the Occident are both seen as peripheral defenses for one whole land mass. It is largely in the inland areas of this land mass, in the contiguous and merging hinterland of the "Sino-Russian Rear" where Sinkiang is found, that China and Soviet Russia have been forging the modern iron of their resistance to Axis devastation.

However it may seem on first thought, this "Sino-Russian Rear" is in fact not at all remote from America, nor is the concept alien. For now that the pattern of the war has become clearer one can realize that the Axis nations have so far been unable to achieve their ends for two main reasons: (1) that resistance has persisted in the Eastern Hemisphere and particularly in the area there *behind* the Chinese and Russian war fronts of Asia and Europe and (2) that *behind* the Eastern Hemisphere the United States has been developing her ocean-sheltered resources of the North American continent partially in support and partially in leadership of that resistance. In these two major "rears"—the American and the Sino-Russian—are held principal keys to United Nations victory and future world freedom. Though far apart in terms of miles the two "rears" are close in spirit and aim, and the talents of the peoples in one need to be transferred back and forth for application to the resources of the other.

The concept of the "rear," as well as its expression in terms of a fighting-building "Sino-Russian Rear" and a fighting-producing "American Rear," though until now almost unrecognized in the Occident, has actually permeated most United Nations war strategy so far. The "rear" idea was really first applied by Soviet Russia, when she built up her Central Asian and Siberian "wastelands" under the Soviet Five-Year Plans. But as a kind of tactics, it was first utilized in war by Nationalist China. After the Extraordinary Session of the Fifth National Congress of the Kuomintang in Hankow during March, 1938, Nationalist China reorientated her warfare to *K'ang-chan Chien-kuo* ("Resistance and Reconstruction"): i.e., *K'ang-chan tsai Ch'ien-fang; Chien-kuo tsai Hou-fang* ("Resistance at the Front; Reconstruction in the Rear"). In war terms this has meant resisting the Japanese at the *war front* in the best fashion that primitive weapons would allow while new industrialized and militarized bases were reconstructed in the *war rear*—in the Chinese Far West. Soviet warfare has, with benefit of longer planning and of observation of China's experiences, since June, 1941, been similarly patterned, although with greater emphasis on the offensive. As a consequence the heart of the Eastern Hemisphere—a vast Chinese and Russian bulwark extending from the Urals and the Caspian Sea in Soviet Russia to the eastern edge of the rugged Chinese Far West, on the south along the mountains fringing Iran and Afghanistan and passing east to include the Tibetan Plateau, and on the north enfolding the Russian Arctic, the Siberian snows and the Mongolian steppe—has been fashioned as a rugged inland "rear" on the *reconstruction* and spirit of which almost a billion of our allies are basing their *resistance* to the Axis today.

Britain's Imperial Defense for a time and on a different scale had the same kind of "rear" basis after 1939; the large dispersal of her resources for industrial and military production and training went to the other members of the British Commonwealth. "Defense of the Western Hemisphere," the American thesis of 1940 and 1941, was based on like principles. Although elaboration concerning the scheme may not have been expressed precisely in this way, the American defense plan did envisage the British, Chinese, and Russian "fronts" and "rears" alike as fitting into a global scheme for United States benefit according to which she herself would be the principal "rear."

Conceptions of "front" and "rear" were immensely simplified by the Japanese onslaught which, between December, 1941, and May, 1942, laid waste areas of East Asia, from Hongkong and the Dutch East Indies to Burma. The Eastern Hemisphere had been brought within range of Axis encirclement and there was grave fear of what effect that might have upon the Americas. Immediately any "resistance-island" in the Eastern Hemisphere became obviously precious to America, and the two most sizable United Nations "resistance-islands" of the globe became those of the United States herself (protected by the Atlantic and Pacific Oceans and continental resistance beyond those waters) and the inland Asiatic frontier between China and Russia (behind desperate fighting lines). In another sense, the ocean edges of the world became the *war fronts* or fighting peripheries and the hemispheric land interiors became the *war rears* or production centers from which the *war fronts* were to be supplied.

This exposes bed-rock fundamentals. The United Nations for maximum efficiency in their joint prosecution of this war on the continental peripheries must be able to maintain unimpeded supply lines between the two great world rears—the American and the Sino-Russian. So far the war against the Axis in the Eastern Hemisphere has been mainly one of resistance. Until that resistance is transformed successfully into offensives and into final victory in Asia as well as Europe, the Axis will continue to threaten world peace and security. "Fringe" offensives will be helpful in part, and that is why bases in Britain, bombing raids on Western Europe, the winning back of part of the Solomon Islands, the offensive in Italy, and successes elsewhere are positive factors. But it would be a mistake to classify "fringe" actions for more than what they are. It would, further, be wasteful not to employ for long-range military-supply and production purposes, and to the utmost, the outstanding United Nations resistance-island in the Eastern Hemisphere—

the Sino-Russian Rear of inland Eurasia. In Sinkiang, an area peculiarly indebted to both Nationalist China and Soviet Russia and yet something apart from either, the United Nations are now at last offered an opportunity for just such action.

For today the innermost recesses of Central Asia are once more accessible. General Sheng Shih-ts'ai, Governor of Sinkiang, has arranged in Chungking with Generalissimo Chiang Kai-shek for the opening up of the province. Hundreds of new settlers have already arrived, a vast new development program is under way, and the whole Chinese Northwest is astir with activity.

European members of the Axis were among the earliest to recognize Sinkiang's value as an entree to China, and it is well that they do not have the opportunity that lies open to the United Nations today to work with this province. When German and Italian diplomatic relations with Nationalist China were severed in 1941, Germans leaving Chungking reportedly prophesied they would return by way of Turkestan. The German drive from Berlin southeast to the Caucasus from June, 1941, to December, 1942, probably was dictated at least as much by this hope as by the temptation of Russian oil. For direct Nazi contact with China via Russian Turkestan and Sinkiang might have written a new formidable story in Far Eastern politics, and German attempts to collaborate with Wang Ching-wei then might have made him more than a Japanese marionette. With German military might severely taxed in Europe, that danger now seems past. The roads through Sinkiang fortunately have been opened, not to the Axis, but to the United Nations. They are accessible for military supply to China; and the region through which they pass is at the same time the new frontier region which the Chungking government is vigorously planning to develop.

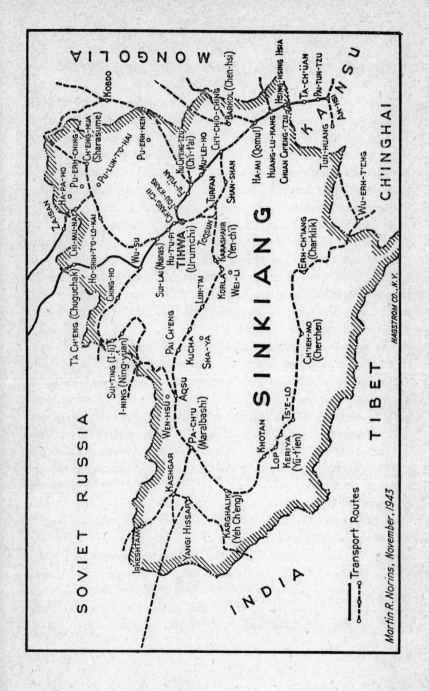

Transport Routes

Martin R. Norins, November, 1943

HAGSTROM CO., N.Y.

II

SINKIANG: THE LAND AND THE PEOPLE

SINKIANG or Chinese Turkestan is a spacious attractive land of about 550,000 square miles, approximately two and a half times the size of France. Yet the province is inhabited only by about four million persons, or an average of less than nine per square mile. By way of contrast Kiangsu Province, which contains Shanghai and other teeming port cities, is one-fourteenth the size of Sinkiang and yet, before the war, had a population density more than one hundred times as great!

By nature a distant and self-contained area, Sinkiang is enclosed on three sides by mountains and on one side by desert and barren terrain. On the west are the T'ien Shan (Heavenly Mountains), the Pamirs, and the Karakorum Mountains; to the south, the lofty K'unlun Mountains of Tibet; on the extreme north, the little visited Altai ranges; and on the east, the Gobi of Mongolia and the Tsaidam wastelands of Western Ch'inghai or Kokonor.

The interior of Sinkiang does have vast expanses of desert. But the T'ien Shan extend from west to east through the center of the province, the Manas and the Tarim River systems moisten immense parts in the north and south respectively, and there are not a few luxuriant, well-watered oases at the bases of her encircling and bisecting mountains. The forested slopes of the Altai ranges and the northern T'ien Shan, the fertile regions alongside the Manas River in the north and throughout the Tarim River basin in the south, and the numerous dot-like oases in the interior—these form the bases for provincial cities and east-west communications.

In early times Chinese often referred to what is now Sinkiang as *Hsi Yü* ("The Western Regions") or as *T'ien-shan-nan-lu* and *T'ien-shan-pei-lu,* i.e., a "Road South of the Heavenly Mountains" and a "Road North of the Heavenly Mountains." These two latter names fitted the natural caravan highways which progressed westward from Chinese Kansu Province on either side of the Heavenly Mountains, weaving along and through the watered and cultivated areas.

Triangle

Sheep numberless as the stars. The shepherd, riding back and forth among his flocks spread out over a half mile, finds moving them from one pasture land to the next a slow process.

Life centers around the village pool in this village south of the Tien Shan.

Lattimore

Bleak winter settles over the valley of the Urumchi River.

Lattimore

Panoramic view of a typical settlement in the verdant Tekes valley, where cultivation is possible. For the rest there are the grasslands.

The houses in the valley are of log and mud. The summer grazing grounds are on the steep hill at the left.

Travellers must often ford the Tekes and other rivers when the spring thaws come and there is no bridge.

Cantilever bridge across the Tekes River. Deep and swift-flowing mountain streams such as the Tekes makes travelling dangerous as well as difficult.

Mr. Willkie is welcomed by General Sheng Shih-tsai, Commissioner of Military Affairs in Sinkiang Province.

The chief of the Tekes Kirghiz with the Lama on his left and the ranking priest on his right.

The sun lays down patterns on a Kashgar street.

A Kashgar mosque where the faithful turn for rest and prayer.

The market place is important for the exchange of wares and gossip in Kashgar.

The snow has come and the nomads must seek other grounds for their flocks.

The nomad spends the night in his temporary shelter which he sets up each evening.

Travellers come into Yarkand at a fast trot.

Lattimore

But life moves more slowly in the city itself.

Lattimore

Sinkiang, "farther than any country from the sea," was once traversed by an old trans-Eurasian Silk Road. Medieval caravans, of Marco Polo's time and before, threaded their way laboriously along it in almost endless lines bearing goods from West to East and back. First high over the jagged Karakorum and Pamir Mountains, then in a gradual winding descent, went the old Silk Road, and along it coursed the trade and embassies of antiquity. Once at the watered bases of Sinkiang's snow-tipped mountains, the trail became covered with string upon string of desert camels, who plodded from oasis to oasis until, past the ancient kingdom of Khotan and the waters of the now-vanished Lob Nor, they wended their way eastward out of Sinkiang to the court of old Cathay.

Advent of fifteenth-century maritime travel turned traders to the sea; and the old caravan trek lost its one-time prominence. Central Asia, which had served as a natural land gateway between Europe and the Orient, was left to lapse into petty internal tribulations, slumber, and finally stagnation. Not until 1931, when Japan began World War II by her invasion of Manchuria, was this remote Sinkiang hinterland at last roughly awakened.

Up to then Sinkiang Province was a picturesque but ill-esteemed old-style Chinese dependency, a frontier land of Central Asiatic tribesmen ruled over by a minority of "Han" Chinese officials. It was an open land of lean Kalmuck nomads and hardy Kirgiz frontiersmen, of Kazakh cowboys galloping like mad across the steppes, of rugged mountains and luxuriant oases and ancient ruins buried in the Takla Makan, a land of mosques and lamaseries and century-old irrigation ditches, of "Turban Heads" and Tung-kans; in short, a land of perhaps the most colorful mixture of race and custom and habitat that ever did exist. Market day in a bazaar might find dark bearded Uighurs from Kashgar in long, bright-colored coats together with veiled and white-cloaked women, a crowd which perhaps would include booted Kirgiz, so-called Aryan Sarikolis from the Taghdumbash Pamir, perhaps outcast unveiled Dulani women from Maralbashi, and a scattering of foreigners from Afghanistan, India, and Russian Turkestan.

Like all frontiersmen, the people of Sinkiang are given to tall tales.

33

A Sinkiang pilgrim, so the story goes, set out from Ha-mi one day early in this century to see the wondrous iron bridge that an American company had built over the Yellow River near Lan-chou, Kansu. Midway on his journey out of the province and down the panhandle corridor of Western Kansu this Sinkiang man, Ma by name, came upon a Lan-chou countryman also named Ma. From early childhood this second Ma had heard such unbelievable stories about the Ha-mi melons grown in Sinkiang that he was at last setting out to see them for himself. Sipping tea at a roadside inn, the two passed the time of day and soon waxed friendly.

"So far as our Iron Bridge is concerned," stated the Ma of Lan-chou, "it is the highest yet. At this date last year a man fell over the side and, when I left, his body had not yet reached the water."

"H-m-m," murmured the Ma of Ha-mi. "Yes, that's high. But as far as our melons are concerned, you are wasting your time traveling all the way to Ha-mi to see them. They grow to such a size, you know, that by this time next year they will be with you in Lan-chou."

Sinkiang (*Hsin-chiang*) has often been called the "New Dominion," and to Chinese, exaggerations notwithstanding, this "new" frontier land has for centuries been full of the wonderful, the picturesque, the bizarre, the new. In the olden days one who brought Ha-mi melons to the capital of the Middle Kingdom would merit special favor, and even today the clippers that soar across Northwest China from Sinkiang to Szechwan inevitably carry a few, now and then, as rare delicacies for the people of Chungking. A rice kernel a half inch long is said to have been developed in the Sinkiang oasis of Aqsu during Manchu Dynasty times, the grapes of Turfan have long been considered unequaled in sweetness and perfection, and today it is the fabulous wealth of Sinkiang's undeveloped natural resources that is inspiring wondrous tales.

Like a legend, the news of riches in Sinkiang has run through China in the past decade—and not without reason. For the North Road and South Road are both plentifully supplied with mineral goods. Certain strategic materials are not present, it is true, but in the North Sinkiang triangle bounded by the three Regions of I-li, T'a Ch'eng, and Tihwa alone, resources are available in such an abundance as can furnish the foundation for a thriving industrialization.

Iron, coal, copper and gold have been found near Sui-ting (I-li). Henceforth this important center on the Soviet-Chinese border may take its prosperous tea and fur trade for granted and brag, instead, of blazing furnaces. T'a Ch'eng (Chuguchak), a frontier locality on the road from the Turksib Railway and probably the only city to have boomed more than Sui-ting, is already boasting of the iron vein one hundred and thirty miles long which runs right through the town, and of the Black Oil Mountain nearby. The oil appears abundantly in the form of springs and is especially black and thick. It is probably a tar, for it gets hard and has been used in the laying out and paving of the new provincial highways. There is coal too, not far away. But miners are nothing new for T'a Ch'eng; in the eighteenth and nineteenth centuries there were thousands of them prospecting in the fifty square miles or so of gold mines roundabout, or so the old people say.

Tihwa (Urumchi), the provincial capital, with a population judged at around 100,000, dominates both the North and South Roads: hence its military and political importance. Nowadays, not to be outdone, it has also been showing great industrial promise. Most of its houses are heated with oil or coal produced in the vicinity. One visitor to Sheng Shih-ts'ai's headquarters saw a piece of coal so huge that it took two men to carry it.

Farther south, Kashgar (Su-fu), largest oasis in Sinkiang and hub of both transport and political interests from the neighboring lands of Northwest India, Afghanistan, and Soviet Turkestan, is also blessed with natural resources. Kashgar oil, though often merely "scooped out" by primitive means, has long provided the city with gasoline, kerosene, machine oil, and grease. Even Ma Titai, old-school Commander-in-Chief of the Kashgar district at the close of World War I, guessed at the worth of the oil in his domain. He put most of his personal army to the task of tapping wells for him, and almost negotiated a deal with Soviet Russians of Ferghana for modern machinery. The Russians had said they would supply the machinery and would personally see to its being escorted to Kashgar, when Ma's plans hit a snag. His ambitions had come to the ears of Lieutenant-Colonel P. T. Etherton, local British Consul-General and Political Resident, who made haste to point out "that the advantages to be gained were out of all proportion to the danger incurred. . . ." The Titai is said to have agreed, the Russians are said to have been "checkmated," and (unsaid) the industrial development of Kashgar was retarded for another stretch of years. This is a sample of the sort of thing that has long been holding back Sinkiang development.

Yet it is doubtful whether the tribesmen of the Sinkiang steppes and oases spent much time yearning for progress as such. They clung to their time-honored ways, and a thousand years more or less seemed to bring little change or concern. For Sinkiang did have color and charm —charm especially of a human, a warm temperament. A perfect host might sometimes put his wife or pretty daughter at the disposal of an overnight guest but paradoxically the modesty of a woman was protected by a face veil. A wealthy khan might expand his harem until it almost rivaled that of Yakub Beg, self-made "King of Kashgar," who maintained three hundred favorites in state and always took at least four with him on his trips to outlying areas. At Sinkiang merry-makings, as befitted a nomad's paradise, mare's milk was quaffed with gusto and horse meat was regarded an expensive luxury. A fortune-teller was always ready to deal out prosperity for the throng of a local bazaar; somewhere near by a tambourine would jingle merrily; and a samovar was usually singing its own happy song. Uighur, Mongol, Kazakh, and Son of Han, all and more, mingled, yet maintained their own traditions; and religion ran the gamut—from Mohammedanism, Lamaist Buddhism, and ancient Manichaeism to Christianity.

But in the old Sinkiang, as has too often been the case elsewhere, along with the enchanting and the bizarre there were poverty, cruelty, and crime. The Sinkiang peasant in most cases made his home in a dirty, mud-wood hovel or, on the steppe, in a primitive, tent-like abode. It was at times hard going for him to scrape up enough food on which to feed himself and his family, and often he took to begging and to thievery, only to be apportioned harsh punishment. It was not unusual for a servant, caught stealing, to have his fingers or part of his tongue cut off. A magistrate of former days, who was angrily aroused by the unusual number of crimes in his district, had all the suspected criminals rounded up and then, merely as a precaution, ordered the tendons of their ankles slit. A murderer once was allotted a terrible punishment. Stripped naked under a hot sun, he was thrown to the hard earth of a compound yard and fastened there with wooden pegs driven through his body. His torturers then secured a live rat under an inverted pot on his mid-section, and left him to die while the sun's rays beat down upon him and the rat ate through his abdomen. Almost as horrifying is the case of the Moslem who came upon his wife with her face unveiled talking across the compound wall to a male neighbor. The husband immediately drew his sword and cut off her head. Throwing it over the wall, he told the neighbor that he could thenceforth have her for good.

Political corruption, too, in former days was rife. The tax burden on the common man was unbearable, and officialdom squeezed for selfish gain. Tax methods were irregular and, since they usually varied from locality to locality, systematic check was difficult. On paper an official would report that he was maintaining a strong force of military but, actually pocketing the monetary difference out of his budget, would only keep about him a fraction of the number of troops reported. Nepotism was commonly practiced and, even if the ugly truth concerning some particular instance did come to public attention, usually little was done about it. Since Han Chinese officials were a small minority and since the people whom they were governing were strange in language and customs, native headmen often obtained important intermediate posts by which they, too, kept their pockets illicitly lined.

Out of this paradoxically alluring and yet repellent atmosphere came finally the Sinkiang uprising of the 1930's and the emergence of a young, well-educated Manchurian Chinese leader by the name of Sheng Shih-ts'ai.

III

SHENG SHIH-TS'AI AND THE "NEW NEW DOMINION"

WHEN SHENG SHIH-TS'AI was offered direction of Sinkiang destinies, history began to record a courageous new chapter—for long a secret and maligned one—in the annals of human emancipation. For Sheng urged that the province discard the old-style dependency tradition and, by adopting a great new six-point charter, cast in her lot with progress. By his Six Great Policies he aimed at reviving long-submerged cultural aspirations of Sinkiang native races and at bringing about revolutionary Sinkiang reconstruction. This he tried to do within the limits of nominal control of the Chinese Republic, at the price of favoring "radical" Soviet ideas, and at the cost of offending other less far-sighted Chinese, as well as many assertedly "foreign imperialist" interests. He has, in brief, made the province into a New Sinkiang *(Hsin Hsin-chiang),* a remarkable "New New Dominion."

Sheng, a moderate-sized, handsome man, with an exceptionally full crop of dark hair and a thick, descending mustache, started out for the region late in the 1920's. Yang Tseng-hsin, warlord master of the province since abdication of the Manchu Dynasty, had been assassinated in July, 1928, and his place taken by the weak, avaricious Chin Shu-jen. Provincial General Secretary Lu Hsüeh-tsu had gone from Sinkiang to Nanking on business, and had been requested by Chin to look around while there for a man of military background possibly suited to build up the army of the frontier province. Sheng Shih-ts'ai was the man Lu selected.

Born in K'ai-yüan county of Liaoning, Manchuria, in 1893, Sheng Shih-ts'ai had been reared "in a small family" and amid conditions of "poverty" and "cold." How he managed an education with such meager resources is not clear, but he attended primary and middle schools, and even had some university training in Nanking. There he studied European history under Chang Chi-luan, the late editor of China's most famous newspaper, *Ta Kung Pao.* Sheng never seems to have forgot-

38

ten his old teacher, and that is probably one of the reasons that the *Ta Kung Pao* has often been able to reveal more information concerning the New Sinkiang than other Chinese journals.

Though Sheng started out to be a student of the arts, the trend of events in China led him, midway in his career, to study military science also. It was after a period of attendance at a university in Japan—where he and his biographer, Tu Chung-yüan, became friends—that Sheng returned to China and entered the then famous military academy at Shaokwan (Ch'ü-chiang) in Kwangtung Province. Li Ken-yüan, an old-time Yünnan militarist-revolutionary, was in charge and guided the young student through the academic ropes. On graduation, Sheng was given an introduction to Kuo Sung-ling, one of the prominent war lords of his native Northeast China.

General Kuo made Sheng a *Hsiao P'ai Chang* (Second Lieutenant) and rapidly promoted him until he became a *Ying Chang* (Battalion Commander). Then he was permitted another period of study, this time in a Japanese military academy. He had not been in Japan long, however, when he was called back to China to join in a military *Putsch*. It failed, and as a consequence General Kuo was killed. Sheng, having lost his benefactor and himself become involved in difficulties, returned to Japan "to read books." While there he received financial backing from none other than Generalissimo Chiang Kai-shek. As a consequence, it is said, he has since referred to himself as "The Student" when signing telegraph messages addressed to the Chinese national leader.

Soon after his Japanese military training had been completed, Sheng Shih-ts'ai joined the Generalissimo in the northward march against the war lords of Pei-p'ing or Peking as it was then called. He was shortly given a post in the office of the Chinese General Staff but was not happy there and decided to try his luck on the Chinese frontier. On first thought, probably due to his past tutelage under a Yünnanese schoolmaster at Ch'ü-chiang, he considered going to Yünnan. The attractions of the vaster and richer territory of Sinkiang, however, ultimately won him.

Not the most pleasant introduction to Sinkiang awaited Sheng. He had met Lu Hsüeh-tsu in Nanking through the offices of a mutual friend, and Lu was persuaded to recommend him to the Sinkiang Military Governor. But when Chin Shu-jen learned of Sheng's background he seemed to fear to take him on; Chin wanted a subordinate, not a possible rival. It was only through third party pressure that Chin agreed to give Sheng his chance. Then, just as the young appointee was about to leave Eastern China, Sino-Russian hostilities over the Chinese Eastern Railway broke out and interrupted normal air transport through Soviet Russia via Vladivostok. Since it was by that route that Sheng had planned to travel, he was forced to spend eight months in Pei-p'ing "reading" again until communications were restored. When the line was at last reopened, he flew through Siberia to his destination; there he was temporarily lodged as a guest of Lu Hsüeh-tsu, who had been his traveling companion. But Sheng did not get to see Chin Shu-jen until over a week had passed; for Lu and the military governor had had a quarrel almost as soon as Lu arrived.

At last Sheng was assigned a position with the General Staff in the Office of the Border Defense Commander of Sinkiang. Not a particularly attractive "boost" for one with Sheng's background, the assignment found him nevertheless immediately setting to his tasks. By 1930 he had worked himself up to the position of Chief of the General Staff in the Office; then, when revolt broke out in Ha-mi, he was made Commander-in-Chief at the Front.

Chin Shu-jen, a man weaker than those before him and yet covetously retaining the old exploitation methods, had attempted to monopolize taxes on Sinkiang foreign trade and had given his sons extensive regional authority. This combination had caused such resentment that, apparently with some Japanese instigation filtering in through Mongolia, it surged up in a swelling tide and flung the waves of civil war over the province. The incident which finally precipitated his downfall came with the death of the Mohammedan Prince of Qomul in 1930.

Qomul, the Moslem city known to Chinese as Ha-mi, as late as 1930 had been still under only nominal Chinese suzerainty. But when its prince died his son was "received" into Chinese protective custody; then the ancient principality of Qomul was legally abolished and the region broken down into three Chinese counties, Ha-mi, I-ho, and I-wu. From those, according to the existing Chinese law, certain taxes were automatically due to the provincial government and to other Chinese government authority. This alone might have been enough to rouse the Moslems of the old principality, for up to then they had not been accustomed to pay such taxes. But to make matters worse a party of eighty Kansu refugees had been brought by Chin Shu-jen to Sinkiang and allotted some of the Moslem land in the "new" I-ho county. Finally, one of the "infidel" tax collectors tried to marry a pretty Moslem girl. In their fury the Moslems killed the tax collector and the eighty Kansu refugees. The small nucleus of Mohammedan rioters gradually accumulated "thousands" more, and open revolt against the Sinkiang administration began.

The whole affair was an expensive demonstration of Chin Shu-jen's ineptitude for the office of Sinkiang Provincial Chairman. The old Prince of Qomul had been thoroughly hated by his own people, and his demise need not have created such an outbreak. Yet, once the revolt had been started, it assumed devastating proportions.

Two of the rebels went to Kansu and solicited help from Ma Chung-ying. With some four hundred Moslem comrades from Kansu to help him, Ma marched forward into Sinkiang. This was one of the far-famed Ma's of the Tung-kan (Tungan) clan. Born at the town of Hochow in Southern Kansu, he had entered the Ch'inghai army of one of his namesakes, Ma Pu-fang, at the age of seventeen. After a time he had gathered his own Moslem Chinese army about him and swiftly brought his name to notice in Kansu military affairs. So prominent had he become by the spring of 1930 that Chiang Kai-shek had permitted him to enroll in the Nationalist military academy at Nanking for a three months' indoctrination course. When he returned to the Northwest, however, his ambitions brought him rapidly into difficulty with other prominent leaders of the region. He had just suffered a military defeat at the hands of Ma Pu-fang when the call came from Ha-mi.

Ma Chung-ying entered Sinkiang as a liberator, and at first recruits came by the throng to his army, the official 36th Division which

Nanking had authorized him to command. He attacked Chen-hsi (Barkol) successfully, and then Ha-mi and Ch'i-chio-ching. Though partly victorious in these latter encounters, he was wounded and temporarily retired to refuge in Kansu. He returned to the fray in May, 1932, chiefly assisted by another Moslem, Ma Shih-ming. Chin Shu-jen then directed Sheng Shih-ts'ai, already promoted to the post of Commander-in-Chief at the Front, to march against the rebels. Sheng was so successful that two of the Moslem leaders, Yulbaz and Khoja Niaz by name, fled from the province. Ma Shih-ming, however, had marched to Shan-shan and launched a counter-attack in the winter of 1932. His forces soon were approaching the outskirts of Tihwa, the provincial capital.

At this time over a thousand of the refugee troops of the Northeast Resist Japan Army from Manchuria—then continuing a journey back into China via Sinkiang—began to march down from T'a Ch'eng (Chuguchak) to defend Tihwa. Ma Shih-ming, noting this, withdrew his Moslem forces to San-tao Pa, which commanded access to the rice-producing areas on which Tihwa was dependent. Chin Shu-jen therefore ordered Sheng Shih-ts'ai to take the new forces with him in an attack on San-tao Pa and later Fou-k'ang, another Moslem stronghold. Sheng had just chased the Tung-kans out of San-tao Pa when there came a new turn of events.

A heavy slaughter of Han Chinese had been going on in many centers elsewhere in the province, and within the provincial capital there was a great rice shortage. Chinese military and civilian leaders alike, therefore, had by this time begun to resent the continued fighting; Tihwa had even come to feel that if Chin Shu-jen were ousted from his post as Provincial Chairman the warfare might subside. White Russian troops, constituting a sizable portion of the soldiers upon whom Chin counted for protection, were at the same time restless about poor treatment they had been receiving. This unhealthy state of affairs came to a climax on April 12, 1933, the occasion of the "Four-Twelve" Affair, when these same White Russians announced that Moslems were attacking the city. A mob, entering the gates of Tihwa, rushed forward in a direct attack on the provincial government headquarters. In the midst of this pandemonium Chin Shu-jen fled out of the city. Provincial military responsibility thus fell directly on Sheng Shih-ts'ai's shoulders.

Tu Chung-yüan, whose account in Chinese of the New Sinkiang has been exceptionally revealing, continues with the story in this way:

> After Chin Shu-jen had fled, the White Russian Army captured both Chin Shu-hsin, his son, and Commander Ts'ui Chao-chi. Ultimately Chin Shu-hsin was killed because he tried to flee during his trial.
>
> It was evening in the city when the White Russian Army opened the meeting. Liu Wen-lung, Provincial Commissioner of Education, was chosen Provisional Chairman of the Provincial Government. Cheng Jun-ch'eng, leader of the Manchurian Northeast National Salvation Army, was named Provisional Chairman of the Military Affairs Commission, and twenty-four men, including Ch'en Chung, T'ao Ming-yüeh and others, were selected as members of a Sinkiang Provincial Government Maintenance Committee. Liu Wen-lung posited three principles for the meeting: Protection of Chin Shu-jen's life and property; Protection of the Consulate; and Maintenance of order.
>
> At the time Cheng Jun-ch'eng was outside the city and did not know what had taken place, so Yang Hsüeh-yüan was sent to get him. Cheng, after declining his appointment three times, finally consented to accept it temporarily. But it was known Chin's appointment of Sheng Shih-ts'ai indicated the latter had considerable power, and some feared that Sheng might help Chin Shu-jen. Pai Yü-hsiu was appointed to see Sheng about taking over Chin's office . . . but was wounded. At the time both Sheng Shih-ts'ai and Yang Hsüeh-yüan were at Cheng Jun-ch'eng's headquarters, and all three of them entered the city together. Cheng continually argued that he and his troops were guests of Sinkiang, and that he could not accept appointment in the province. The people therefore selected Sheng as Provisional Border Defense Commander . . .

Young Sheng Shih-ts'ai, rich in military background, recognized this opportunity for what it was; his military successes had already won him acclaim and the Sinkiang capital was looking for a new military leader. Though Cheng Jun-ch'eng, leader of the Manchurian contingent passing through Sinkiang, might have been first choice, he did not feel free to accept provincial military command. Perhaps Sheng helped persuade him to decline. Sheng was the most eligible leader left and, accordingly, was selected.

43

Sheng Shih-ts'ai had been placed in a difficult position, and at first there seemed little that he could do. The Tung-kan armies of Ma Chung-ying had cut him off and were bleeding the countryside of Eastern Sinkiang of its sustenance. Everywhere along the road from Ha-mi to Tihwa there was "misery, debris, devastation!" At Ha-mi the shops were closed, their fronts barred with sinister wood shutters. The village of T'ou-p'u had become merely "heaps of clay." At Ch'i-chio-ching the streets were littered and stinking with the bodies of dead horses shot in battle. Movement on the thoroughfares of Turfan had ceased, its commerce was paralyzed and there, too, the shops were shuttered and bolted. Ma Chung-ying had become the "autocrat of Eastern Sinkiang" from Ha-mi to Korla and west as far as Kashgar; by June, 1933, he had entered even Ch'i-t'ai (Ku Ch'eng-tzu) "unhindered" and had begun to push from there towards Tihwa. Behind him, though, he had left a wake of pillaging and poverty. The ruthlessness with which he and his men plundered the countryside and the people earned him hatred even from countless fellow Moslems as well as from the Han Chinese.

Sheng directed the Northeast Resist Japan Army to continue the march against Ma, who was as a consequence forced temporarily into a retreat; but he recovered enough to reform his men into ranks and to capture Turfan. From there, where the North and South Roads of Sinkiang come closest to juncture, he controlled access to both East and South Sinkiang. This news came as a severe jolt to the capital, for revolt had also broken out further north at I-li (Sui-ting), under General Chang Pei-yüan. Representatives of the Chinese National Government took this opportunity to attempt negotiation of a peace between Sheng and Ma. Nanking sent first General Huang Mu-sung, then the late Lo Wen-kan. But both were unsuccessful. Sheng was amenable, yet requested that Ma make Ha-mi his headquarters and take orders from the provincial government; to this Ma would not consent. Instead, at the turn of 1934, he once more marched his armies toward the capital which had just sent its main force in the direction of T'a Ch'eng to put down the Altai uprising of Chang Pei-yüan.

At this point Sheng Shih-ts'ai arranged with Soviet Russia to import large amounts of war materials—trucks, armored cars, machine-guns, ammunition, and even airplanes. With these and the help of Russian troops from the Altai area, the government forces captured Hsi-hu, on the Altai road, and compelled General Chang to flee ultimately toward an ignominious suicide. Then Sheng turned once more to press home his attack on Ma Chung-ying. Had the Russian matériel not been obtained, Ma might have won the battle of Tihwa. As it was, the Tung-kans were forced to flee back all the way to Toqsun; and Sheng's armies began to block their enemies off, both outside Turfan and in the vicinity of Karashahr (Yen-ch'i). Ma's position quickly became so desperate that he began a long retreat to the southwest in the direction of Kashgar. Sheng's airplanes harried the retiring forces with bombs at Turfan and again at Korla, and it was only by the narrowest margin that the Tung-kan leader squeezed past those towns to Kucha. From there he fled to the comparative security of Kashgar in April, 1934. Yet he was forced to leave even that refuge, for troops of the Northeast Resist Japan Army marched in within four months. Ma is said to have been escorted over the Chinese frontier into Russia, and his whereabouts have since then seemingly been swallowed up in mystery.

Sinkiang was not, however, sorry to see him depart, after the four years of warfare. The desperate people were instead only too ready to heed proclamations which were dropped from Sheng Shih-ts'ai's airplanes urging the populace to make "genuine submission" in return for "rehabilitation" and "safety." An army of Kirgizes, Turkis, Torguts, Taranchis, and White Russians, according to words ascribed to one of the tribesmen himself, had at last been formed "to drive Ma and the Tungans out of Sinkiang." All who followed Sheng Shih-ts'ai had been promised, too, that "a new era" had begun for the province; that General Sheng was going to reorganize Sinkiang administration and bring "order, peace, and security."

On first coming to power in 1933, Sheng Shih-ts'ai concerned himself principally with the handling of dissident factions; soon, however, he issued declarations of radical administrative policy, and then introduced a first, and in due course a second, three-year plan of provincial reconstruction. His program was not at first so effective in South Sinkiang as in North Sinkiang, and his accomplishments have been less noticeable there. But at that, under his administration Sinkiang Province boasts of its modern innovations, such as electric light, telephone, and wireless improvements, of airplane and widespread automobile transportation, of motion pictures, daily newspapers, and of rapidly spreading literacy. These are all the more remarkable in view of the relatively remote terrain to which they have been brought.

This is the way in which Tu Chung-yüan summarizes the great changes in Sinkiang:

> From the time of the "Four-Twelve" Affair Sinkiang has changed politically, militarily, and socially. This change has been the result of a great upheaval, and it is only due to his acquaintance with international affairs, politics, and his personal experience in Sinkiang that Sheng Tu-pan has been able to cope with it. The people of China have long mistakenly felt that they deserve to govern in Sinkiang as a great people over lesser peoples. Has not this mistaken idea, which existed not only during the administrations of Yang Tseng-hsin and Chin Shu-jen but which was derived from the code of Tso Tsung-t'ang and Liu Mien-t'ang, has not this mistaken idea really aimed at the military subjugation of Sinkiang? Such might have passed muster formerly but not today. With the boundaries of Sinkiang and Soviet Russia touching for several thousand Chinese miles and with the Soviet kind of socialism and liberty already having been made available to the lesser peoples of Soviet Russia, how is it possible for a ten per cent Han minority to subjugate successfully in Sinkiang an over eighty per cent Moslem majority? . . .

Shortly after his election as Provisional Border Defense Commander of the province, Sheng issued an Eight Point Proclamation which set the early keynote for his conduct of government. Establishment of Racial Equality and a Guarantee of Religious Freedom were primary and secondary in the proclamation. Its other six points were: Equitable Distribution of Agricultural and Rural Relief; Reform of Government Finance; The Cleaning Up of Government Administration; The Expansion of Education; The Promotion of Self-Government; and The Improvement of the Judiciary.

It is more than coincidental that the Eight Point Proclamation made no mention of ties to Sovietism and that its first two guarantees were those of Equality and Religious Freedom. It is just the kind of a proclamation which might have been issued in an early, purely Chinese, attempt to conciliate the rebellious Moslems. Nor does it seem by chance that next emphasis was placed on aid to agriculture and the rural areas, for that has been a leading part of Sheng Shih-ts'ai's accomplishments. Reforms in government finance and administration also were particularly applicable in a period following the avaricious rule of Chin Shu-jen. The remaining three points, dealing with education, self-government, and the judiciary, are more abstract; but they too were practicable planks for a Sinkiang political platform.

But the Eight Point Proclamation does not seem to have received the continued stress that has been placed upon another, a complementary, set of principles of the New Sinkiang.

Once, as Tu Chung-yüan puts it, Sheng Shih-ts'ai ". . . had eliminated internal rebellion, unified Sinkiang, and firmly established government authority," he ". . . invoked his Six Great Policies . . ."

The Six Great Policies of the New Sinkiang are: (1) Anti-imperialism; (2) Kinship to Sovietism; (3) Racial Equality; (4) Clean Government; (5) Peace; and (6) Reconstruction. In them the unique character of the New Sinkiang is to be found. As a unit these principles constitute a magnificent charter, a message which may even match that of the Magna Charta of Britain, the Bill of Rights of the United States, and the Roosevelt-Churchill Atlantic Charter for the effect it has already had and can have in Asia in the battle for Chinese emancipation. For here, in the heart of Central Asia, a colony had cast off her fetters, risen and shouted forth the dogma upon which she was to stand or to fall. Upon it she built a new civilization for herself, and her message is one to which the world well may listen.

IV

ANTI-IMPERIALISM

A FRONTIER, it has been written, is by its own nature usually an unsettled region. There rough, unscrupulous men come to seek quick, easy riches; and there the good living of peace, education, responsible government, and material comforts is often either lacking or only ostensibly proffered from the embattled mansions of outlaws or despots. Usually confronting another country, the frontier is the place which feels most suddenly and severely the shocks of changing political and military relationships in the world: the slightest overt military incident on an international frontier time and time again has been the spark to set nations aflame with war. Multiplied a hundred-fold or more is this disquiet and tension when a frontier lies helpless and unprotected at the crossroads of world empire.

Such a frontier has Sinkiang been. Tu Chung-yüan writes:

> Behind the facade of the racial and cultural complex of the province every imperialist force has sought to cause dissension and division. A certain imperialist force, for instance, has increasingly fostered independence for South Sinkiang, and Japanese imperialism has helped the Ch'an Hui [Turban Moslems] promote a Mussulman state. If this matter is not put foremost, if it is not struck a decisive blow, if all the people of the province are not cautioned about it, then all Sinkiang government will share a like fate.

A nineteenth-century outpost for the commerce of China, Russia, Britain, and Japan, Sinkiang has seen her borders patrolled incessantly by the armies of the first three while her steppes and oases have been infiltrated by the counter-agents of probably all four and more. The pulse of life in Sinkiang might be said to have been timed almost literally to beat with the tread of a marching frontier guard. One day it was bruited about that the Russians were plotting to march through Sinkiang to Lhasa and Bombay; the next, that the British coveted Sinkiang as a road to Urga; a third, that Japanese would use Sinkiang as a base to set the Moslems of the Middle East in revolt! Nor has

48

it only been these. China has had great difficulty in defending this frontier during the nineteenth and early twentieth centuries, yet she herself probably began imperialism in Sinkiang some two thousand years ago. And she had to compete even then with the nomads of Siberia, Mongolia, and Turkestan. It is through "Anti-imperialism" that the New Sinkiang has attempted to arm herself against all this.

Chinese Imperialism in the Western Regions

The "Anti-imperialism" of the New Sinkiang may well have been, in the first place, a reproach for Chinese imperialist frontier policies of the past. For Sinkiang Province was not always Chinese territory. The area appears to have been inhabited in ancient times by a number of separate independent clans, principalities, and states which Chinese gradually came to know collectively as the *Hsi Yü,* or "Western Regions." By conquest, and often by repression, of the natives of these Western Regions, Chinese were among the first to acquaint them with imperialism. A related, but slightly different, approach to this point is made by Owen Lattimore in his study, *Inner Asian Frontiers of China:*

> The history of the Chinese in Central Asia . . . is a history of imperialism, of conquest. The Chinese could not here expand, adding contiguous region to contiguous region as they did in their advance toward the Yangtze and beyond, but had to subjugate and dominate from afar. They had, moreover, to compete with the imperialism of the steppe, which also attempted to assert its control over the oasis world. The record of the Chinese in Central Asia is therefore by no means continuous; in fact, their effective control has been estimated at only about 425 out of about 2,000 years, divided into a number of periods, of which the present Chinese rule in the province of Sinkiang is the fifth major period.

China seems to have had earliest contact with the Western Regions during the Han Dynasty (B.C. 206-220 A.D.). The Hsiung-nu (Hun?) nomads of Mongolia had been raiding the Chinese frontier, and the Chinese Emperor, Han Wu Ti, wanted to outflank them with bases in the Western Regions. He didn't get those bases at first; but through an emissary, Chang Ch'ien, he did initiate Chinese frontier activity in Central Asia. By the end of the first century A.D. a Han general Pan Ch'ao had expanded that activity so successfully in a military sense that "more than fifty kingdoms" of the Western Regions had "sent hostages," and countries as far away as Persia were regularly sending "tributary" missions to the Chinese throne.

China did not retain this position permanently. Some three to four hundred years later, Chinese of the Sui and T'ang Dynasties had to play off "western Turks" (apparently a people of the Western Regions) against the "northern Turks" (probably a people then in present-day Mongolia) to regain mastery of Turkestan. In this period, during the reign of the Emperor Hsüan Tsung of the T'ang Dynasty (713-756), Chinese power extended as far as the sites of Kashmir and Gilgit (in present-day Northwest India).

But this was the limit to which Chinese westward expansion was then to go, and later it even met with severe reverses. When the Sons of Han did carry their authority back to Turkestan, it was centuries later and then they were mainly henchmen to their own "barbarian" overlords: the Mongols in the thirteenth, and the Manchus in the seventeenth century. What memories must have been left the people of Sinkiang by plundering Mongol hordes of Genghis Khan! And by the Manchus! In 1750 during the reign of Emperor Ch'ien Lung, their armies laid waste the Altai region and annihilated 600,000 inhabitants. A century later they slaughtered numberless Moslems in the "pacification" of such Asiatic revolts as that of Yakub Beg of Kashgar.

Nor, for almost a quarter century after Chinese revolt from Manchu rule in 1911 and 1912, did Sinkiang have an opportunity to dissociate the idea of Chinese rule from that of stern military conquest. The administration of the first Republican governor of the province, Yang Tseng-hsin, aroused so much resentment that he was assassinated on July 7, 1928. Once his firm hand was withdrawn unrest again stirred; and it was thus that the Sinkiang civil war which brought Sheng Shih-ts'ai to power broke out in the 1930's.

In the later days of the Manchu Dynasty, meanwhile, a new imperialism had come to Sinkiang. The expanding Russian Empire had not been slow to profit from her proximity to China, and in the Treaty of Kuldja of 1851 she gained her first sizable foothold in the Sinkiang economic door. The treaty, kept secret for a time, was made public in 1861. It gave Russia the right to send agents into the region, permitted Russian commercial dealings with Kuldja (Sui-ting or I-li) and Chuguchak (T'a Ch'eng), and foresaw the opening of a Russian consulate at Kuldja. In the Treaty of Peking, November 14, 1860, this beginning was enlarged to permit the opening of another consulate, at Kashgar.

Then came the Yakub Beg revolt of the 1860's and an upset in the Central Asian balance of power. The Turkestan frontier was so "disturbed" that in 1871 Russia occupied points on the Chinese side, promising that her forces would be evacuated as soon as China had restored order. There was doubt at the time as to Russia's true intentions, and all might not have gone so well subsequently had China's army under Tso Tsung-t'ang not been successful in its bitter campaign to "pacify" the Moslem uprising. Russia, unable in 1881 to challenge the victorious Chinese, reluctantly signed new conventions with China. By these the Tsar, in return for a monetary payment, ultimately gave back much of the Chinese territory he had occupied. A *modus operandi* was achieved by which China, among other matters, recognized the Russian right to open consulates at Kuldja, Chuguchak, Kashgar, and Turfan, and assented to creation of other Russian consulates at Ha-mi, Tihwa, and Ch'i-t'ai (Ku Ch'eng-tzu) should commercial relations warrant.

British Imperialism

Russian ambitions in Chinese Turkestan in the time of the Tsars had, however, additional reactions farther south. It is not too surprising that, once Russian troops had moved across the Sinkiang frontier in 1871, authorities of the British Empire tendered political "recognition" to the "government" which the rebel Yakub Beg had then organized at Kashgar. The British felt their "preserve" in nearby India was being "threatened" and as a consequence "countered" Russian action both by recognizing the Beg and by taking a more active interest in "trade" with South Sinkiang.

Sinkiang-Indian trade had been under way for some time, but the British Government became officially committed to its furtherance in 1876. This policy, they found, could not be pursued satisfactorily without dispatch of an armed force to pacify the Northwest Frontier of India. In taking this step, they trespassed on what Chinese feel was and is their ground. Thereupon, say Chinese, when in 1884 a British force marched into "Kanjut" *(K'an-chü-t'i* or *Kan-chu-t'e)*—the site of the Gilgit Agency and Hunza Valley of modern Northwest India— outright English "aggression" against Sinkiang began. Subsequently a British agent and a British consul were established at Kashgar. This South Sinkiang metropolis became a focus for British activity which, under the aegis of the Indian trade agent, the British consul, and native *aqsaqals* (headmen), was carried on mainly as an intra-Mohammedan affair. It became, consequently, subject to a persistent suspicion on the part of Chinese non-Moslems.

Manchu Commercial Efforts

That the Russians and British were attempting to dominate Sinkiang trade became apparent to China by the closing years of Manchu rule. In a limited and tardy way the Manchus attempted to strengthen administration in the province, therefore, and to foster new development of intra-Chinese trade. New colonizing blood was poured into the veins of Sinkiang. At the same time went manufacturers and ideas; and from the province came jade, gold, furs, skins, and a number of other items. The avidity with which foreigners in Tientsin and Shanghai sought the furs, skins, and wool especially helped, and by the beginning of the twentieth century Chinese traders were bringing these goods out of Sinkiang in such amounts that she was beginning to experience a new prosperity. But the process of itself could not develop to satisfactory proportions, due to the then current weakness of the

Manchu position in China as a whole, as well as to the physical limitations set by the necessary journey.

The Convenience Factor

Traditional routes from China Proper into Sinkiang not only have always been fraught with danger and difficulty, but they have also been excessively long. Negotiation by primitive means of some 1,500 miles of hard travel over desert and mountain areas formerly was required for the journey from Pei-p'ing to Tihwa; there were, in addition, the following distances from Tihwa to selected outlying Sinkiang trade centers near the Russian and Indian frontiers:

Sui-ting (Kuldja)	360 miles
T'a Ch'eng (Chuguchak)	375 "
Aqsu	927 "
Kashgar	1,375 "
Khotan	1,644 "

Yet, compare those distances with the mileage along main trade routes by which there was travel from modern communication centers in Russia to key points in Sinkiang. A French writer, M. Castagné, has shown that from:

Andizhan to Kashgar by Irkeshtam through Terek Pass is	427 miles
Pishpek (Frunze) to Kashgar by Narinsk through Chatir Köl is	346 "
Alma-Ata to Sui-ting (Kuldja) by Khorgos is	534 "
Semipalatinsk to Chuguchak (T'a Ch'eng) by Sergiopol is	400 "
Zaisan to Sharasume is	160 "
Zaisan to Chuguchak is	160 "

M. Castagné also points out how the Russians were economically favored over even the British when he explains that from Leh, in Northwest India—along a customary British trade route—it is respectively 460, 530, and 619 miles to such key commercial points of South Sinkiang as Karghalik, Khotan, and Keriya. The British routes, besides, went over some of the most difficult mountain passes in the world, some replete with blizzards and terrific heights; at least one over 18,000 feet.

These remarks show, without need of further elaboration, that the main centers of Sinkiang have been relatively much more convenient to centers of Russian Central Asia than to those of British India or, to a much greater extent, those of Eastern China. They also show how Russia's favored geographical position could shortly turn Sinkiang trade in her favor.

The Emergence of Tsarist Leadership

For a generation the Tsarist Government had wielded considerable commercial influence in the Kashgar region of South Sinkiang; and the proximity of the Russian Turkestan railways and highways was felt only less by degree in the Altai and T'ien Shan areas of North Sinkiang. According to Gabitov, a Soviet writer, a real shift toward Russia in Sinkiang trade came in the period immediately following the Russo-Japanese War of 1904-1905. Up to then nearly all the wool of Tihwa and Tarbagatai (T'a Ch'eng) had gone into Tientsin across Su-chou and Lan-chou. But in 1905 the freight prices jumped, and Tientsin imports of Sinkiang wool were diminished. This started a shift which took the goods from Tihwa across the Chinese-Russian border to Semipalatinsk and on to the east coast of Asia via the Trans-Siberian Railway. This export route made good use of the relatively comfortable trek from Tihwa to the Russian border via the Manas River valley. In the early years of the twentieth century this avenue of trade became the most important for Sinkiang. Large and small livestock and raw materials for Russia herself also went this way, but some other Sinkiang products—cotton, silks, and a certain amount of wool from the Khotan, Keriya, and Yarkand areas farther south—entered Russia along the Kashgar-Irkeshtam-Osh road. In return Russia sent Sinkiang finished manufactures, silks, iron (including plated and rimmed iron), barred steel, earthenware, perfumes, and sugar. Henceforth, with the exception of the earliest period of Soviet government in Russia, Sinkiang-Russian economic bonds gradually grew stronger. By 1930 Soviet engineers had completed the Turksib Railway, which reached almost to the Chinese frontier; thus Russia gained another great advantage over her rivals in the markets of Sinkiang. Total recorded Sinkiang-Soviet trade in 1930 had already jumped to over 32,000,000 rubles, and in 1931 Soviet Russia reportedly obtained new and considerable trade and communications privileges in the Chinese province. When the revolt of Sinkiang Moslems during 1930-1933 led to the emergence of Sheng Shih-ts'ai, Soviet Russia extended him such substantial aid that he was able to institute sweeping changes in the territory under his administration.

The Soviet Position: One Chinese View

There are Chinese, such as the writer Chiang Chün-chang, who have intimated that the Soviet record in Sinkiang has been merely a continuation of old Tsarist imperial policy and who hint that Sheng Shih-ts'ai has been merely an instrument in the hands of Soviet Russia. Chiang, whose opinion does not necessarily represent that of most Chinese, appears to feel that Soviet as well as Tsarist Russia has been an "aggressor" in Sinkiang. His argument (in public print, 1937-1939) has been that Soviet Russia began to make great headway in Sinkiang after the assassination of Yang Tseng-hsin and after Chin Shu-jen (by specific agreement in October, 1931) had welcomed the importation of Soviet arms into the province. When Sheng Shih-ts'ai's influence had succeeded that of Chin Shu-jen, Sheng got Soviet help in overcoming provincial opposition, and relates Chiang, "has since then been one of the Soviet brood." "Sheng Shih-ts'ai has engaged Soviet advisers in his army," has not conferred "with the Ministry of Foreign Affairs," and has not sent "duplicate copies of treaties for the Executive Yüan to keep on record," Chiang adds. Though information on the extent of the authority which is held by such Soviet advisers as have been in Sinkiang is not clear and is largely based on foreign reports, Chang Chün-chang continues, it is to be feared that Soviet Russia has been sending many Kazakhs across the Soviet border into Sinkiang and has planned to have part of Sinkiang enter Soviet Kazakhstan. At the same time, he says, she has reportedly prepared Sinkiang Moslems to form a "Moslem Soviet under Soviet Russia."

These last accusations of Chiang Chün-chang are notably absent from Tu Chung-yüan's writing, and that Tu takes quite a different point of view is clear. But Chiang's statements ought not, on that account, to be eliminated from consideration completely. Their existence emphasizes that, in the recent past at least, certain influential Chinese have been suspicious of Soviet Russian intentions toward Sinkiang just as Chinese used to be suspicious of Tsarist Russia and of other powers. Since "Anti-imperialism" precedes "Kinship to Sovietism" among the Six Great Policies it is not unreasonable to feel, then, that these Policies have from the first at least been linked with a certain amount of reservation in regard to Soviet Russia. No doubt some Chinese would adhere to the following: To the degree that what Chiang Chün-chang calls Soviet "aggression" may come into too sharp conflict in Sinkiang with "Anti-imperialism" as Tu Chung-yüan conceives it, to that same degree, Sinkiang "Kinship to Sovietism" may very well be weakened. In a word, "Anti-imperialism," so far as Sinkiang is concerned, all along has been a warning to Soviet Russia as well as to other powers.

Other "Aggressors"

Yet Sinkiang "Anti-imperialism" seems to have been formulated as a reaction not only to past policies of the Chinese and Russians, but also to former ambitions of the British and others as well. Chiang Chün-chang has been more outspoken than Tu Chung-yüan about this matter. Whereas the latter has hinted mainly that a "certain" imperialist force "has increasingly fostered independence for South Sinkiang," Chiang has bluntly called the English an "aggressive force" aiming to establish an "independent government" "around Kashgar." He has even cited a "Turkish" report that British have "already" spent a considerable sum in the "South Sinkiang Movement," and he has named an A-k'un-pa-yeh-fu (Akonbaiev?) Trading Company as the supposed center for an English-sponsored Moslem movement in the province. He has even expressed his concern over the religious and other connections between the people of South Sinkiang and the people of Turkey. It is apparently his belief that France had hoped to help develop an unbroken overland empire from Syria to Indo-China through seizure of Sinkiang, and he also suspects that foreign trade interests—notably German—have been approached in Afghanistan in regard to a Sinkiang movement for Moslem independence. Such Chinese imputations may very well be exaggerated, yet they ought not to be ignored. So far as the principal Axis powers are concerned, by 1939 when war broke out in Europe, all three had openly become active sponsors of Islamic revolutionary activities with direct or indirect effect on Sinkiang Moslems.

Japan—the Foremost Imperialist

Of all these "imperialist" threats to Sinkiang, the foremost in recent years has undoubtedly been that originating in Japan. Chiang Chün-chang has reported not only Japanese sponsorship of a Moslem organization in the Altai region, but even Japanese military support of Ma Chung-ying's revolting forces during the Sinkiang insurrection of the 1930's. Since 1931, when Chinese troops were routed in Manchuria and fled through Siberia to Sinkiang, Sheng Shih-ts'ai has emphasized that the Japanese is the worst form of imperialism. This point of view has since pervaded the entire atmosphere as is strikingly evident now in Sinkiang's co-operation with the rest of China and the United Nations. When Japan attacked Manchuria on September 18, 1931, and began World War II, she set forces in motion which were to be felt not only in Manchuria but on China's whole inland frontier. From Manchuria, if unchecked, Japan might have had easy access to caravan routes which cross Outer and Inner Mongolia and which in normal times enter Sinkiang and Northwest China. Had she been able to master those overland passages she might have broken down the whole inland structure of Chinese Northwest defenses. Sheng Shih-ts'ai knew this, and as a consequence he quickly declared his opposition to Japanese imperialism. In at least this one respect he might well have been thinking along the lines of Marshal Tso Tsung-t'ang who in the nineteenth century said:

> Great weight should be given to Sinkiang as a protection to Mongolia. For as it protects Mongolia, it ensures that the power of the

capital and the forearm of the Northwest work in unison. It also ensures that there is no break in the country's topographical defenses. But if Sinkiang is not strong, then Mongolia will not be at peace. Moreover, then bandits might outflank the whole Kansu, Shensi, and Shansi frontier. In such an emergency those places might be defended, but not victoriously. In such a case, Sinkiang would be a direct north gate to the mountains, and there would not be a day of rest or sleep.

Thus, there was little question in regard to Sinkiang support for the Chinese National Government's resistance to Japan—especially after signature of the Sino-Russian Pact of Non-Aggression in August, 1937. In October, 1938, an All-Sinkiang Congress in Tihwa pointed out that Japanese machinations in Inner Mongolia had also been unsuccessfully aimed at Sinkiang. The Congress pledged not only ten airplanes for the Chinese Air Force, but also that Sinkiang would oppose "Japanese imperialism" and keep open an overland route for Chinese international communications.

The "Anglo-Americans"

Just to keep the record, it is well to know also that the New Sinkiang's open opposition to "imperialism" has not forgotten the Western Hemisphere. After the outbreak of war in Europe in September, 1939, the editorials of the *Sinkiang Daily News* referred not only to the Germans, Italians, and Japanese but also to the "Anglo-Americans" as members respectively of "imperialist" axes. This editorial line, in print before Germany attacked Soviet Russia in June, 1941, and before China formally entered into war against Germany, Italy, and Japan, resembled that followed by the Soviet Russian and Communist press in general.

An "Anti-imperialist Balance"

This, then, is what "Anti-imperialism" has meant to the New Sinkiang. The questions involved have not been simple. One might suggest, however, that at least up to 1942 the New Sinkiang was for the most part trying to promote her own self-interest by "balancing" the "weights" of political affinity to China and economic kinship to Sovietism on an "Anti-imperialist scale." The spread of Axis aggression, since the attack on Soviet Russia and the bombing of Pearl Harbor, undoubtedly affected this. It made the problems of the Sino-Russian "balance" temporarily less pressing than the question of whether the preponderance of international "weight" was to be finally on the United Nations or the Axis side of the larger, world military, "scale." This may even prove to be the main factor which has facilitated new Chinese, British, and American activity in the province. A unique opportunity seems incidentally to have been offered the United Nations with whom the province is now co-operating. Theirs is now the chance to demonstrate in practice and on the spot whether they, too, are or are not "Anti-imperialistic" in the Sinkiang sense.

V

KINSHIP TO SOVIETISM

SOME OBSERVERS have mistakenly interpreted Sinkiang adherence to "Anti-imperialism" as evidence that this Chinese province had fallen under Soviet Russian domination. Their view may even have seemed superficially substantiated by the way the New Sinkiang openly admitted her "Kinship to Sovietism." Why did the administration of Sheng Shih-ts'ai do this?

"The Soviet Russia of today is not the same as the old Russian Tsar," says Tu Chung-yüan, in giving a partial explanation. "She does not have aggressive designs . . ." Chao Lieh, another Chinese writer, echoes this sentiment in an August, 1941, *Kuei-lin Ta Kung Pao* feature article, but gives more stress, first to foreign trade and, second, to Soviet help in Sinkiang reconstruction. He adds, also, that a certain kinship necessarily has been forged between Sinkiang and Soviet Russia due to their contiguous frontiers.

There has, indeed, been "Kinship to Sovietism" in Sinkiang. By some strange quirk in Sinkiang history, originally "aggressive" processes affecting the province have brought in their wake progressive and even "radical" ideas as well as material advances for the populace. These changes came for a time almost in spite of what Chinese from China Proper, and probably others from abroad, could say or do; and they may largely be explained by a gradual drift in Sinkiang, dating from Tsarist days, toward close economic relations with Russia. Yet this evolution has not prevented the merging of the Sinkiang political program with that of Nationalist China.

The Difficulties of Early Soviet-Sinkiang Relations

It has been mentioned that, when Republican Chinese overthrew the Manchu Dynasty in 1911-1912, Sinkiang administration became the responsibility of Yang Tseng-hsin. In at least one sense the advent of his regime was fortunate. Yang's firm seizure of autocratic powers prevented political disintegration in the province, which, nominally at least, remained Chinese and did not fall into alien hands. Otherwise the old life of Sinkiang might have ended earlier in an even worse internal scramble than that of 1931—possibly Sinkiang might even have become openly a part of the Tsarist Empire. As events turned out, Yang watched the borders of his province closely and maintained cordial but not servile relations with Russia. The Bolshevik Revolution of 1917, however, created a new situation.

Unrest within Russia had manifested itself in Turkestan as early as the Kirgiz insurrection of 1916, and by the next year the Sinkiang-Russian border was severely disturbed. Gabitov indicates that the first reaction was a swiftly increasing surplus of wool. This piled up on the Russian side of the frontier, because of a lack of transport facilities to send it on to Russian and third-party markets. By 1918 the over-supply had halted much of the Sinkiang trade with Russia, and by 1920 that trade had ceased almost completely. Chinese probably were secretly relieved that revolution had upset the Tsarist tendency toward expansion in the direction of Sinkiang, but Governor Yang at first pursued strictly a policy of watchfulness. He virtually closed the Sinkiang-Russian frontier; Nazaroff, a Russian "white" who tried to escape from Russian Turkestan to Kashgar, has given a clear account of the difficulties encountered by anyone attempting to cross into

Chinese territory. By 1920 the formerly strong Russian colony in Kashgar had dwindled to only twenty-three persons.

So far as relations with the rest of China and with Russia were concerned, Governor Yang's position soon became so powerful that he could afford to dictate. Therefore it is not surprising that the terms of the following agreement which he is said to have concluded with Soviet authorities in 1920 are harsh:

1. Offices for commerce and foreign affairs will be established respectively in Russian Turkestan and in Chinese Turkestan;

2. China will have two of these offices, in the Province of Semirechia and at Verkhneudinsk; and in virtue of the principle of equality and reciprocity, Russia will have two—at I-li and at I-ning;

3. The Russian offices will inform their agents who conduct trade between I-li and Russia that they will be subject to the regulations of the general tax of Sinkiang and to the tariff of the Chinese Maritime Customs;

4. All the imports and exports must go by way of Nikang [? sic]; merchandise which takes any other route will be considered contraband and will be subject to seizure;

5. All commercial litigation between the agents of the two countries will be adjudicated by the local tribunal;

6. The agents of both countries must show their passports in passing the frontier. Questions relative to civil and military (Russian) refugees will be settled amicably.

7. The Russian representatives declare that the general amnesty decreed by the Government at Tashkent for reasons of humanity is inviolable, and that in consequence all Russian civil or military refugees in Chinese territory will be permitted to re-enter their country without fear of molestation. China engages to return them to their homes to take up once again peaceful occupations.

8. Russia will be authorized by the Government at I-li to attach an agent to the Office of Commerce and Foreign Affairs and two or three attachés charged specially with treatment of the questions relative to repatriation of the civil and military refugees; this mission will end as soon as the task is completed. The question of sequestration or confiscation of all private goods appertaining to Chinese will be regulated amicably.

9. The Russian representatives declare that, since they have not the power to treat on questions of this order themselves—until the Government at Tashkent has set up a Commission to study the question—it

is best that each claim be made the subject of friendly and direct arrangements between both governments. The Russian representatives nevertheless agree to bring before the Government at Tashkent a measure in accordance with Chinese claims.

The above stipulations, rendered in the Chinese and in the Russian languages, have been approved by the representatives of both parties each of whom is keeping a signed copy.

The most conspicuous points of this document are its local character, the new limitations on the type and extent of Russian representation in Sinkiang, the restriction of trade to one route, and the provisions stipulating return to Russia of refugees in China. Negotiations apparently were conducted between authorities of Sinkiang and Russian Turkestan, not between the Government of China and the Government of Soviet Russia. Instead of the former Tsarist right to seven consular establishments in Sinkiang, by the agreement Soviet authorities are only alloted offices for commerce and foreign affairs at Sui-ting (I-li) and nearby Ning-yüan (I-ning). Only trade via North Sinkiang is apparently provided for, and none via South Sinkiang. Finally the refugee problem, one which the White Russian-Bolshevik differences had been making difficult for Sinkiang authorities, is thrown back on the Soviets. The agreement does, however, open the way to a resumption of trade—of potential benefit to both sides. Moreover, irrespective of the restrictions in the treaty Russian agents appear to have transacted business in Sinkiang shortly afterwards from T'a Ch'eng (Chuguchak).

In 1921 Soviet authorities made a good beginning toward recouping the former Tsarist commercial position, only to lose the trust of Chinese tradesmen a year or so later. For instance, the Siberian foreign trade organization, Sibvneshtorg, opened offices at Semipalatinsk and sent an agent to T'a Ch'eng. According to Gabitov, 8,500 head of large cattle and around 169,000 sheep were successfully contracted for. The last payment on the contract was made by December of the same year, only two months after the last delivery of the cattle. This placed Sibvneshtorg on a strong basis in Sinkiang, and even livestock on credit became available to it rapidly. But in 1922 the Semipalatinsk division of Sibvneshtorg went under the control of what was then

called Kirkrai, whose name indicates a "Kirgiz regional" organization. Apparently weaker in resources and interested in local and
temporary advantage more than long-range commerce, Kirkrai soon
undermined this sound beginning.

In the fall of that same year the T'a Ch'eng representative of the
local Soviet foreign trade agency, Kirvneshtorg (presumably a foreign
trade subsidiary of Kirkrai), entered into five contracts with Sinkiang
Chinese to purchase livestock. The price was one ruble twenty kopeks
banked silver a pood, live weight, for both cattle and sheep. The
account was carefully detailed and compensation was to be made in a
barter-like fashion thus:

> 40% in manufactured goods
>   (mostly cotton)
> 25% in silver
> 18% in iron and iron manufactures
> 7% in green tea (brick)
> 7% in various crockery
> 2% in sewing thread
> 1% in glass

The cattle were taken from the market and pastured for the winter
in accordance with the agreements; but the Kirvneshtorg payments
were held up long after the cattle were delivered. In fact several traders
from China were not paid for their livestock until June, 1924; and then
many of them received payment only because they themselves traveled
all the way to Moscow to get it.

"Similar dealings," wrote Gabitov in 1925, ". . . undermined every
trust in Kirvneshtorg . . ." There were other Soviet attempts to revive the trade between 1922 and 1924, but they had little success.

Trade Shifts and Advocated Reforms

While Soviet economic relations were thus muddling along in the
north, the Soviet Government "was entirely unrepresented" in South
Sinkiang. Considerable anti-Soviet political agitation even emanated
from there. This, in turn, was accompanied by a striking shift in
trade. A considerable amount was diverted from the Kashgar-Osh

route into Russian Turkestan to trails connecting Kashgar with India, especially that via Yarkand and Ladakh (Ladok). American, British, German, and Japanese firms busily began opening offices in Sinkiang, and some of these even got as far north as Tarbagatai (T'a Ch'eng). While the main point of origin for the new trade was British India, some commerce came from Tientsin. A British firm, apparently called Agrico, even entered into an arrangement with the Russian organization Sibsel'soius of Novo-Nikolaevsk to send goods in transit through Semipalatinsk and then by Russian railway to Tientsin. These western and Japanese firms had certain very real advantages over Soviet Russia in this period. They could pay without any considerable delay, and they could pay in cash; the Russian traders, on their part, were continually delaying payment, were hampered by the Red "red tape," and often broke their contracts.

Yet even in that early period farseeing Soviet students of Central Asian economics envisaged a day when Russian trade could surpass that of other powers in Sinkiang. Gabitov advocated a number of reforms and innovations which, he concluded, would restore Russian commercial prestige. His well-considered and now historically significant recommendations included the following:

1. The transfer of the local agent of the foreign trade office from Kirkrai to Turkkrai. (This change was intended to ensure impartiality as to which area of Russian Turkestan was to be allotted a specific item of Sinkiang business.)

2. More speedy completion of a railway line from Tashkent.

3. Punctual payment of all contracts, in any case for the next one or two years, until Russia had re-established her credit.

4. The production of manufactured goods of every sort so that Russians could compete with the Japanese in the sale of cheap items in Sinkiang.

5. Reduction of cartage rates from the borders.

6. Those dealing in the area to have full knowledge of the local border and of its commercial likes and dislikes, and to maintain friendly relations with the local Chinese population.

"Under the spur of these improvements," Gabitov concluded, "it is safe to say that Russia will quickly regain her former place here in commercial relations. For, under such circumstances, English and Japanese competition with Russian goods should be exceedingly difficult."

A New Diplomatic Gain

Opportunity for Soviet Russia to regain standing in Sinkiang at last came with the opening of diplomatic relations between China and the Soviet Union in May, 1924. Not only did the Soviet Government soon reopen consulates and establish a consulate-general in the province, but commercial relations became greatly improved.

The opening of the first Soviet consulate in Sinkiang, that at T'a Ch'eng (Chuguchak), took place in December, 1924. The red flag was raised in the presence of a number of persons, including the Chinese administrator of the circuit and the Soviet consul. Some months later another Soviet consulate was opened at Sharasume (Ch'eng-hua), and a Soviet consulate-general established at Tihwa (Urumchi). By August, 1925, a Soviet consul had also taken up residence at Kashgar. China on her side utilized the new friendly relations to establish a consulate-general at Semipalatinsk, in Kazakhstan, and consulates at Tashkent, Andizhan, Zaisan, and Alma-Ata.

Though these events were a part of the increasing Chinese-Russian cordiality from 1924 to 1926, they were to have special meaning for Sinkiang-Soviet relations. For by August, 1927, bloody conflict had broken out between the Chinese Nationalists and the Chinese Communists in Central China. This quickly put a strain on the friendship that had for such a short time existed between China and the U.S.S.R. Yet Sinkiang authorities, irrespective of Central China policy, appear to have desired to keep close ties with Russia. How strong those ties had become is suggested in the following commitment assertedly made on December 28, 1927, to the editor of a Semipalatinsk newspaper:

The dark reaction in Central China has taken on frightful proportions in the unprecedented manifestations against Chinese workers and against the representatives and representations of the friendly republic of the U.S.S.R. This fact is grievous to us, for we are the official representatives of the Chinese Republic. In order to make known precisely the true situation we judge it our duty to explain that the Consulate of Semipalatinsk has nothing in common with Central China and is not able, consequently, to take upon itself the responsibility for events which have occurred recently in Central China. This consulate is dependent upon *Western China* which does not wish, in any case, to sever its friendship with the U.S.S.R.

It is true that we are supposed to be dependent also on the Government of Peking, to the degree where the acts and instructions of the latter will not be directed against the interests of *Western China*. In the opposite case, we do not consider ourselves obliged to remain obedient further to the Government of Peking, particularly in the case where its acts are able to involve a rupture of diplomatic relations between *Western China* and the friendly republic of the U.S.S.R., relations with whom are so dear and are so necessary for us, from the point of view not only of commerce but also of politics. We testify once more that the friendship of the two republics is esteemed and appreciated equally on the two sides; we find an example of this in the fact that from the first days of the recent events in Central China, the local authorities expressed their faith and friendship for us and placed an armed guard near the consulate in order to defend us against provocations of isolated individuals. The indissolubility and solidarity of the friendship between *Western China* and the U.S.S.R. is equally confirmed by the fact that we have in the U.S.S.R. five Chinese consulates from *Western China* . . . and that the U.S.S.R. possesses five consulates in *Western China* . . . in keeping with most friendly and most pacific relations. These mutual relations and the friendship between *Western China* and the U.S.S.R. should be eternal and immortal.

This document was cited in the official Soviet newspaper, *Izvestiia,* on January 8, 1928. It appeared over names which have been identified in translation as those of the Chinese Consul-General at Semipalatinsk, Lu Chan-pin, and the Secretary of the Consulate, Tien Shen-chi.

In 1927 China's Revolution had not yet brought about complete unity, and seats of so-called Chinese national government existed in both Central China and North China (Peking). In that regard, this unique declaration states: first, that Sinkiang ("Western China") assertedly had "nothing in common with Central China" in 1927 and, in case of a conflict of interest, did not even feel obliged "to remain obedient" to the "Government of Peking"; second, that Sinkiang in

1927 did "not wish, in any case, to sever its friendship with the U.S.S.R."; and third, that the Chinese Consulate-General at Semipalatinsk and the "five" other Chinese Consulates in the U.S.S.R. (apparently a reference to those in Russian Turkestan at Semipalatinsk, Tashkent, Andizhan, Zaissan, and Alma-Ata) were in 1927 all "dependent upon" or "from" "Western China." Since this representation was published in *Izvestiia* and seems to have been signed by the Consul-General and the Secretary of the Chinese Consulate-General at Semipalatinsk, it may with good reason be considered official. Those who have criticized Sheng Shih-ts'ai and the New Sinkiang for "Kinship to Sovietism" may well be referred to this declaration as a most outstanding bit of evidence that such kinship has been a broad historical tendency and has not been "conceived' merely since 1933.

The "Seven-Seven" Affair and Chin Shu-jen

Yet seven months later—on July 7, 1928—Sinkiang Governor Yang Tseng-hsin was assassinated. Sinkiang remembers this date as the "Seven-Seven" Affair and has given it a place in the history of provincial emancipation comparable in importance to that of the later "Four-Twelve" Affair.

Blame for Yang's murder has been placed on Fan Yao-nan, a brilliant young man who was then Sinkiang Special Commissioner for Foreign Affairs. With many of the details lacking, it is of little moment here to speculate too much on the internal politics involved. But the fact that the crime was committed at a time so proximate (1) to the Semipalatinsk declaration on "Western China" (Sinkiang) foreign policy and (2) to the anti-Communist and anti-Soviet demonstrations at Nanking, ought not to be ignored. All was not well in 1928 so far as Tihwa-Nationalist attitude toward Soviet Russia was concerned.

Dr. Sven Hedin testifies that Yang's successor, Chin Shu-jen, attempted in the early years of his brief regime (as Yang Tseng-hsin for a time had done before him) to close off outside access to Sinkiang. But a combination of factors, including popular dislike of Chin himself and the incidence of the Moslem revolt of 1930 and 1931, so weakened his position that he in turn also fell back on Soviet Russia for aid.

In October, 1931, when the Tung-kan rebel Ma Chung-ying had successfully captured Barkol (Chen-hsi) and Ha-mi, Chin signed a new agreement with the Soviets. By it he permitted the opening of Soviet trade agencies in Tihwa, T'a Ch'eng, Sui-ting, and Kashgar and of outlying offices in Aqsu, Kucha, Yarkand, and Khotan. By the same document he also permitted unrestricted movement in Sinkiang for Soviet trade representatives, provided for reduced custom duties on Soviet goods, and initiated new Sinkiang-Soviet telegraph and radio privileges. Sinkiang is supposed to have received in return only (1) a limited right for two-way transit of goods of Chinese origin across Siberia from Sinkiang to Eastern China and back, and (2) an intimation that the Soviet Government would send specialists to train the Chinese of Sinkiang in the fields of electrification, communications, rural economy, and animal husbandry. For signing this treaty without authorization and for not reporting it to Nationalist China's Ministry for Foreign Affairs, Chin Shu-jen was later sentenced to imprisonment in Nanking.

The new agreement did not save the situation for Chin, nor did it end Sinkiang civil war. As we know, Chin fled from Tihwa and left his one time "underling," Sheng Shih-ts'ai, to pacify the Sinkiang people. Sheng soon found his military difficulties increasing so much that he, too, at last called upon Soviet Russian troops to aid him in suppressing the rebellion. It is known that Soviet Russian personnel and military aid were sent him; more than one "neutral" eye-witness has testified that such actually happened.

Why Soviet Aid to Sheng?

It is not difficult to understand why Soviet Russia should have been interested enough in Sinkiang events to give Sheng Shih-ts'ai substantial help in suppressing provincial revolt. Owen Lattimore was a sound prophet for the time when he wrote for publication in 1930 that ". . . Chinese control of Chinese Turkestan, though maintained with admirable ability, is only maintained as it were from month to

68

month . . . A struggle for the succession to power . . . would precipitate Russian control, if not formal Russian rule."

Re-establishment of formal Soviet political relations with Sinkiang under Yang Tseng-hsin had given Soviet foreign trade interests a grand new opportunity; and completion of the Turksib Railway, on the Soviet side of the frontier, in 1930 climaxed this. The new railway could bring Moscow's latest products to the doors of Sinkiang in but a few days, and therefore Soviet trade could successfully overcome all competition—including that from the Chinese and British. By 1930 Sinkiang was already falling economically into the hands of her Soviet neighbor; and the Ha-mi insurrection left Chin Shu-jen too weak to resist the trend.

When civil war came, it threw the province not only into military and political, but even into financial, chaos. Sinkiang money was then principally fiat paper currency, with little value once public confidence had been lost; and the civil war indeed destroyed public confidence in it. To a certain extent the evil might have been alleviated by shipment of real goods out of the province and by deposit of the foreign or Nationalist Chinese currency receipts in foreign banks or other banks elsewhere in China. But, since Soviet Russia had gained a near monopoly on Sinkiang trade, outside currency could be obtained for Sinkiang inhabitants practically only by Soviet sufferance. Through her control of Sinkiang trade Soviet Russia had gained a hold on Sinkiang finances as well.

Nor did Soviet Russia have reason to consider her favored position in Sinkiang lightly. Between 1923/24 and 1930 inclusive, Sinkiang annual exports into the U.S.S.R. had risen from 3,015,000 to 16,033,000 rubles; and annual imports into Sinkiang from the U.S.S.R. had leaped from 418,000 to 16,027,000 rubles. This meant a rise in the total annual trade from 3,433,000 to 32,060,000 rubles. Moreover, up to that date, in tonnage as well as in value of visible items of trade, Soviet Russia had continually received more from Sinkiang than she had returned. That situation even continued from 1931 to 1937 inclusive, so far as recorded bulk is concerned, though it altered at times in respect to recorded value. It was not merely the rubles that could be realized from what Sinkiang had or would buy—not merely the wool, the cotton, sheep guts, livestock, and horses that came across the border—that made Sinkiang so valuable to the Soviet Union. Japanese occupation of Manchuria in 1931 had upset the whole strategic orientation of Northeast Asia; and a new, dynamic Soviet interest in Sinkiang development was a logical counter. A new aggressive force had thrust herself upon the Asiatic continent and, from the Soviet point of view, had endangered not only the Soviet Maritime Province and Mongolia but the whole Russian strategic position in Northeastern and Central Asia. For Manchuria is but a part, the easternmost sector, of a vast and interrelated Inner Asian living space which includes Mongolia and Turkestan and which quickly reacts in each of its distinct parts to political changes in any other part. Specifically, from Manchuria there is in normal times relatively easy access to the caravan routes which cross into Sinkiang from Outer and Inner Mongolia. Should Japan master or influence those, Russia would be completely outflanked in Asia. Already by 1933 Japanese designs on Jehol and Inner Mongolia had been revealed, and they were thought to have been reflected in the Sinkiang war. Had China herself been able to consolidate Sinkiang strongly in opposition to Japanese intrigues, perhaps Soviet concern would have been less. But the flight of Chin Shu-jen in 1933 left instead a Sinkiang political chaos which Soviet Russia could ignore only at her own peril.

The specific technique by which Soviet aid was given Sheng Shih-ts'ai has not been adequately revealed. But without an attempt at too complicated an analysis, it can be indicated by a glance at the record of Soviet-Sinkiang commerce since 1923. The steady increase by bulk in total Soviet import-export trade with Sinkiang from 1923/24 continued till 1931 and 1932, when sharp drops were registered. After 1933 on trade again rose. The bulk rise in 1933, practically all of it, represents Sinkiang shipments to Soviet Russia; that in 1934 mostly Soviet shipments to Sinkiang. The trade figures after that show a steady rise by bulk on both sides. By 1936 and 1937 total import-export trade had jumped to over 60,000,000 rubles in value and to over 50,000 tons in bulk—in sharp contrast with the record of around 3,000,000 rubles and 13,000 tons in the year 1923/24.

There may be no positive proof gained, but it is nevertheless worth while to point out: (1) that 1931 and 1932 were the years of the initial great strain of the civil war and years when Soviet-Sinkiang trade might therefore be strongly hit; (2) that in 1933 Sheng Shih-ts'ai together with his Manchurian and Russian aides had already begun to regain control of the trade route from Tihwa to T'a Ch'eng on the Russian border and so might be able to utilize that route once again; (3) that 1934 was the crucial year for the province and that during that year considerable Soviet aid came to Sheng Shih-ts'ai, who as a consequence was able to repulse his arch-rival, Ma Chung-ying; and (4) that Sinkiang political "unity" is said to have come in 1936, by which time a new prosperity in Soviet-Sinkiang trade relations had become obvious. The temporal relationship thus shows a rough correlation in the shifts of Sinkiang politics and war to trade in the same period.

Exact information on the nature of Soviet aid to Sheng Shih-ts'ai and of Soviet participation in Sinkiang affairs has up to now been quite successfully kept from most public knowledge in the Occident. But, in describing Soviet-Sinkiang relations, Chinese stress Sheng Shih-ts'ai's desire to "revive" Sinkiang through provincial reconstruction. Since his plans required backing in the form of capital and talent, it is said, he turned at first to Soviet Russia.

As a matter of fact, he probably had almost nowhere else to turn in the 1930's; besides he was in debt for Soviet help in suppressing the insurrection. And by 1933 trade with Soviet Russia had grown to be so important that to turn elsewhere might have seemed contrary to the economic interests of his province.

The Soviet Position: A Second Chinese View

Up to this point, the argument fits in with the explanation previously given for Sinkiang's concern over possible Soviet Russian "imperialism" in her region. Yet, whereas Chiang Chün-chang has carried it on from this stage to hint that Soviet Russia as well as Tsarist Russia has been an "aggressor" in Sinkiang, Tu Chung-yüan insists, instead, that "Kinship to Sovietism" has been anything but insidious. Tu admits that in Sinkiang specialists in animal husbandry, doctors in hospitals, pharmacists of the provincial pharmacy, and instructors for the provincial Military Officers Academy and for the provincial Air Force have come from Soviet Russia. But, he inquires, does that mean Sinkiang has gone "Red"? Did not Soviet Russia, at the beginning of her national reconstruction, get assistance "from thousands upon tens of thousands" of "capitalist" experts? Yet wouldn't it be difficult to say Soviet Russia is "White"? According to Tu, there has never been Soviet political control in Sinkiang. If Soviet Russia had "controlled" Sinkiang politically, would she have tolerated the White Russians who still remained there? Have not the Three People's Principles textbooks of Sinkiang been identical with those elsewhere in Nationalist China? Are not the military and administrative authority of Sinkiang still in the hands of China?

"Kinship to Sovietism" and Chinese Nationalism

It appears that up to Sheng Shih-ts'ai's accession to power, Sinkiang's concern with the Chinese National Revolution and its *San Min Chu-i* (The "Three People's Principles" of Nationalism, Democracy, and the People's Livelihood) was not too serious. Sinkiang was geographically and economically a great distance from most other Chinese provinces, her leaders were devoted almost exclusively to selfish acquisition of wealth, and the Chinese Republic's then existing national political structure was not mature in Sinkiang. Since 1933, however, the year of the "Four-Twelve" Affair, Sheng Shih-ts'ai has altered this. As politics have taken on national stature elsewhere in China, Sheng Shih-ts'ai's background and interests have carried Chinese political organization and support of the Three People's Principles in a new way into the far Northwest. Remembering Japan's invasion of his Manchurian homeland in 1931, Sheng Shih-ts'ai has also warmly supported China's resistance to the aggressor; and having seen the needs of his own administrative region, he has particularly devoted himself to its reconstruction. Thus his work has fitted neatly into both the basic revolutionary program of the Three People's Principles and the wartime program of *K'ang-chan Chien-kuo* or "Resistance and Reconstruction." True, Sinkiang's Six Great Policies of Anti-imperialism, Kinship to Sovietism,

Racial Equality, Clean Government, Peace, and Reconstruction are unique. But they are not so strange to the ideals of China that they do not keep within the bounds of Nationalist principles, of Chinese political unity, of successful resistance to Japan, and of freedom from Soviet Russian domination.

This view is further supported by a brief glance at the manner in which Sinkiang's interprovincial and international record has evolved since 1934.

Sinkiang and World Affairs, 1934-1943

It was largely Soviet help which enabled Sheng Shih-ts'ai to gain mastery of Sinkiang, but in 1934 Chinese authorities from Nanking still had been able to attempt negotiation of the civil war and formation of a compromise administration. Since Soviet troops had operated with the White Russian forces already in Sinkiang, it is obvious that their restoration of order had been a "coalition measure" and not an attempt at immediate Soviet annexation. Soviet military aid is, in fact, said to have been withdrawn as soon as order began to appear though "Kinship to Sovietism" remained important in Sinkiang affairs. By 1936 Sheng Shih-ts'ai had established a "unified" government in all Sinkiang.

Outbreak of open Sino-Japanese hostilities in July, 1937, made Sinkiang an obvious region for Chinese-Soviet compromise. The treaty signed by both Governments in August, 1937, guaranteed there would be no Russian aggression against China; and a through overland truck and air route, between eastern China and Soviet Russia, through Sinkiang, was thereby made practicable. Sinkiang's three-year plan of reconstruction was instituted with Soviet advices in the same year. By the fall of 1938, when China had been forced to retreat from Hankow into the west, Sinkiang's new truck highways provided assurance that China would not be internationally isolated in her Northwest. At that time Tihwa even telegraphed a resolution to that effect, pledging that the province would keep open China's international communication lines, would intensify efforts to help fulfill the national Resistance and Reconstruction program, and would work with the rest of China to-

73

ward ultimate victory over Japan. Other Chinese negotiations culminated in signature of a new trade agreement with Soviet Russia on June 16, 1939. By it, though not expressly mentioned in the text, the use of Sinkiang's international communication lines was underwritten.

But Russia's Treaty of Non-aggression with Nazi Germany in August, 1939, introduced a new guardedness into Sino-Russian relations. The march of Soviet armies into Poland, Finland, and the Baltic countries after the opening of European war gave rise for a while to a fear that Russia might at the same time be considering initiation of a "forward" policy against China through Sinkiang. This fear was evidenced in late 1939 by a noticeable falling off of the truck traffic that had already begun to pass between Russia and China along the Sinkiang-Kansu motor road. China concentrated exceptionally heavy numbers of soldiers in the northwest provinces of Shensi, Kansu, Ningsia, and Ch'inghai. This was a wartime precautionary measure, but many of the troops were only ostensibly training for the Sino-Japanese war front to the northeast and east. Final ratification of the Sino-Russian trade agreement was, moreover, delayed until early 1940.

Sinkiang, through her policies supporting both Soviet Russia's actions in the west and China's resistance to Japan in the east, however, became more important than before in the role of a kind of Chungking-Moscow "middleman." At this time the *Sinkiang Daily News* was interpreting the policies of both of the benefactors of the province as aspects of a "Eurasian" front for "peace" and "anti-imperialism." It was also following the then current Soviet line of deriding the so-called "imperialist axes" in the world. This attitude neared its high point at the close of 1940 and early in 1941. When signature of the Tripartite German-Italian-Japanese Alliance was announced on September 27, 1940, the *Sinkiang Daily News* commented to the effect that the contradictions between the "two imperialist forces" of the German-Japanese-Italian Axis and the "Anglo-Americans" would soon bring an open clash between them while an armed peace would persist on the Eurasian "peace" front.

Yet, as throughout the war, Sheng Shih-ts'ai evidenced continued support of the Chinese Nationalist Government. On December 8, 1940, he joined other Chinese leaders in condemning the Wang Ching-wei Chinese puppet regime which had recently been recognized by Japan. At the turn of 1941 also, when differences between the Chinese Communists and the Kuomintang over the New Fourth Army seemed to have approached a breaking point, he reiterated his position. He told a *Ta Kung Pao* newspaper correspondent (1) that Sinkiang was devoting her whole strength to transport work and reconstruction in order to hasten Chinese victory; and (2) that all parties and cliques in China should continue in their united resistance to Japan.

Whether or not this was an attempt to maintain a "balance" between Sinkiang's political affinity to China and her economic kinship to Sovietism, it was soon to be proved insufficient. For Soviet Russia and Japan signed a non-aggression agreement on April 15, 1941; and by an accompanying joint declaration Soviet Russia formally recognized "Manchoukuo" in return for Japanese recognition of the Soviet-sponsored "Republic of Outer Mongolia." The new agreement and declaration were sound business for Soviet Russia, who thus became more free to face the Nazi attack when it came on June 22, 1941. Somewhat differently they offered Japan more freedom for activities in Southeast Asia and Pearl Harbor, both of which she attacked on December 7, 1941.

But the easing of Soviet-Japanese tension over Manchuria and Outer Mongolia did not erase the basic contradictions on which the Asiatic policies of the two countries had been based. For the inner Asian flank of Sinkiang and Inner Mongolia was left formally unaccounted for. In these zones either power might possibly attack the interests of China (and less directly the interests of each other) without violation of any public agreement. This, in turn, made Sinkiang more desperately concerned than ever with the strength of Chinese defenses on her east, in West Suiyüan and Ningsia (Inner Mongolia), not to mention the provinces of Shensi, Shansi, and Kansu. The Soviet-Japanese accord postponed any final decision in the area, but at the same time it made possible the intensification of Japanese intrigues on the less protected Sinkiang frontier farther inland.

This, with other factors, has now drawn Sinkiang closer than ever to the fold of Nationalist China and has even helped effect a significant shift—perhaps temporarily—away from Soviet Russia. Sinkiang's anxiety concerning the recently exposed areas on her eastern borders was matched in 1942 by Nationalist Chinese interest in wartime development of precisely the same region. Such interest, instigated by the Japanese threat to Southwest China from Burma and Western Yünnan and possibly backed by ample monetary credit from the United States, has brought a new and stirring Nationalist activity in all Northwest China including Sinkiang. At present, therefore, there appears to be (1) the closest expression to date of Sinkiang-Nationalist co-operation in internal Chinese affairs; and (2) at least a temporary substitution of Nationalist Chinese influence in the Sinkiang area for that of Soviet Russia. It may still be too early to say conclusively whether this change has or has not been accomplished without serious international differences. Press dispatches of October and November, 1943, in connection with Russian "withdrawal" from Sinkiang suggest the shift has been carried out "without unpleasant incidents of any kind," "peacefully, with the minimum of possible friction." Yet more recent (though scanty) dispatches (issued under Ulan Bator and Chungking datelines) state that both at the close of last year as well as in March of this year, small armed clashes took place on the Sinkiang-Mongolian frontier. During the incidents in question, it is alleged, Soviet as well as Chinese airplanes went into action when a question arose as to Chinese treatment of Kazakh nomads in the Altai area. These incidents do not, however, necessarily warrant hasty assumption that a change in Sinkiang policy has come which will be permanent; neither need they prove that the whole structure of "Kinship to Sovietism" in the New Sinkiang is in the process of destruction. The unfolding pattern is, instead, another clear demonstration that "Kinship to Sovietism" has not meant Soviet Russian political domination over Sinkiang, which has on the contrary retained and strengthened her political ties with the Chinese National Government.

VI

RACIAL EQUALITY

THOUGH ESTIMATES of the Sinkiang population have run from as low as one to as high as six million, since the present Sheng Shih-ts'ai administration came to power the local people speak of their population as "four million persons." The great majority of these "four million" appear to be a combination of so-called Turkic-Tatar and "Alpine" racial stocks. The remainder are divided between a "ruling" group of so-called "Han" Chinese, a group of "Tung-kan" or Moslem Chinese, and groups of other minorities which include Manchus, Mongols, Kirgiz, Kazakhs, Tajiks, and Russians.

So far as Occidentals are concerned, "Racial Equality" in Sinkiang might, in general, mean justice and equal opportunity for and between these little known ethnic groups. So far as Sinkiang herself is concerned, however, it would seem to mean mainly a military, political, economic, and social readjustment between a minority of "Han" Chinese overlords and a majority of Chinese subject peoples. The "Han" overlords of Sinkiang, it turns out, are the "Chinese" with whom the Occident has normally been acquainted; under their rule in times past the natives of Sinkiang were not given their full measure of freedom and equality. The fact that old-style Chinese rule has been in recent years confronted with the neighboring system of Soviet Russian cultural autonomy, has in the main forced the need for change.

The Moslem Wei-wu-erh

Most of the Turkic-"Alpine" ethnic groups in the province speak a relatively pure Eastern Turki tongue and believe in Mohammedanism. This majority, whom Chinese from farther east have given a name which may have a rather derogatory meaning—*Ch'an-t'ou* (Chanto or "Turban Head")—are to be found almost everywhere and yet each local group has in a way been able to retain or to develop some claim to distinctiveness. Thus there is a tendency to call the people of Kashgar "Kashgarliq;" those of Turfan, "Turfanliq," those of Korla (K'u-erh-lo), "Kuerhliq," those of Ha-mi (Qomul), "Qomuliq," and on and on. There has also, however, been a countertendency to associate these exceptionally localized Turkic and "Alpine" ethnic types as a whole with the Uighur race that flourished anciently in the Sinkiang area. Since Sheng Shih-ts'ai came to power in Sinkiang, these *Ch'an Hui* (or Chanto) have been given the name of *Wei-wu-erh,* a Chinese transliteration of "Uighur."

It is not clear precisely what the earliest racial stock inhabiting the Western Regions, or present-day Sinkiang, was. Investigation has disclosed the existence of relatively ancient independent peoples in the Altai region, perhaps as early as the third century B.C., and one pioneer student of the subject has described their history as being "mysteriously wrapped up" in that of the Uighurs "from the far south of Mongolia. . . ." The Uighurs are supposed to have been a light-haired and blue-eyed people and in them, it is insisted, is to be found the "origin of the Turkish race who, later on, overflowed all Central Asia and made an Empire on the shore of the Bosphorus."

Some of these Uighur peoples of Sinkiang seem at one time to have believed in Manichaeism—the doctrines of the Persian, Manes—but they were willing to try their religious luck elsewhere. They became in turn Nestorian Christians, Buddhists, and finally and most permanently, Moslems. In the eighth century—when almost simultaneous Tibetan and Arab attacks had forced the Chinese armies of Kao Hsien-chih to fall back in retreat from Turkestan and when the Arab forces were advancing successfully under Qutaiba to the edge of the Pamirs—the Uighurs gradually turned to Islam. As the T'ang Dynasty's military standing declined in Turkestan, its nominal subjects—the Uighurs—began to carry on for it the burden of colonial rule. The Uighur prestige grew so swiftly that, before the tenth century was well under way, they wielded the balance of power in Turkestan from their capital at Bishbalik, near the site of the present Sinkiang capital, Tihwa. During this period they served almost as an overland bridge for the introduction of Mohammedan culture into China. The Uighurs themselves derived considerable cultural benefit from their newly gained strategic position; and their language, Turki, was established permanently in

Sinkiang from this time on. Under their kindly patronage a cosmopolitan scholarship developed in the Western Regions, and to it Arab, Khitan, Mongol, Persian, and Tibetan, as well as Chinese, contributed. The vestiges of learned tomes, once impressive shrines, and even whole cities that are buried in the sands of the Takla Makan are evidences even now of this once flourishing native culture.

Authorities of the New Sinkiang have been re-awakening the pride of the Wei-wu-erh people of today on the basis of this ancient kingdom's grandeur, and these Wei-wu-erh may indeed be the modern heirs of the Uighur traditions. Tu Chung-yüan, who is one of those who openly calls the Wei-wu-erh the original settlers of the province, says that they are distributed throughout the south and in much of the north, being especially strong around Ha-mi, Kucha, Kashgar, and Khotan.

One of their principal centers is Kashgar. Perhaps these people are not as strict as some other Mohammedans in their observance of the principles of the Koran, but they do have great reverence for many Islamic rites and observances. They are of the Sunni sect, one of the two great branches into which Islam was split in 645 when the Caliphate was assumed by Ali, the Prophet's son-in-law, in the midst of a dispute over the succession which has remained heated ever since. Whereas the Kanjutis across the border in Northwest India are Shias and follow a leader who traces his lineage to Caliph Ali, the Wei-wu-erh of Kashgar are among the most loyal Sunni Moslems in Chinese Turkestan.

The Wei-wu-erh have deep-set eyes and high noses, and Chinese are inclined to group them racially with the Turks. The girls are often exceptionally beautiful, with eyelashes inclined upwards and with jet hair topped by cheery pompoms and quaint petite caps. Maturity comes early in Turkestan, and often these girls marry before they are fifteen. Betrothal is pledged by a girl's father and mother, and the ceremony is performed by the local *A-hung,* or priest. There is understandable gaiety on the occasion, and considerable piping and drumming. The bride finally is borne on a donkey to the house of her future husband for completion of the ritual. If the husband and wife do not prove to be compatible they are, like all Moslems, permitted to divorce. "In case the husband separates from his wife," Tu Chung-yüan explains, "the household goods are entrusted to the wife; if she separates from her husband, she does not get the household goods. A son is the property of his father; a girl, the property of the mother. After a half year's separation, it is not improper to remarry."

Marriage and divorce in Turkestan, in fact, not so long ago came with a frequency that was alarming. Go-betweens of a city could customarily find a bride for almost any newly arrived traveler. One story, which gives a hundred days as the waiting period before new nuptials, credits a certain rather gay young lady with marrying a man in one locality, divorcing him ostensibly as a result of a dispute, and then receiving the requisite official document testifying she was again free. After one hundred days she married again, loved, quarreled, and divorced even more rapidly, and thus obtained another document. Now having two such papers in her possession, she traveled to another town where she began her amours and marriages once more and *ad infinitum,* for by this time she always had authority in her possession entitling her to a man in advance of the stipulated one-hundred-day period.

Yet unfaithfulness *per se* in a lady has more frequently brought humiliating punishment. The face of one such untrustworthy wife was given a dusting with soot, and she was then seated backwards upon a donkey. The butt for all types of abuse and invective, she was led thus from bazaar to bazaar and her wickedness exposed openly to the populace.

The Wei-wu-erh tribesman is a picturesque figure in his long, bright-colored cloth coat. This garment has long sleeves which he pulls down over his hands in place of gloves in winter, and it is tied about the waist with a kerchief. His cap is usually of common cloth but sometimes of velvet with fur around the edges. Beneath his coat he wears pantaloons usually reaching down to within about six inches of his feet, which are often encased in leather boots with detachable slippers. The ladies are often dressed similarly, but in beautiful vari-colored and gaily designed wraps or in cloth coats of white or some light color. These, as in the case of the men, hide trousers. The face veil sometimes has fine lace work and a delicately embroidered fringe. Not all the

Wei-wu-erh ladies bother with the convention of the veil, however, and some merely keep it thrown off the face and trailing down the back.

Good food is the watchword of the Wei-wu-erh of Kashgar, and his restaurants and shops are well provided. An abundance of melons, mulberries, plums, pears, pomegranates, peaches, and apricots, are seasonably available; and they are sold from open stalls in the local bazaar. *Mantu,* a dish of small meat dumplings, is a favorite repast, and there is also an abundance of steaming soups, fresh salad greens, and a local style of doughnut. The principal diet is, however, mutton and rice. This is accompanied by cooked onions, turnips, spinach, or potatoes. The common man usually partakes of only two meals a day, but feasts have been known to begin in early morning and to end only at sunset. What delightful, varied-tasting Chinese dishes can be served at Kashgar banquets! A few samples of such festive dishes are: ducks'-egg soup, stags' tendons, sharks' fins, bamboo shoots, wild duck, preserved eggs, all manner of pungent sauces, roasted mutton, sweet-sour fish, and many, many kinds of chicken—boned, broiled, roasted, fried in quarters, chopped, and sliced and fried in strips.

There are also many types of Wei-wu-erh entertainment. In the narrow streets a fortune-teller, sitting cross-legged, will ever be ready to promise good fortune for a few cents. The tea-shop, where the Wei-wu-erh, unlike the Han Chinese, drinks his tea with sugar, is another congenial spot. Theaters were for a long time unknown, but a Chinese performance is nowadays a pleasant diversion; and Soviet motion pictures have also been brought to town. There is dancing, too, but it is not the kind common to the Occident; and it is for the men. Only in rare instances do the women join in the dance. Kite-flying is popular with the young Wei-wu-erh, while the most strenuous sport for the adults is the game of *ulagh.* This is played on horseback in teams and has a distant resemblance to polo; the object, though, is to retrieve the carcass of a goat or a sheep. It is a wild, uproarious, racing *melee,* and the source of endless excitement and laughter.

"Han" Chinese

Tu Chung-yüan states that the "ruling" Chinese (he calls them "Han" by way of contrast to the rest of the population) constitute about ten per cent of the people of Sinkiang. It is doubtful if the exact number who live in Sinkiang is known, but Owen Lattimore indicated in 1934, at the start of Sheng Shih-ts'ai's administration, that they numbered one to two hundred thousand and were mostly distributed in the north. These are, in a sense, the "Chinese" with whom the Occident has long been familiar. But often they are descendants of men who came to Sinkiang as criminal exiles. Other Han Chinese migrated there as merchants. Many came as a "gravy train" along with appointment of a leading official from their home region. Tso Tsung-t'ang, who "pacified" the Chinese Northwest near the close of the Manchu Dynasty and was mainly responsible for formal establishment of the province, was a Hunan man and brought many Hunanese into Sinkiang with him. In like manner, Yang Tseng-hsin, who had a long term as governor at the turn of the twentieth century, brought many from his native province of Yünnan. Chin Shu-jen later added more from Kansu.

These Han Chinese became mainly the administrators, the soldiers, the traders, the businessmen, the shopkeepers, of their communities. Shansi men have been noted as money-lenders, Pei-p'ing and Tientsin men as general merchants, and Hunan and Hupeh men particularly as dealers in brick tea. Chinese entering Sinkiang from the east did not often become farmers except for a few, such as those who fled from dire poverty in Kansu and Shensi. Usually the Han have located in the larger cities of the province, and the great majority have settled around Tihwa and Sui-ting and some in Kashgar, farther south.

Han Chinese organized and maintained much of the trade which passed through Sinkiang from the Occident to the Orient and back in olden days. Theirs was principally a commerce in tea, silk, and spices, and the commodities for which these things were exchanged, such as furs, skins, jade, and rare metals. Due to troublesome factors of distance and topography, as well as of war and politics, this remained for the most part a luxury commerce, and was always too precarious of itself to support the outlying frontier. The "foreign trade," it has been said, went "over the heads" of the native population. It did so because it was largely a Han-Occidental, and not so much Sinkiang-Occidental, commerce.

Today at last Han Chinese appear destined to settle on the land in Sinkiang. If successful this should be a substantial gain to the province and should give their colonization more permanence than that of previous days. Yet, the question of what land is being allotted to these Han Chinese will merit most careful handling. For allocation of native soil to "outlanders" has long been a touchy subject in Sinkiang.

The Tung-kan: Chinese Moslems

Among the Han Chinese of Sinkiang there are a large number who adhere to the Mohammedan faith and yet are distinct from the other Moslems of the province. These *Han Hui* ("Han Moslems") are also known as *Tung-kan Hui* or often just as *Tung-kan* (Dungan). The name, Tung-kan, has been explained in many ways. Chiang Chün-chang says it is of Russian origin and means "Mohammedan Offenders of the East" or "Offenders of the East." Another variation, *Kan Hui,* according to Chiang, means "Mohammedans of Kansu" and indicates that many of the Tung-kan hail from there. Probably the Tung-kan are offspring of Central Asians who wandered into Kansu and married Chinese women. Owen Lattimore concludes that, in a kind of reverse migration, they were sent back into Chinese Turkestan during Manchu Dynasty times in order to offset Mongol influence. They are quite distinct from the "head-binding," or turbaned, Wei-wu-erh; the two groups have often opposed each other violently, and before China's resistance to Japan it was said that they had in common only their religion.

One finds the Tung-kans not only in Sinkiang but throughout the Chinese Northwest, particularly in Shensi, Kansu, Ningsia, and Ch'inghai. As a racial group they are said to be of greater virility than the regular Han Chinese; they are of a fine, sturdy stock and are particularly noted for their soldiery. They are also devoted Moslems. The most usual surname among them is Ma, the Chinese character for horse, which may represent a Chinese attempt at transliterating the sound "Mohammed." The saying that *Wu Ma,* "Five Ma," rule the Chinese Northwest, shows how strong the power of the Tung-kans has been in modern China.

Many of the Tung-kans have traditionally settled in Ha-mi, Kara-shahr, Sui-ting and Tihwa. It was Moslems from Ha-mi, near the Kansu border, who summoned the Tung-kan leader Ma Chung-ying from Kansu to lead the revolt of the early 1930's (see pp. 40-5). As a consequence of the civil war Tung-kans are now scattered almost throughout South Sinkiang. In 1935 when they gave up Kashgar they were assigned their own "domain" at Khotan, which they had previously fortified and made the focus for their abortive Mohammedan state. Some of them may even still be under arms. Recent news concerning the Tung-kan armies of Central Asia has not always been freely available, but reports have said they have been strongest in the outlying towns of Southern Sinkiang—Posgam, Karghalik, Guma, Khotan, Chira, Keriya, Cherchen, and Charklik. The 1942 appointment of Ma Pu-ch'ing, famous Tung-kan leader of Shensi and Kansu, as Pacification Commissioner of the Tsaidam Marches of Western Ch'inghai, is of interest in this connection. For the attitude, belligerent or otherwise, of the Chinese Tung-kans of neighboring provinces carries great weight among their kinsmen in Sinkiang.

Manchus and Manchurians

Manchus came to greatest prominence in Sinkiang during the expansionist periods of the Ta Ch'ing (Manchu) Dynasty of China. K'ang Hsi (1662-1722) and Ch'ien Lung (1736-1795) sent thousands of Manchu "Bannermen" to fortify the Turkestan frontier. Thus Sinkiang was garrisoned at one and the same time against Imperialist Russian aggression and against uprisings of the Tung-kans.

These Manchus at one time were scattered throughout the larger cities of Sinkiang but today they appear to have been mostly assimilated into Han Chinese ways of living. Two of the most notable exceptions have been the Sibo and Solon peoples in the Sui-ting and the T'a Ch'eng areas. The Sibos (Hsi-po) and the Solons (So-lun), though from Manchuria, actually are of Tungusic origin, only indirectly of Manchu stock and distinct from the other Bannermen who for the most part made up the Manchu military organizations sent into Sinkiang. Most of the Bannermen gradually lost their identity because they had not held land or engaged in trade in Sinkiang, but not so the Solons and the Sibos. They settled on the land and colonized in a resolute way.

The Japanese invasion of Manchuria in 1931 has brought many Manchurians into Sinkiang as refugees. These took a prominent place immediately in the life of the New Sinkiang, and they have constituted a considerable numerical addition to those already in the province.

Since Sheng Shih-ts'ai is a Manchurian, his administration has offered this people another unique role in Sinkiang, comparable to that of the Bannermen of previous days. Sheng and those of his blood, for one thing, can serve as "middlemen" between the Han Chinese from other provinces and the Wei-wu-erh. For another, by helping in the reconstruction of Sinkiang they can be preparing a formidable supply base in the "rear" by which their Manchurian homeland may ultimately be liberated from Japan.

The Mongols

Genghis Khan's Mongols, who in the thirteenth century subjugated Chinese Turkestan and long were dominant there, now amount to only about five per cent of the Sinkiang inhabitants. Picturesque in their role as nomadic horsemen, but not so picturesque in their susceptibilities to drink, the Mongols of Sinkiang constitute one of the great ethnological curiosities of the world. They have a great past to look back to; yet how they have changed! They once possessed the vigor and strength to sweep across all Asia in conquest and even to terrify Europe; they set up vast kingdoms and in the heyday of Kublai Khan, the Mongol Court at Peking was liberal and cultured, a great patron of the arts. But for four hundred years the Mongols have been under the religious whip of the Lamaist church, and only now in the twentieth century are they gradually rebelling, under the spur of ideas introduced from Soviet Russia.

A fascinating figure they cut as they swagger about in long varicolored gowns, large over-sized knee-boots, and broad-brimmed and cone-topped hats. They are persistent drinkers, and can have a rousingly good time on almost anything intoxicating from *arak* or Russian vodka to a rare imported brandy. The rough, unkempt Kalmuck Mongols of the Tekes Valley of North Sinkiang are especially devil-may-care fellows; but they have, at times, got amazingly rich from their countless horses and sheep.

A vast sweep of nomad devastation, which won them the throne of China and carried their warfare as far west as the Danube, brought the Mongols to Chinese Turkestan. What is now both Chinese and Russian Turkestan, once those areas were subjugated, came under Jagatai, second son of Genghis Khan, and he and his successors remained in power for almost two centuries. But in 1368 the Yüan (Mongol) Dynasty in China was overthrown by the House of Ming and soon afterwards Turkestan also seceded from Mongol rule. Thus temporarily the Mongol star seemed to have set, and differences between the peoples of Mongolia proper and those in the Altai area (the Western Mongols) set in.

One of the subordinate leagues of the Western Mongols, the Ölöts (Eleuths), soon came into military prominence in Turkestan under a Khan by the name of Galdan. Galdan's nephew, Rabdan, gave the name of his branch of the Ölöts—the Jön Gar (Jungars, sometimes written Dzungars, Zungars)—to the kingdom when he succeeded to the Mongol possessions. The name has since stuck in geographies as Jungaria (Dzungaria or Zungaria), and it has reference to the part of Sinkiang which lies between the T'ien Shan and the Altai, i.e., North Sinkiang. These same Ölöts took advantage of political differences to the south of them and came to dominate South Sinkiang, Ch'inghai, and Tibet for a brief historical period; this epoch has even been viewed by one Chinese historian as a "Golden Age" for the Western Regions. Yet the fount of Ölöt power, for the Ölöts as for others of the Western Mongols, was Jungaria and the steppes, not the oases of South Sinkiang, where Uighur (present Wei-wu-erh) civilization appears to have persisted. For Mongol life has been the phenomenon of nomadism, and life in South Sinkiang has been that of the isolated, petty agriculture of the oasis. The power of the nomad is his mobility, and he requires extensive pasturage for his cattle; yet the life of oasis agriculture is essentially fixed and in South Sinkiang it seems to have continued with little change despite the death and flux all around it. It has been demonstrated that the Mongols only ruled South Sinkiang, and did not occupy it as they did the territory between the T'ien Shan and the Altai. The contrast in living conditions of the Mongol nomad and the Wei-wu-erh man of the land is even today one of the noticeable differences between life in North and South Sinkiang.

Today the Mongols are mainly represented in Sinkiang by the Unen Susuktu, the Bato Setkhiltu, and the Ching Setkhiltu Leagues. The Unen Susuktu League, composed of Old Torgot Mongols, is numerically the most important of these three. Its representatives are to be found around Ching-ho and Wu-su in North Sinkiang and Karashahr on the southern slopes of the T'ien Shan. The Bato Setkhiltu League, modern representative of the Hoshots, also is located around Karashahr (Yen-ch'i). The New Torgot, New Hoshot, and Orianggai Mongols of the Ching Setkhiltu League are to be found in the Altai region, especially in the vicinity of Pu-erh-ching. In addition there are two groups of Ch'ahar Mongols in the Borotala Valley between Tihwa and I-ning, and a concentration of Olöt (Eleuth) Mongols in the I-li Valley, many of whom are also known as Kalmucks.

Mutton, *kumis,* and cheese are what mainly fill the Mongol larder. But, for the fastidious, that cheese would present a terrific trial, so filled is it with hair and sundry other debris. Nomad that he is, the Mongol lives in a felt tent, called a *yurt,* and his wealthy neighbor has great numbers of these—curious, collapsible, uncomely habitations. If devout, he dedicates one or more of his sons to the Lamaist priesthood, where celibacy is supposedly required. In accordance with this tradition, entrance to the Kalmuck monastery is usually forbidden to women; but on certain rare religious festivals each year women are said to be admitted. Then, the story goes, the Mongol Lamaist forgets his vows in a wild, sensual Bacchanalia.

The Mongol woman wears a cloth skirt, often brocaded, a blouse of brocade also, a wide saucer-shaped hat and thick sturdy boots, that are life-long items of apparel. Innumerable necklaces and bracelets of precious stones and long false braids which she makes of horse hair or, if she can afford them, even of human hair, are also part of her costume.

There is, on the whole, a stirring, Wild West attractiveness about her appearance, this Kalmuck Mongol, even as she goes about the tasks of preparing cheese, chopping wood, or milking.

Nor is she necessarily an ignorant woman. A Mongol princess of Tihwa, for example, has studied English in Pei-p'ing, French and medicine at Brussels, and in addition speaks Russian as well as her native tongue. The problem of so-called Oriental conservatism, according to this woman's views, may have originated in a desire to be undisturbed. But she, and other Mongol intelligentsia, are alert and modest enough to admit that out of the creativeness of the Occident new light is being shed on how man might best live; from the history of such as she and her ancestors, the Occident has in its turn much to learn.

The Kirgiz

Another of the fascinating ethnic groups that roam the Sinkiang mountains and steppes are the Kirgiz. They are the people whom a legendary white Prester John is said to have ruled in the Middle Ages, and they are supposed to have introduced the Christianity of Nestorius to Asia. The Kirgiz are related to the old Uighurs also, it seems, and were powerful in the Altai region in the centuries just preceding the Mongol invasion. They, like the Mongols, are horsemen; but their homeland is in the steep crags, the narrow mountain trails and not so much in the steppes. Those who now live in the Pamirs fringing South-west Sinkiang have their own legends of origin. It seems that there were once *kirk kiz,* "forty maidens," who became pregnant and so gave birth to the Kirgiz people. One version of the story is that they had intercourse with a red dog; another, that they dipped their fingers in a magic stream; a third, that the foam of Lake Issyk Kul served as the needed sperm.

Moslems of the Sunni order, the Kirgiz vest their tribal government in the hands of elders whose dicta are strictly respected. These elders adjudicate a multitude of questions such as those of petty thievery, pastoral boundaries, and property settlements. No foreigner is supposed to witness a Kirgiz court, which often meets in an ante-room of an *ak-ui* or *kirga*—the native tent dwelling. Adjournment of the court is signalized with a loud sounding of the table and a solemnly sworn oath. The vow resounds fiercely through the *ak-ui,* and then justice has been done.

Kirgiz scoff at the thought of grubbing at the soil, but they are hardy, courageous men who mount patrol on the lofty Pamirs. They have a keen sense of sight and can spot small objects from miles away. Falconry is the great sport for those who are the wealthiest, and the usual quarry is a type of hill partridge, the *chikor.* Sometimes the young women as well as the men become adept at this. Big game is limited, but at times the Kirgiz do hunt the now rapidly vanishing *ovis poli,* or long-horned mountain sheep, when it can be found. A sport they especially like is *baiga,* a contest like the *ulagh* of the Wei-wu-erh. In *baiga* some forty or fifty mounted sportsmen strive with each other to retrieve a dead carcass of a sheep or goat. One of the contestants dashes forward and hurls the carcass to the ground while the others wait. Then, in a thundering onrush of dust and shouts, the remainder of the players lunge toward the game. They resort to all manner of tactics to get to the recumbent prize—they beat an opponent's mount if it is in the way, they unhorse each other, and they ride their steeds like champions. Such confusion and bedlam; but it is rare, beautiful excitement.

A long coat stuffed with wool and cotton is worn by the Kirgiz over trousers tucked into high boots, while a fur piece with ear coverings (or an embroidered round cap) keeps his head warm. His woman is attired alike, but she wears a turban precariously high on her head. The gala Kirgiz occasion is a wedding, and divorce is not common. According to his religion a Moslem is permitted four wives, but a Kirgiz is usually not rich enough to afford more than one. Hilarity and celebration, not sadness, characterize the funeral ceremony of the Kirgiz. The basis for this, they point out, is that the dead are giving away to their heirs the wealth that has been amassed during a lifetime of labor; festivity, consequently, is in order. At the funeral the dead person is placed on a hill-top, interred with food, clothing, and a certain amount of money in a high, walled tomb. The sustenance is supposed to feed him on the way to the hereafter. This, like certain other rites of the

89

Kirgiz, who, for example, have occasionally been found to worship fire, is said to be a vestige of Shamanism.

The Kirgiz are split up into many small mountain dwelling groups and often are not able to keep in touch with others of their race. In recent years, however, some have become educated to a more modern, more urbanized life.

Kazakhs

Chinese, it may be said, do not usually make distinctions between the Kirgiz and another people of Sinkiang, the Kazakhs. The latter are also Moslems and are widely distributed between the T'ien Shan and the Altai. They speak Turki, are notorious as raiders, and are famous for their wild horsemanship. Tu Chung-yüan says that Kazakh children of five or six are already well trained to ride horseback. "There are none," he says, "at the age of ten who do not have unusual talent such as enables them to tell the sickness of a horse, to control the animal, to stand on its back, to bend from the horse to pick up things, to straighten up quickly, and above all to ride as though glued on the animal. Such feats as these are performed by Kazakh soldiers in Soviet motion pictures."

Tu reminds his readers that Sino-Russian boundary demarcations have put one branch of the Kazakhs under Russian and the other under Chinese political authority. This has made it difficult to draw a rigid racial line on the frontier, and Kazakhs riding across the steppes to raid an innocent herder at times have created border incidents. As Tu states, "The Kazakh people are very strong but also very lazy, and outside of tending cattle, often do not have any occupation. So some, when winter comes, take to the life of a lancer. A few steal cattle and horses, and many kill men and take their goods. For this is only an outgrowth of their military talent, and they lack any other way in which to use it. Wouldn't one think that, if these excellent warriors were persuaded to attack the enemy in this time of Resistance, each would do the work of a hundred?"

As in many another Chinese racial problem, however, there is a mixup concerning information about the Kazakhs. Russians, who have a separate group named similarly (the famous Kazakhs, or Cossacks of the Russian cavalry), have called one type of this Turkestan nomad the Kara-Kazakh and another the Kirgiz-Kazakh. C. P. Skrine, a British authority, even describes the Kara-Kazakh as a branch of the Kirgiz. Yet Owen Lattimore emphatically states that the Kirgiz and Kazakh are not the same, that the Kara-Kazakh is actually purely and simply Kazakh and calls himself that, while the Kirgiz-Kazakh is purely and simply Kirgiz and looks down upon the Kazakh as inferior. The Kirei, an outstanding people of former Turkestan history whom Douglas Carruthers has identified as Kirgiz but who, Mr. Lattimore indicates, are Kazakh, are said to have been probably the "purest Turks of all . . ."

Some Other Peoples of Sinkiang

There are still other ethnic groups in Sinkiang, including a large section of White Russian refugees who fled from their native land in the early years of the Soviet Republic, a considerable number of Soviet Russians, and other foreigners. The Tajiks or Sariquolis, found in a "few secluded mountain regions" of the Pamirs and especially in the Sariquol area, are said to be a nearly pure specimen of the so-called *homo alpinus* and do not speak Turki. Other types include two groups of South Sinkiang known as the Habdals and Dulanis, a colony of Turki stock known as Taranchis who are settled in the I-li Valley, and the Uzbeks who appear to be mostly migrants from adjacent Uzbekistan.

The "Fourteen" Races of Sinkiang

The authorities of the New Sinkiang in recent years have tried to popularize the idea that there are "fourteen racial types" among all these people of the province. These the Chinese name as *Han, Man, Meng, Hui, Wei-wu-erh, Ha-sa-k'o, T'a-chi-k'o, T'a-lan-ch'i, T'a-t'a-erh, Ko-erh-k'o-tzu, Wu-tzu-pieh-k'o, Hsi-po, So-lun,* and *Kuei-hua.* The inclusion of such a primarily political and geographical term as Han and religious category as Hui (both already briefly discussed) would tend to eliminate this as any "scientifically" worked out ethnic list. The same comment applies to the *T'a-t'a-erh* (Tatar), the *Ko-erh-k'o-*

tzu, or Khalkha (both related to the Mongols), the *Hsi-po* (Sibo) and *So-lun* (Solon). The other types mentioned might be identified in their order as Manchu, Mongol, Uighur, Kazakh, Tajik, Taranchi, Uzbek, and White Russians. It is worth while to notice, however, that in the list of the fourteen racial types the name Tung-kan is not mentioned except as it is "swallowed" up in the general categories of Han or Hui. This may be (though it probably is not) due to the equating of the name Tung-kan with the name Hui or (more likely since Wei-wu-erh also are identified as among the category of Hui) to a looseness of racial classification. Yet might not the omission actually be a way of evading mention of a pressing problem and an actual negative indication that all is not yet completely well so far as Sheng and those particular Chinese Moslems are concerned?

Though there has been a certain looseness of expression throughout the fourteen-fold list, so far as Chinese usage is concerned no real error has been made. *Min-tsu,* the Chinese term translated here as "race," literally means a "clan of people," "a tribe," even "a nation." As "clans" or ethnic types the fourteen groups mentioned here certainly deserve to be distinguished, though they may not all represent "races." In fact the naming of them is especially valuable as indicative of the kinds of "people" that are locally prominent now among the Sinkiang "peoples" themselves.

Policy: Old and New

It was the resentment of most of the people in this tremendous racial mixture over the former treatment accorded them, which confronted the administrative authorities of the New Sinkiang almost from the first. "Formerly," Tu Chung-yüan writes, "the people were permitted to read only Han books . . . and even if they read those they were not permitted to hold office, but could serve only as half-slave translators. As a result, none of the races wanted to do such work. In the Yang-Chin period force was used to make some do it. But . . . just as soldiers had to be hired in the interior, so only poor persons could be hired to do the reading."

Since Sheng Tu-pan began to stress "Racial Equality," Tu says, change in the traditional policy has come:

. . . each race and every educational institution has received help from the government; and, though reading of Han books is required, each race can also read its own literature. Since this has happened readers have multiplied like the spread of mist. Government positions have since been opened to all the educated, and the self-respect of each race has been restored . . .

The unfortunate omission of detailed information relating to the place or lack of place of the Tung-kans under this policy, leads one to feel that the Tung-kan question may not even yet have been solved in Sinkiang, and in this respect the policy of "Racial Equality" as practiced in the province may possibly be vulnerable to criticism. Yet, otherwise, the policy seems to have been intended for all racial types in Sinkiang and has become more and more widely effective. During the autumn of 1938, for instance, the "fourteen" ethnic groups of the province met as a body at the All-Sinkiang Conference in Tihwa. Even more long-run evidence which Tu Chung-yüan gives of progress toward solution of the racial questions in Sinkiang is to be found in the broader base of education. Not only is "Racial Equality" practiced in the schools but the cultural contributions of each racial group in the province have been particularly emphasized through organization of what Sinkiang calls Cultural Progress Societies. Both of these developments are described in more detail in the chapter on "Reconstruction."

"Racial Equality" has been, withal, a praiseworthy experiment and it could have great promise for this province. It has affirmed in a land where race and mixture of race have for centuries brought sharp contrasts and rich interchange as well as bitter conflict, that henceforth in Sinkiang there was not to be discrimination against either minority or majority because of lineage. It has promised that each clan may develop its own cultural heritage to the fullest, and that no one clan or combination of clans shall impose its or their way of life forcibly upon any other clan. It has posited for all groups of men, any one group of men, and any one man, equal bestowal of both benefits and duties of society. Surely in such a concept, among the others of the Six Great Policies, could not the peoples of Sinkiang and of all the United Nations well find an intimate community of interests?

VII

CLEAN GOVERNMENT

SINKIANG as a Chinese province has existed for less than three-quarters of a century, and even during that period it has been not so much a province as a Chinese outpost and dependency. The changes in Sinkiang since Sheng Shih-ts'ai came to power have brought a new administrative pattern, one which has been summed up in the Six Great Policies as "Clean Government." This new political structure came partially as the result of close ties to Sovietism; but it has never meant surrender of Sinkiang autonomy to Soviet Russia. "Clean Government" has been, instead, an effort to improve upon old Chinese institutions and upon the treatment formerly allotted to the Sinkiang natives.

Han Relations with Ancient Sinkiang (Western Regions)

The degree and type of influence which China has exerted in Sinkiang has in a sense varied with the good or bad fortune of effective Chinese control over that dependency. For the purposes of this study the Han (B.C. 206-220 A.D.), T'ang (618-907), Ta Ch'ing or Manchu (1644-1912), and Republican (1912-present) epochs have been selected as periods which modern Chinese themselves view as outstanding for effective Chinese influence in Sinkiang. Though there has been considerable difference in particulars, up to the inception of Sheng Shih-ts'ai's administration there ran through them all a like—though in many ways maturing—thread of colonial policy.

In Han times when Chinese first began to assert their colonial influence in Central Asia they sent gift-bearing, sometimes militarily escorted, diplomatic missions to the numerous petty states of the Western Regions. Once they had opened cordial relations in this manner, they followed with intermarriage between Chinese and members of a particular ruling family or principality of the outlying area. Then came exchange of hostages between the Han and the outlying state. When the Han had thus become established in the Western Regions, they entered more seriously into local politics and began where possible to enthrone puppet or at least "loyal" princes. Political manipulation was followed, or accompanied, by military demonstration where it was needed and where it was possible. The policy of letting "barbarians rule barbarians" early became a cardinal feature of Han-Turkestan relations and, in many ways, it has remained so. This was important in an area so distant as the Western Regions, and in ancient days was practiced to the extent of utilizing one colonial principality in military compaigns against another and to the extreme of "permitting" native personnel to administer localities—though this often seems to have been "allowed" in cases where it could not have been prevented. In instances of severe difficulties whole populations were shifted to distant areas or, where deemed necessary, depopulated by the sword.

The pinnacle of Han administrative achievement on this frontier was the creation of the office of the *Tu-tu*. His job, Chinese history states, was to "watch" a particular outpost. He was, it is evident, an all-around colonial executive and the ancient Chinese counterpart of the Occidental Military Governor of a dependency in the pre-Pearl Harbor epoch.

T'ang Improvements

Where T'ang Chinese considerably improved upon the Han was in their attempt to convert much of the Western Regions into the administrative units used in China Proper—the *chou* and *hsien* (department and county). This meant application of customary Chinese law to the Central Asian frontier, but it did not mean abolition of the office of the Tu-tu. He still administered outlying areas. His duties, however, became in some cases more closely allied with the regional and local government machinery of China Proper than previously. By the new arrangement, also, executive machinery in the Western Regions became exceedingly complicated and broad. At one time this machinery was centered in the Tu-tu prefecture *(Tu-tu Fu)* at An-hsi (in present-day Kansu), with power said to extend from Khotan to Persia, and the following units under its direction: sixteen "states," eighty departments, one hundred eleven counties, and one hundred twenty-six military departments *(chün-fu,* also called *chi-mi chou* or "restrained" departments).

The situation that faced the Ch'ing Dynasty was, however, considerably different. By the Ta Ch'ing period the Khitans and the Mongols —in particular the Ölöt Mongols—had accustomed the North Road of the Western Regions to a system of widely effective overlordship. Moslem influence, on the other hand, had consolidated itself in the south. Chinese, therefore, spoke of "Four Ölöt Leagues" on the North Road and of a "Moslem League" on the South Road. These regional distinctions were complicated further by the fact that the Ölöts were exceptionally ambitious and had been expanding from the Altai southeastwards across Turfan and Kokonor as far as Lhasa.

In tackling this problem the Ch'ing first attacked Ölöt power on the southern flank, in Tibet; after ousting the Ölöt party from power there, they devastated the Road North of the Heavenly Mountains (*T'ien-shan-pei-lu*) and wiped out that Mongol stronghold. They then turned to subjugation of the weaker Moslem League in the south.

To ensure that order could be maintained, more than twenty thousand Manchu soldiers were imported into the Western Regions and stationed at I-li (Sui-ting), Yangi Hissar, and Kashgar. I-li became the central military headquarters, and a complicated new system of control was set up. It included at least a hundred special emissaries for handling tribute relations, military affairs, and rationing of food, besides a special office for Moslem affairs. All in all, the early Ch'ing emphasized military, more than political, activities in the Western Regions. The innumerable ramparts and petty military stations (*ch'eng-pao*) constructed are concrete evidence to that effect. Not only had the Ch'ing rulers resented Mongol strength in the Western Regions; they had begun to view with alarm the rise of Islam in Chinese Central Asia and to sense danger from Europe.

Tso Tsung-t'ang, who was drawn out to the Western Regions by Moslem rebellions of the late nineteenth century, made many new administrative changes there. It was he who stressed the importance of, first, Urumchi (Tihwa) and Aqsu and, second, I-li (Sui-ting) and T'a Ch'eng for control and defense of the area. He also suggested irrigation projects, more extensive colonization, and a land survey. But most important, Tso recommended that the Western Regions be consolidated into one province, *Hsin-chiang* ("The New Dominion") or Sinkiang. By this he at last crystallized the Sinkiang frontier, on the one hand for China and on the other hand against the empires of the modern Occident. Actually the regional lines—that is to say, China's more rigid northwest national boundary and the framework for the province of Sinkiang—cut across the natural grain of traditional Central Asian life and jarred the nomad, the farmer, and the merchant there. The strategem, with local squabbles within Europe indirectly assisting, did help to counter the threats of imperialism, primarily that of Tsarist Russia.

But for at least three reasons Tso Tsung-t'ang's recommendations did not suffice. First, his major emphasis was upon the old-style Ch'ing military control which could not stand up in the face of the weapons Europe was even then beginning to fabricate. Second, his constructive measures do not seem to have been far-reaching enough in scope or in execution or to have provided suitable means of binding Sinkiang to China Proper through economic ties. Finally, the ebb of Ch'ing power which brought Republican revolt and the fall of the Dynasty in China by 1912 was bound to be felt keenly on the far-flung Sinkiang frontier.

Under the Early Republic

Tu Chung-yüan speaks of administration in Sinkiang during the early years of the Chinese Republic in this manner:

. . . The Yang [Tseng-hsin]-Chin [Shu-jen] period was lengthy and greedy. The politician did not believe in working but only in officiating; even when he was officiating he aimed only at making money. This arose from the fact that Yang and Chin were basically that type. In general if a person were to come to Sinkiang from the interior it was not asked whether he had qualifications or not, whether he was talented or not. All that was necessary instead was that he be of an "experienced" temperament or perhaps that he had served in an office of a military governor or of a provincial government for eight to ten years so that it could be seen he had been reared in the atmosphere of slavery. . . . Or, again, if he were appointed, say as a county magistrate or as a tax collector, it was only desired that he collect eighty to one hundred thousand dollars in a year's work. Can one ask that a man's talents be developed in this type of government atmosphere? Since the culture of other peoples of Sinkiang had been submerged so much, the Han official became like a god, and if a magistrate were appointed for a county in South Sinkiang he need not have been especially greedy to receive fifty to sixty thousand from the Moslems on one visit. Therefore all people coming to Sinkiang from the interior had such hopes. But now it is not possible!

The "Clean Government" of the New Sinkiang

In the face of provincial discontent over the old Sinkiang administrative system, Sheng Shih-ts'ai set about in 1933 to institute reforms. It would have been surprising indeed if prevalent and all too customary Chinese foibles—of "squeeze," "rotten gentry," and excessive taxes, for instance—had been completely eradicated under his policy of "Clean Government." Since almost no first-hand data, such as reports from any long-time Occidental resident in the province, are available it may be some time before what may or may not have been accomplished along these lines can be fully known. But so far as Tu Chung-yüan is concerned, the changes have already been praiseworthy. Former abuses concerning salaries, "gifts," and taxes by office-holders in the province have been checked, he says, by a provincial commission which is required to enter accounts in regard to all public moneys in the records of Sheng Shih-ts'ai's own office. Sheng himself has set a leading example in governmental unselfishness, according to Tu, by accepting a monthly salary of less than $100 Chinese for his work. Mrs. Sheng, an administrator of a girls' middle school, is held before the reader's eyes as a model also because she gets a monthly salary of only about $10 Chinese. Such examples, Tu points out, are in sharp contrast with the practices of past administrators.

In regard to the type of administration in the New Sinkiang, this much can be also said. The province is governed under a "committee" system similar to that in other provinces of China. Members of a provincial committee are appointed by the Executive Yüan of the Chinese National Government, which also ratifies the appointment of one individual from among their number to the office of Concurrent Provincial Chairman. Sheng Shih-ts'ai was appointed to that post in 1940, and he has given it more and more of his attention since the decease of the former Provincial Chairman, Liu Wen-lung. Actually, so far as power is concerned, Sheng Shih-ts'ai seems to have dominated Sinkiang since 1933 through his military strength; the effective participation of other members in the provincial committee seems to have largely been subject to his approval, and in many respects the ratification of his and their appointments by national authorities has been mostly a matter of form.

Statements as to the administrative organization of Sinkiang areas do not always jibe. But Tu Chung-yüan writes, and other authorities seem to substantiate, that there are nine principal administrative regions in the province: Tihwa Ch'ü (including the capital of the same name), I-li Ch'ü, T'a Ch'eng Ch'ü, Ha-mi Ch'ü, A Shan Ch'ü, Yen-ch'i Ch'ü, K'o-shih Ch'ü, and Khotan Ch'ü. According to Tu there are administrative officers over these, each of which includes a number of counties. There are, he states, seventy-two counties in all Sinkiang.

It is hard to tell how effectively this *Ch'ü* and *Hsien* (Region and County) system has been working in Sinkiang. In the past such governmental forms have worked better in the oasis settlements than in the outlying pastures, but have on the whole been subordinated to varying local tribal customs when the two systems came into practical conflict. Where relations between provincial officials and non-Chinese-speaking races have become too complicated, native headmen speaking Chinese have in the past served as "middlemen."

So far as the national allegiance of Sinkiang is concerned, let any doubts be immediately dispelled. The name of the province indicates that it is a part of the territory subject to the laws of the Chinese National Government and the officials and people of both Sinkiang and the Chinese Republic as a whole operate accordingly. Both as Commander-in-Chief of Border Defense and as Provincial Chairman in Sinkiang Sheng Shih-ts'ai is formally an appointee of the Executive Yüan of the Chinese National Government. The fact that he is allotted and accepts such national titles is significant evidence that neither he nor the National Government wants Sinkiang and her officialdom to be other than Chinese in name.

The Chinese National Government may not, it is true, always have been able to do what it liked in Sinkiang since Sheng Shih-ts'ai achieved power. It appears, from Chinese testimony, that Sheng has in the past negotiated with foreign powers without conforming to customary national procedure, and that his administration has often excluded Chinese of other provinces from Sinkiang territory and has found ways at times to circumvent—if not necessarily to disobey— National Government regulations.

This situation gave a certain credence to distasteful accusations in regard to Soviet Russian influence in the province. After China and Soviet Russia signed their Non-aggression Agreement in 1937 Tokyo quarters fanned rumors that China had been forced to give up Sinkiang as a concession to Soviet Russia. Since then—and especially at the turn of 1939 and 1940 when Russia was advancing her armies into Poland, Finland, Esthonia, Lithuania, and Latvia—like sources often hinted at the "invasion" of Sinkiang by Soviet troops.

I have no first-hand evidence by which I can prove that such reports are false, but I believe in their falsity. I saw many Soviet Russian "volunteer" troops in Lan-chou, Kansu (adjacent to Sinkiang Province), when I was in China in 1939 and 1940, and there could have been more such troops in Sinkiang. But in late 1939, on the other hand, I also visited Sining, Ch'inghai, which is west of Lan-chou and between Kansu and Sinkiang, and I did not see Soviet Russian troops there. After weighing available evidence, I do not believe that Soviet Russian troops have been in "occupation" of Sinkiang or have been "controlling" it during the years since Sheng Shih-ts'ai summoned their aid to put down Sinkiang rebellion. I do not even believe that they were "occupying" it before the widely publicized reports of October, 1943, came forth proclaiming the "withdrawal" of Soviet Russia from Sinkiang. It is admitted that there have been many Soviet advisers in Sinkiang in a number of capacities, civilian and military, in that period; and among them there may have been Soviet "volunteer" soldiers and aviation pilots. But there is not justification for saying that such "volunteers" and advisers ever made Sinkiang a Soviet dependency.

Indeed the evidence seems to demonstrate that, far from being a Soviet Russian "puppet," Sheng Shih-ts'ai has been one of the most far-sighted, enlightened, and independent military leaders of modern China. The Chinese colonial record in Sinkiang was not very praiseworthy up to Sheng's appearance on the scene. He was able to assay the needs of the situation and the resources at his command; he was also competent enough to make constructive use of opportunities offered him. The Six Great Policies and especially the program of Sinkiang reconstruction which Sheng Shih-ts'ai fashioned out of the rough clay of the Moslem revolt of the 1930's indicate that he has had at heart the interests of both Sinkiang and China. That he has been able to turn these interests into a positive program which did not completely sacrifice China's title to the province but which brought to Sinkiang instead much of the best qualities of both China and of neighboring Soviet Russia is truly an amazing achievement, too long unappreciated by the outside world.

It was inevitable that Sheng Shih-ts'ai's New Sinkiang should have been influenced by Soviet Russian ideas, personnel, and materials. Developments in neighboring Soviet areas had so drawn the attention and admiration of Sinkiang people by 1933 that a feeble Chinese version of an outmoded military or economic imperialism not only might have fallen flat but might have flung the province—politically as well as economically—into Soviet Russia's perhaps embarrassed lap.

Sheng Shih-ts'ai is no puppet and the New Sinkiang is no political dependency of Soviet Russia. Sinkiang instead has incorporated Chinese ideas of loose political authority with the Soviet creed of cultural and economic autonomy. From the two has come a unique Chinese frontier political economy. From them also the basically non-Han Chinese people of Sinkiang have gained new opportunities of livelihood, and by the combination much of the old bitterness between Han and non-Han has been removed.

VIII

PEACE

BEFORE SHENG SHIH-TS'AI had brought the New Dominion into being, civil war had stamped mercilessly through Chinese Central Asia. The Swedish explorer, Sven Hedin, who was in this region a decade ago, has written of the "marauders" in Sinkiang Province at that time who "stole" and "looted everywhere" and of the "utterly terrified" civilians. Nor were those circumstances without previous parallel in Sinkiang. Probably nowhere else in the world has there been such a locale for historical turmoil. Along her North Road especially, there have been for millenniums almost unending waves of conquest, brigandage, rapine, and fire. From the days of the Hsiung-nu in Han Dynasty times to those of Ma Chung-ying between 1931 and 1934, the sight of the armed horseman sweeping fiercely across desert trails to slash at his foe must time and time again have inspired a terrible fear in the souls of the populace. Turk, Tibetan, Arab, and Kirei, Khitan, Mongol, and Manchu, each "barbarian" in his turn has slashed a path of blood and destruction across the steppes in order to establish his own rule of force over Central Asia.

Little wonder that for centuries the Men of Han and Tang could see no peace in Turkestan but an armed one. Where law was mainly one of might, the vigor of a Pan Ch'ao and the steady arm of a Kao Hsien-chih might have seemed for China a justifiable military means with which to subjugate the restless borderland. The ruins of Bishbalik stand for the glories of peace and culture which the native Uighurs once maintained in Sinkiang; and yet Bishbalik, too, is forever a monument to the prowess of Uighur warriors who themselves once staunchly stopped the flow of wantonness in Asia. Kara-Khitai has been immortalized as a medieval Khitan kingdom of North Sinkiang, yet it was founded in the Altai mountains by the battling of an exile band from Northeast China. Even the Ölöt Mongols—who under Galdan and Rabdan established what one Chinese historian has viewed as a "Golden Age" for the Western Regions—even their accomplishments came at the cost of bristling armor and ruthless suppression. The Manchus in their turn dominated the Western Regions by force; for they were compelled first to drive the Ölöts back from Tibet and Eastern Sinkiang and then to lay waste the North. When Sinkiang Moslems of the nineteenth century revolted, the armies of Tso Tsung-t'ang suppressed the uprising by some of the bloodiest campaigns in history.

If not the military struggles of these earlier days, then at least the desperate civil wars of the 1930's, described earlier in this volume, have been enough to make the slogan of "Peace" welcome to the Sinkiang masses. "Peace," Tu Chung-yüan says, has been to Sinkiang what Lenin's "Bread and Peace" was to Soviet Russia. It was maintenance of "Peace," probably as much as anything else that enabled a new and promising day to dawn for Sinkiang.

IX

RECONSTRUCTION

PERHAPS ONE of the most convincing actual proofs that "Peace" was brought at last to Sinkiang is revealed in what her new administration has accomplished. Sheng Shih-ts'ai's record of "Reconstruction" may not be one of unlimited attainment, but it is certainly one of creditable progress.

Chinese say that Sheng did not succeed in establishing a "unified" Sinkiang government for three years. Numerous taxation and currency stabilization problems remained unsolved, and there was still not complete political cohesion. In 1937, however, he instituted a three-year plan of reconstruction under Soviet Russian guidance, and by 1941 the second such plan was well under way. Two institutions, a Foreign Trade Company and a Local Resources Company, have transacted most of the Sinkiang business, and, on a profit-for-the-province basis, have dealt with and for a network of local cooperatives. All provincial banking is said to have been monopolized by a Sinkiang Commercial Bank. Together with a Reconstruction Commission, these organizations have been at the core of the new provincial economy. What the administration of the New Sinkiang has been able to do on the basis of this arrangement—in terms of admittedly incomplete and in many cases generalized or proximate data—is indicated below.

Education

Tu Chung-yüan, himself one-time Chancellor of Education in the New Sinkiang, suggests that, second to political equality, the border has long wanted educational equality as the means to gain true autonomy for the racial groups of Sinkiang. The New Sinkiang accordingly made expansion of education fundamental to her reconstruction program. That is the basis upon which the number of students in the province reportedly leaped from less than 3,000 before 1933 to well over 150,000 by 1936. By August of that year around 2,300 educational institutions are said to have been established in Sinkiang. These included one college of law and political science, several middle schools, probably over two hundred primary schools, around one hundred so-called people's schools, and from one to two thousand private schools. There is good reason to believe that by 1943 there was an even greater number of educated persons and educational institutions.

There has also been, apparently distinct from the above-named institutions, a new and special kind of emphasis on education of cultural minorities and majorities. This has largely been effected through what are called Cultural Progress Societies. In 1936 these existed for the Wei-wu-erh, Ha-sa-k'o, Hui, Meng-ku, T'a-t'a-erh, Kuei-hua, and Han. Figures on the next page suggest the extent to which the work of the first three mentioned societies has been carried.

Students, no matter whether in attendance at the University, at a middle school, or at a primary school, are aided by the provincial government. In the case of the University, the Normal School, and the "First Middle School," students have even been given "pocket money."

Society	Wei-wu-erh	Ha-sa-k'o	Hui	Totals
Central Office	1	1	1	3
Regional Branches	8	5	3	16
County Branches	41	8	14	63
Village Branches	23	?	?	23+?
Total Educational Institutions	1,980	207	37	2,224
Total Students	129,649	10,194	2,700	142,543

Currency and Finance

For currency stabilization and a practicable operating budget, Sinkiang Province has persistently required outside financial help. Not only was this true in the old days of the Chinese Empire but it was particularly true in the period just before and during Sheng Shih-ts'ai's rise to power. In the 1934-1941 period Sheng met the situation mainly by internal reforms and aid from Soviet Russia. But he has not yet got the problem licked.

For decades after the province was established, Sinkiang operated on a substratum of financial subsidy. The first annual grant came from the Manchu government and amounted to 600,000 taels. This was gradually increased until in 1905 it had risen to 2,980,000 taels. With the abdication of the Manchu Dynasty and the establishment of the Chinese Republic in 1912, the old subsidies—one year excepted—were discontinued. Various measures were taken in an attempt to cope with the new situation, but the principal method used for many years thereafter was issuance of provincial notes. These notes in turn began to bring on Sinkiang inflation. By 1934 that inflation had become seriously disturbing to the provincial economy.

Sinkiang has had a wide variety of mediums of exchange. Formerly, in addition to paper notes, these included silver coins, stamped silver "shoes," irregular bullion, and at times tea or even sheep. Paper provincial notes were first circulated in 1899, and were backed by a Tihwa cash reserve. Later "oil cloth notes" *(yu-pu piao)* were also issued by provincial bureaus at Sui-ting and Kashgar. These had a sixty per cent note and a forty per cent bullion backing. Yang Tseng-hsin, military governor immediately after abdication of the Manchus, even permitted additional notes to be issued to make up for discontinuance of the imperial subsidy. It was, however, during the governorship of Chin Shu-jen and the years of the Moslem revolt that the gradual devaluation in Sinkiang currency became most alarming. In the period, 1912-1929, three Sinkiang dollars (taels or *liang*) at the lowest would exchange for one dollar of Chinese Nationalist currency (*yüan*). Yet by 1934 the Sinkiang note issue had grown so excessive—it is said to have amounted to more than 1,200,000,000 taels—that one Chinese Nationalist dollar at times would buy more than 4,000 Sinkiang dollars. How well Sheng Shih-ts'ai's administration met this serious predicament is suggested by the report that a Sinkiang Province dollar by 1942 had become worth six Chinese Nationalist dollars—although, to be sure, the Chinese Nationalist dollar had by then itself lost value through severe inflation.

Many Chinese writers attribute the change in the provincial monetary situation to Sheng's numerous reforms. Among such reforms, the 1939 reorganization of the Sinkiang Provincial Bank into a commercial bank with an expanded field of operations is especially notable. This new Sinkiang Commercial Bank began to issue new notes, took steps to improve and to unify Sinkiang currency, and undertook to withdraw old notes from circulation. It has been remarkably successful in carrying out this program, and the Sheng Shih-ts'ai administration does deserve praise in this connection. But it would be a mistake not to realize that the greater exchange value of the Sinkiang dollar is in part due to at least two other major factors: (1) Sinkiang's protected geographical position at the rear of the Chinese War of Resistance; and (2) Soviet Russian credits. Chao Lieh, a Chinese authority on Sinkiang to whom I have already referred, gives these credits particular emphasis. By 1941, he writes, Sinkiang is said to have borrowed a total of 15,000,000 rubles from Soviet Russia. Though this money went for many purposes, such as purchase of machinery and trucks, one of its most important functions was to serve as backing for Sinkiang currency. It is doubtful if Sheng could have come near stabilization of his province's monetary unit in the years 1933-1941 without such credits.

An indication of confidence in Sinkiang finance is seen in the report that over $5,444,000 Chinese were subscribed in the province for her 1941 Reconstruction Bond Issue. Yet this does not necessarily mean that she is financially solvent. Quite the opposite is suggested by Chinese comment of November, 1942, that the Sinkiang budget of that year showed a considerable deficit and that the achievement of a budget balance is still considered one of the most serious current problems before the provincial government.

Agriculture and Irrigation

Because of their basic importance to the life of the province, agricultural and irrigation developments deserve special scrutiny. There are indications that the Sheng Shih-ts'ai administration has given the problem considerable attention, but the available information is not satisfactory. Under these circumstances it might first be well to consider the following base figures given by Chiang Chün-chang for 1918 cultivated acreage in Sinkiang:

CULTIVATED ACREAGE IN SINKIANG, 1918	
Crop	Acreage
Wheat	480,782
Corn	340,486
Rice	52,790
Melons and other fruit	46,737
Cotton	40,025
Sesamum	33,815
Kaoliang	32,325
Beans	23,040

These figures can hardly serve as a definitive 1918 total of cultivated land for the province; some of the crops may, for instance, have been rotated on one and the same acreage. They do suggest, however, that in 1918 there was a total Sinkiang cultivated area in round figures somewhere between a minimum of 500,000 and a maximum of 1,000,000 acres. If Chiang's figures may be considered typical, they also show that cultivation of wheat and corn has by far overshadowed that of other agricultural products, and that the province does have a history of a considerably varied cultivation. Samuel Chao, an authority on Northwest China, says, in fact, that her natural riches have made Sinkiang the third largest agricultural producing center of that broad region.

In the absence of figures showing increase in cultivated acreage under Sheng's administration, statements as to the improvement of native irrigation facilities are useful—for most of Sinkiang's agricultural development has for centuries been dependent on widespread use of just such irrigation. Under Sheng's first three-year plan twenty-two new irrigation conduits were opened and forty-two old ones repaired. Nine river-deepening projects, two artificial basins for watering of cattle, and the repair and deepening of the locally famous thirty-five mile Hui-yüan irrigation conduit were some of the other tasks undertaken in the same period. By 1940 it was estimated that there were 944 main irrigation canals and 2,335 branch canals in the province. One Chinese writer enthusiastically claims that the cultivable land reclaimed as a result of the improvements mentioned amounts to approximately seventy thousand acres. A more recent survey, available in November, 1942, states that more than 3,000 miles of water conduits and wells have been added to, or repaired in, the provincial irrigation system, making available more than 150,000 acres of cultivable land. While these figures leave an uncertainty about the exact amount of land that actually is under cultivation today in Sinkiang, they do point to considerable emphasis on the problem of land reclamation. The work, moreover, undoubtedly has raised the 1918 base minimum of some 500,000 acres of cultivated land considerably in the direction of —if not beyond—the possible 1918 maximum of roughly 1,000,000 acres.

Ha-mi, Tihwa, Sui-lai (Manas), and Sui-ting in the north and Turfan, Aqsu, Kashgar, and Khotan in the south have all been famous in one way or another for their agricultural or related produce. Tu Chung-yüan claims that agricultural products of Sinkiang are "far superior to those of the interior in body, beauty, ripeness, and size." He then continues, "If one were to plant a Ha-mi melon seed elsewhere in China, the first year's crop would bring a change in the sweetness and beauty of the fruit. By the second year the melons would be unrecognizable so far as quality and taste are concerned." Turfan grapes are exported in dried raisin form to other parts of China; I tried them repeatedly in Kansu Province, and can testify to their delightful taste. The Sinkiang rice, too, is notable for the size and meatiness of its kernel. Chinese from Hunan are said to have first brought rice cultivation to Sinkiang, toward the end of the nineteenth century when they began cultivating the crop along the banks of the Urumchi River. Aqsu, Manas, Wu-su, Sui-ting, and San-tao Pa at present are all rice-growing localities.

South Sinkiang is the principal cotton-growing region, and the crop of Turfan, with an annual yield recently estimated optimistically at some 4,000,000 *chin* (catties), is the best. Flourishing cotton fields abound also at So-ch'e, Maralbashi (Pa-ch'u), Shan-shan, Su-lo, and Korla. In the past Sinkiang cotton was practically all of local origin, but in recent years American cotton seed, imported from Soviet Russia, has begun to predominate. The estimate of one Moslem merchant (as reported in late 1942) put the annual provincial crop of Sinkiang-type cotton between 40,000,000 and 50,000,000 catties.

Around a million catties of raw silk reportedly is produced each year from Khotan, Yarkand (So-ch'e), and Su-lo acreage, and a considerable increase is expected; for the provincial Reconstruction Commission has been importing improved silkworm eggs and extending sericulture plots.

Animal Husbandry

When Chinese Minister of Agriculture and Forestry, Shen Hunglieh, visited Sinkiang in 1942, he and Ch'en Chi-jung, a *Ta Kung Pao* newspaper correspondent, inspected a number of cattle ranches near the Urumchi River. Ch'en on that occasion was told that the technique developed on the Sinkiang ranches in the past five years of cattle breeding could be compared favorably with that of any nation in the world. This achievement, in combination with some of the world's best pasture land, has made animal husbandry vie with agriculture as one of the foremost occupations of the New Sinkiang. Samuel Chao estimates that it is engaged in by one-fourth of the Sinkiang people, and elsewhere it is pointed out that in this field Sinkiang leads all other provinces of China. "The ox of I-li, the sheep of the Altai Mountains, and the horse of the Pa-li-k'un region, all have widespread fame," states the *Ts'ai-cheng P'ing-lun*. Mr. Chao judges the number of domesticated animals in Sinkiang to be as follows:

AN ESTIMATE OF AVAILABLE LIVESTOCK IN SINKIANG

Livestock	Amount
Sheep	12,000,000
Horses	2,000,000
Goats	1,300,000
Cattle	1,000,000
Camels	500,000

"Animal husbandry," writes Mr. Chao, "is concentrated in the northern part of the province where the steppes along the I-li River and the Altai Range provide feeding ground. The Altai prairie is Sinkiang's leading sheep raising district, Suiting [I-li] is famous for cattle, and, with Chenhsi [Chen-hsi or Barkol] and Yenchi [Yen-ch'i or Kara-shahr], also well known for its horses."

He estimates Sinkiang's annual output of animal products, skins, and furs to be:

AN ESTIMATE OF SINKIANG'S ANNUAL OUTPUT OF ANIMAL PRODUCTS INCLUDING SKINS AND FURS

Product	Amount	
Wool	30,000,000	Catties
Camel's hair	2,500,000	"
Horse hair	1,200,000	"
Sheep skins	1,500,000	Pieces
Ermine skins (exports)	100,000	"
Ox hides	60,000	"
Fox skins (exports)	48,600	"
Horse hides	40,000	"
Wolf skins (exports)	11,000	"
Sable skins (exports)	5,000	"

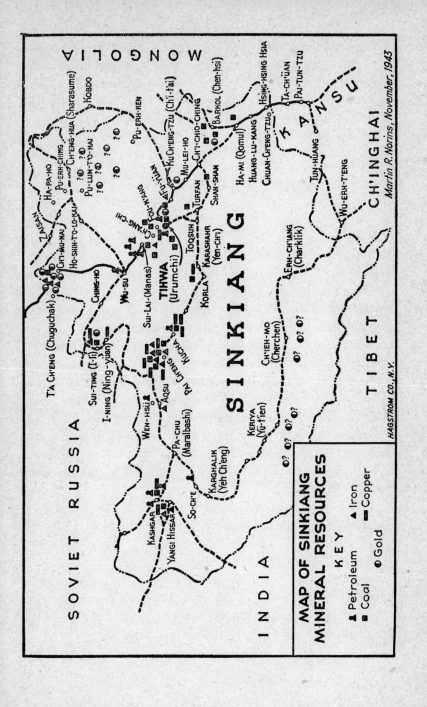

MAP OF SINKIANG
MINERAL RESOURCES

KEY

▲ Petroleum   ▲ Iron
■ Coal   ▬ Copper
        ◎ Gold

HAGSTROM CO., N.Y.

Martin R. Norins, November, 1943

The administration of the New Sinkiang has taken significant steps to assist the peasants in the solving of their agricultural and animal husbandry problems. Field stations have been set up in every county with, among other services, eight veterinary hospitals and one veterinary school. There are province-wide facilities by which farmers may rent farm machinery otherwise unavailable. Experimental irrigation stations, forestry offices, and weather bureaus have all been established under Sheng's administration. These are epoch-making innovations for this once relatively isolated "desert" area.

Mineral Resources

Chinese reports have long testified to the rich mineral potential of Sinkiang Province, but the Occident has only recently attempted systematic study of that testimony. Now it is learned that numerous oil fields have been put into operation in Sinkiang. "Prosperous," though primitive, iron foundries have existed since the time of Ch'ien Lung (1736-1796), and now the Sinkiang iron veins are being rapidly opened. Excellent coal is found near Tihwa, Kashgar, and Yangi Hissar. The gold fields of the Altai Mountains are among the richest in Asia; and good-quality copper ore is being extracted from a number of deposits. Almost virgin mineral riches lie in the soil of Sinkiang, and serious attempts have recently been made to bring them into full utility.

Petroleum. A so-called "Ferghana Series" of oil-bearing strata runs into Kashgaria from Russian Turkestan and extends along the foot of the T'ien Shan past Aqsu to Kucha (K'u-ch'e). What may be an extension of this same series reappears again in the region of the Sinkiang North Road. The extent to which this series now is being utilized is indicated by the next table which names some of the fields of the province.

Samuel Chao gives a figure of 85,000 catties as the annual production of Sinkiang mineral oil. But in the past there has only been fractional utilization of the provincial oil potential; there has not, moreover, been sufficient public information on the more recent developments, which have no doubt shot the figure considerably higher.

Locale	Field	Comment
Kashgar (Su-fu)	Unnamed	4 mi. long & 2 mi. wide; daily yield, 100 catties for 1 well
Kucha	K'o-la-ya-lun	Over 100 catties daily
Manas (Sui-lai)	Lake An-chi Hai	Largest field in Western China; quality oil comparable to Baku product
	Ch'ia-tzu Wan	4 gushers; output, 20-30 catties daily
	Shih-yü Yen	Output, about 50 catties daily
	T'ung-ku Po	9 wells; output, over 200 catties daily
	Po-lo-t'ung-ko	Operations suspended; former yield, 70 catties daily
So-ch'e	Shang-wo-p'u	70-80 catties daily
T'a Ch'eng (Chuguchak) ..	Black Oil Mt.	9 oil springs; possibly a tar; daily yield of greatest spring, 200 catties
Tihwa	Ssu-pen Kou	7 oil fields in Tihwa, 3 abandoned; Ssu-pen Kou & Su-ta-chang, outstanding
	Su-ta-chang	See above
Wen-hsü	T'a-na-k'o	"Hundreds" of catties "regularly"
	Ma-li-li-k'o Shan	
Wu-su	Tu-tzu Shan	4 fields in Wu-su; 32 oil springs, 15 operating at Tu-tzu Shan

Iron. Sinkiang iron is distributed both in the north and south. The vein which runs through T'a Ch'eng is really the largest in the province, though that of Khara Balgasun Mountain near Turfan is historically the best known to Chinese. Prime difficulties with iron mining in Sinkiang have been its seasonal or market fluctuations and, as with so many other resources of the province, the failure to apply scientific mining and production processes. Progress has, nevertheless, been made in uncovering many important deposits. Some of them are named below:

IRON DEPOSITS IN SINKIANG

Locale	Deposit	Comment
Aqsu	K'o-kan-ch'ia	2 deposits | Not high-
	T'ieh-pen-erh-k'o-la-pu-la-k'o	2 deposits | est quality
Ch'ang-chi	Meng-k'o-t'u Ling	
Fu-yüan	Shui-hsi Kou	7 furnaces installed with 600 catties pig iron capacity
Sui-ting (I-li)	So-erh-ko Ling	
Pai Ch'eng	Ming-pu-la-k'o Mt.	
	T'a-erh-ch'i Mt.	Mining area of each
	Ya-se-la-min Mt.	said to be less than a
	Neng-li-ha-t'a Mt.	mile square
	K'o-shih-k'o-k'o-pa-shih Mt.	
T'a Ch'eng (Chuguchak)	K'o-la-t'a-fu-pan to Ch'i-erh Shan	Vein, 130 miles long; largest in province
T'a-pan Ch'eng	Unnamed	
Yangi Hissar	I-ko-jih-ya-yen Mt.	
	A-ha-mai-ti Mt.	

Coal. Samuel Chao asserts that Sinkiang has an annual coal production of about 100,000 tons, while 6,000,000 tons has been the old conservative estimate for what may be a much greater Sinkiang coal reserve. The latter is scattered mainly along the Altai, T'ien Shan, and K'un-lun Ranges. A table of Sinkiang coal deposits which have recently come into prominence is given on the following page.

Gold. Gold resources, too, have long made Sinkiang famous among Chinese; and there is reason. The Altai ("Gold") Mountain deposits of North Sinkiang have proved their value, and other deposits have been found, particularly in the foothills of South Sinkiang. The work

Locale	Deposit	Comment
Barkol (Chen-hsi)	San-t'ang Hu	
	Hsiao Liu Kou	Bituminous
	Kuan-t'an-yao	
Ch'ang-chi	Ch'a-han-wu-su	
	T'ou-t'un Ho	
Fou-k'ang	Big Yellow Mt.	Coal only 10 ft. under-
	Little Yellow Mt.	ground
Fu-yüan	Unnamed	
Ha-mi (Qomul)	San-tao Mts.	Strata over 35 mi. long with coal sometimes 20-30 ft. underground
Sui-ting (I-li)	Hui-yüan	"Coal caves"; "sizeable output"
Karashahr (Yen-ch'i)	Ha-man Kou	Useful for iron smelting
Kashgar (Su-fu)	K'an-chi-kang	2,000-3,000 ton annual yield; smelts iron
Kucha	Su-pa-yi	"Fine" coal
Pai Ch'eng	K'o-p'ing	
	T'i-li-ko Shan	
	T'a-la-k'o	
	Ya-hsiang-pa	
Shan-shan	Ko-ko-ya Mt.	"Extensive" deposits; 5 mines now in operation
T'a Ch'eng (Chuguchak)..	K'u-k'o-ts'ang Mt.	Anthracite; in Tarbagatai Range
Tihwa	Shui-mo Kou	S. Chao says Tihwa coal
	T'ou-t'un Ch'ang	is "best" in province
	Ts'ang-huang Kou	
Turfan	Unnamed	East & West of city; 300-400 workers seasonally
Yangi Hissar	Sa-pa-t'i-k'o	Useful for iron smelting

of excavation in the Altai has been on the increase since 1917 when some 10,000 miners extracted gold valued at over 60,000 taels. In 1942 thousands of miners were said to be operating in the district, though most of the gold mined is reported to have gone to Soviet Russia.

Interesting is the claim that a two and a half pound gold nugget once was mined from the Altai Hou Kou field. The richest of the South Sinkiang gold deposits are in the vicinity of Cherchen and Keriya. Local villagers have contracted for extraction of ore from these deposits, and each year over 3,500 taels are said to be paid for the mining privileges. These are the best known gold fields of the New Sinkiang:

GOLD FIELDS IN SINKIANG

Locale	Field	Comment
A Shan (Altai)	Tung Kou	
	Hsi Kou	
	Ch'ien Kou	
	Hou Kou	
	Chung Kou	
	Ha-hsiung Kou	
	Pan-tang Kou	2½ lb. nugget mined — "Highest" qual.
Barkol (Chen-hsi)	Hsiao Liu Kou	
Cherchen (Ch'ieh-mo)	Unnamed	
Ch'i-t'ai (Ku Ch'eng-tzu)	Unnamed	
Sui-ting (I-li)	Ch'iao-li-k'o R.	
Keriya (Yü-t'ien)	A-ha-t'a-k'o Shan	
	Ch'ia-pa Shan	
	Tsao-li-ya-k'o	
	Yu-mo-chiang Shan	
Sui-tung (?Sui-ting or I-li?) ..	Unnamed	
T'a Ch'eng (Chuguchak)	Ha-t'u Shan	Placer. Between T'a-erh-ta-mu-t'u and Su-erh-t'u Rivers
Tihwa	Unnamed	

According to rumor, gold is so plentiful in Sinkiang that all Moslem families have their own caches hidden away; many of these are individually of unimportant amount, but the sum total is supposed to be large, and some of the caches are said to be "several thousands of taels." One can understand, therefore, why the Sinkiang gold reserve and annual production have been enthusiastically estimated at 31,300,000 and 50,000 ounces respectively. With all due allowance for exaggeration, there seems little question that if the gold latent in this province can be brought forth into the public markets many of China's, let alone Sinkiang's, financial worries will be eradicated.

Copper and other minerals. There are also considerable finds of copper, alum, quartz, gypsum, nitrate, and common salt in Sinkiang. Of these the 40 per cent pure copper ore that has been extracted from one of two great mines near Kashgar, and the copper deposits at K'ang-shan, Pai Ch'eng, Kucha, Tihwa, I-ning, and Sui-ting are notable. These are some of the recently publicized workings of the province:

COPPER DEPOSITS IN SINKIANG

Locale	Deposit	Comment
Sui-ting (I-li)	Wu-ts'ung-tao Shan	
I-ning	Ha-erh-han-t'u Shan	
K'ang-shan	Unnamed	
Karashahr	K'u-erh-tai Shan	
Kashgar (Su-fu) ..	Wu-lan-wu-su R.	20% pure ore
	Su-hun Shan	40% pure ore
Kucha	New Copper Works	
	Old Copper Works	
	Su-pa-shih Copper Works	
Pai Ch'eng	Ho-se-erh Copper Works	
	K'o-t'a Copper Works	
	Kung Po Copper Works	
	Upper Copper Works	
	Lower Copper Works	
T'a-pan Ch'eng	San-chio Shan	
Tihwa	Chai-o-pao	

Industry

Though possibly microscopic in American eyes, the "industries" of Sinkiang deserve, and have been receiving, encouragement. The province has long been known for her handicraft talents in rug-making and silk-weaving, and recently primitive establishments of older days like those for wool-washing and leather-tanning have been improved and supplemented. Tihwa, T'a Ch'eng, and Sui-ting have become principal "industrial" centers boasting of leather tanneries, flour mills, and auto repair and small parts shops. Concentration has, where possible, been put upon the installation of utilities in these and other major cities, and electricity, telephone, and telegraph facilities are now well established. In 1939 it was reported that there were twenty Sinkiang factories of various kinds, including tanneries and mills and a soap factory.

By the close of 1942 a new textile mill capitalized at one million taels was in operation in Tihwa, the province had a sizable iron and steel plant, and new sugar-refining and canning factories were in process of construction. With the aid of a large hydraulic plant the electric power of the province had been increased by this date to 28,000 kilowatts. Public printing offices have been opened at such widely separated points as Tihwa, T'a Ch'eng, Kashgar, Sui-ting, Aqsu, and A Shan, and the *Sinkiang Daily News* is being published in Tihwa.

Communications

Modern communications have made the province aware of the stirring events in the outside world. Telegraph services were opened between 1893 and 1896 when Emperor Kuang Hsü appropriated 240,000 Chinese taels to construct the initial lines and offices. In the period 1903 to 1913 lines were completed which brought the service to Tihwa, Ch'i-t'ai (Ku Ch'eng-tzu), and the Altai region. Successful experiments were made with a radio station at Kashgar and Tihwa in 1921, and a 250-watt station was installed at the capital in 1930. By 1939 radio stations were located at such important towns as Tihwa, Kashgar, Ch'i-t'ai, Ha-mi, T'a Ch'eng, Barkol, Karashahr, Sui-ting, Kucha, and Aqsu. Under the Sheng Shih-ts'ai regime fourteen new wireless and eight new radio stations are said to have been set up. Under his first three-year plan Sheng put through the rigging up of 672 miles of telegraph wire, the repair of 1,379 miles of old lines, and the construction of 1,350 miles of telephone lines. Through these facilities the Chinese and Russian official news services, Central News and Tass, bring up-to-date information to the provincial capital.

Aviation

One of the most significant recent innovations has been the establishment of regular aviation transport to and through Sinkiang. A Eurasia Aviation Corporation line between Shanghai and T'a Ch'eng, opened in 1933, was the first step; but its use was necessarily curtailed by the outbreak of war in 1937. Not until October, 1939, did Eurasia, through the medium of the newly formed Sino-Soviet Aviation Company, open a new service. It ran from Chungking to Ha-mi, whence, through the co-operation of Sinkiang authorities and the Soviet People's Aviation Company, it was continued via Tihwa, I-ning, and Alma-Ata (the latter over the border, in Soviet Kazakhstan) to Moscow. The trip from Chungking across Sinkiang to Alma-Ata totals about 2,584 miles and has become extremely important in United Nations mail and transport services.

Road Transportation

Most significant advances in the New Sinkiang have been those in the field of road transportation. The old caravan routes between China and Russia that run through Sinkiang have been readapted to modern truck travel. The only truck highway in Sinkiang before 1933 is said to have run only a short distance from the provincial capital, and there were then only some twenty military trucks in the whole area. But Ch'en Chi-jung has reported that by 1938 the following truck roads had been completed and put into use in North Sinkiang:

TRUCK ROADS IN NORTH SINKIANG, 1938

Main Roads	Branch Lines	Termini	Distance Covered
Ti-I		Tihwa and I-li (Sui-ting)	450 miles
Ti-Hsing		" " Hsing-hsing Hsia	470 "
Ti-T'a		" " T'a Ch'eng	430 "
	Ti-Tu	" " Turfan	
	Tu-Ch'i	Turfan and Ch'i-chio-ching	1,150 "
	T'a-Ch'eng	T'a Ch'eng and Ch'eng-hua	
Total Mileage ..			2,500 "

Repairs and reconstruction were in addition undertaken over more than 1,875 miles of what is called "dry line" between Tihwa and Khotan (running via Karashahr, Kucha, Aqsu, and Kashgar). A transport control office of the provincial government, which had over 400 trucks of its own in 1938, has maintained control and repair stations on every line and by that date well over the equivalent of $500,000 U.S. currency had been expended on such work. By 1941 it was reported that there were altogether 3,000 trucks engaged in Sinkiang transport work.

Truck transport that has connected Tihwa with Soviet Russia and with other parts of China ran principally from T'a Ch'eng (on the Russian border) through Tihwa to Hsing-hsing Hsia (on the border of Chinese Kansu Province). There has also been important South Sinkiang contact with Soviet Russia from Kashgar to Andizhan via the Terek Pass. On the Chinese side the Sinkiang road system mainly links up with routes that have been under the direction of the Chinese Northwest Highway Administration via the 800-mile Kansu-Sinkiang motor road, which runs from Hsing-hsing Hsia (Baboon Pass) to Lan-chou. The Northwest Highway Administration has had a force—of 1,500 trucks as well as 5,000 drivers and supplementary workers—which maintains lines ultimately connecting up with Chungking. The main Kansu line, a modernization of the old Imperial Caravan Road which used to bear traffic in camels and carts from Sinkiang to Pei-p'ing, represents plans and work extending over the years from 1935 to the present.

Traditionally less well developed and less practicable for truck transport are the caravan trails which lead from Sinkiang (in the south) to Ch'inghai and (in the north) to Mongolia. These have been regularly used for limited local commerce—particularly the stretch from Keriya via Cherchen to Wu-erh-t'eng in Western Ch'inghai—and have great truckage and rail possibilities for the future.

Some Recent Developments

A milestone in Sinkiang modernization was the opening of through telephone connections between Tihwa and Chungking. *Ta Kung Pao* correspondent Ch'en Chi-jung used the line when he was in Tihwa on

October 23, 1942. He has reported that even though reception was weak on the other side, he could hear Chungking clearly. Another sign of the times was the announcement by Chungking postal circles on May 28, 1943, that direct mail service between Sinkiang Province and India had been inaugurated. According to the published report, "After the loss of Burma, all the mail destined for countries by the overland route was sent to Russia where it was re-directed to its various destinations. The opening of the new service has speeded up mail delivery to foreign lands. Arrangements are being made for the opening of parcel service on this overland route."

The wartime fight against inflation and against serious jarring of living conditions has met with considerable success. It is claimed that Price Control Commissions set up "everywhere" have made the Sinkiang price level the lowest in China. Yet wages, correspondent Ch'en Chi-jung has found, are high. Ch'en, walking by a 1942 Sinkiang road construction project about six miles outside of Tihwa, came across laborers who were receiving $12 Chinese a day. He indicates that skilled workers of the province were currently receiving even more.

Serious wage lags in the case of subordinate government salaried employees have been one of China's serious problems in the inflationary years of her Resistance and Reconstruction. This may have been proving difficult for Sinkiang also since many of her government workers, for instance, still receive little more than $200 Chinese a month. But Sinkiang authorities have been meeting the situation for such workers with reductions of social and public expenses, with compensation in the way of reduced prices on commodities, and with small monthly subsidies in such staples as rice, flour, salt, sugar, matches, and oil.

Reports in October, 1943, of Russian "withdrawal" from Sinkiang, have been coupled with increasingly illuminating accounts of new Chinese migration to the province. This can promise a whole new vista of reconstruction developments in the province, and such developments deserve to be watched with keen interest. One of the most immediately noticeable effects has been the announcement on November 10, 1943, of an "ambitious plan" for the modernization of the Sinkiang capital. "During the past three months," the report states, "thousands of soldiers and workers have been working day and night on part of the public works scheduled to be completed by the end of this year. This includes the building of four asphalt roads of over 1000 meters, several macadamized roads of 1500 meters and the modernization of buildings. . . . Over 1,000 old and dilapidated houses are to be torn down and rebuilt, and some 1,800 new houses put up in the new civic center."

The Sinkiang representative on China's National Political Council, Sheng Shih-chi, pointed out during the fall of 1942 that there are no beggars in Sinkiang; I heard the same thing from Chinese Moslems when I was in Kansu Province in 1940. At that time one Moslem, a Lan-chou vendor of Sinkiang raisins and Soviet lump sugar, made pointed examples of one of the city's numerous ragged and grimy child indigents and of a nearby beggar cripple, both whining with hands outstretched. *"Tsai Hsin-chiang mei-yu-liao"* ("That doesn't happen in Sinkiang"), he commented with a shake of the head. Tales that filtered through to Lan-chou in 1939 and 1940 painted Sinkiang in a favorable light indeed. The shortage of labor, the abundance of land and resources, the crying reconstruction needs, and the progressive point of view of the administration in Sinkiang all tend to corroborate Sheng Shih-chi's assertion.

Sinkiang's transformation in the past decade may not appear miraculous in terms of superficial material measurements. The task of domestic reconstruction is not nearly complete; and at least partial credit for what has been accomplished is due to outside aid. Yet, with all this, unswerving and successful application of her Six Great Policies has put the New Sinkiang and the interfusion of frontier races inhabiting the region among the major phenomena of this age. In the years between 1933 and 1943 the province cast aside five centuries of decadence and began to play a unique and vigorous part in modern living. Now, in the midst of a magnificently intermingled old and new—the Sinkiang newspaper hawked in a native bazaar, the phone call to Chungking from a picturesque yamen, an airplane flight over the old Silk Road —the Sinkiang people have shown their eagerness to join in the fashioning of a better world life.

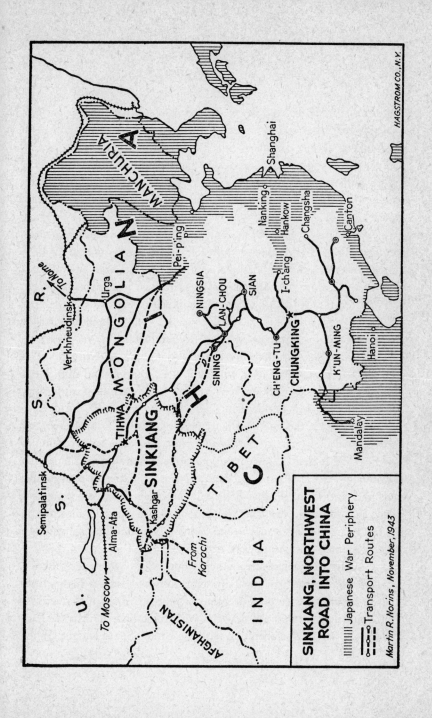

SINKIANG, NORTHWEST
ROAD INTO CHINA

|||||||| Japanese War Periphery

—o Transport Routes

Martin R. Norins, November, 1943

X

WAR REOPENS SINKIANG

SHENG SHIH-TS'AI'S TECHNIQUE, which favored guidance and help from Soviet Russia, had at first required as strict and selective control as possible over all other contact with Sinkiang from the outside. This in the main kept knowledge of what was happening in Sinkiang from the rest of China as well as from the rest of the world. The province, for most purposes, became autonomous and isolated, and with Soviet help Sheng Shih-ts'ai kept it so.

Open warfare between China and Japan in 1937, however, made it necessary for Sheng to allow a limited relaxation of his policy. He permitted Soviet military supplies to come into Eastern China and allowed Chinese wool, skins, tea, and bristles to get out in repayment to Soviet Russia over tightly controlled truck highways running through his province. By 1939 the outbreak of European war also made it advisable and possible to open Chinese-Russian air communications via Sinkiang. But a large measure of the provincial seclusion was strictly maintained. A rigid watch was kept over what strangers went in and out of the province, and strict penalties were invoked by government authorities on trespass of transit privileges.

Now, however, the policy of extreme Sinkiang seclusion has at last been discarded. By the spring of 1942, Japanese pressure on Yünnan Province had forced Chinese attention to the Northwest, and especially to Sinkiang. Soviet Russia, in contrast, was less able to provide the personnel and resources that had been earlier available. Since there is doubt that Sinkiang can longer count on Soviet Russia's direct help, she has turned for assistance to the Chinese National Government and to other United Nations powers.

Nationalist China has already acted dynamically to replace the aid which Soviet Russia gave to Tihwa for almost a decade. In so doing she has initiated a sweeping program of reconstruction in the Chinese Northwest, has emphasized new ties with India and the Middle East, and has shown new co-operation with the United States and the United

Kingdom. This can presage heavy shipment of United Nations goods to China and the Chinese war fronts at last by a revitalized "back door" to Asia.

Generalissimo Chiang Kai-shek himself was dramatically responsible for starting Sinkiang back into world prominence. In February, 1942, two months after Japanese attack on Pearl Harbor, he flew to India and conferred there with British officialdom. His epochal journey took him on February 13 to the Northwest Frontier of India, where he and British companions inspected part of an old Northwest India-Sinkiang transport route. He took the occasion, moreover, to address mountain tribesmen who guard its strategic passes and still pay token tribute to Chinese suzerainty. Almost simultaneously General Chu Shao-liang, military governor of key areas in the Chinese Northwest and a trusted friend of the Generalissimo, traveled to the Sinkiang capital to engage in conversations with Sheng Shih-ts'ai. Shortly thereafter the Chinese National Government appointed a British-educated Chinese, Chaucer H. Wu (Wu Chai-hsiang) to the post of Sinkiang Special Commissioner for Foreign Affairs. The Chungking appointment signalized, first, that control of Sinkiang foreign relations had, probably for the first time since 1927, returned openly to Nationalist authorities in China; second, that predominant Soviet ascendancy in Sinkiang foreign relations might be on the way out.

Chinese announced in July of 1942 that six hundred economic and engineering experts had gathered at Lan-chou, capital of Kansu Province, in connection with proposed development projects for the Chinese Northwest, and that Moslem General Ma Pu-ch'ing had been appointed Pacification Commissioner of the hitherto neglected Tsaidam Marches of Western Ch'inghai, through which it is feasible to lay out one or more routes from South Sinkiang into Kansu. Lan-chou is a key terminus on the Sinkiang-Kansu motor road of Northwest China, and General Ma has long been famous among Chinese for his successful road construction work in Shensi and Kansu provinces. These reports might, therefore, even at that early date have sufficiently hinted at Nationalist China's intentions. Visits subsequently made to Sinkiang by Madame Chiang Kai-shek and Chinese Minister of Economic Affairs

Wong Wen-hao undoubtedly were occasions which helped Chung-king and Tihwa to seal their new bargain. On September 16, 1942, it was announced that Generalissimo Chiang Kai-shek himself had just returned to Chungking after a month's inspection of the Chinese Northwest, and the next day came word that $10,000,000 CNC was being allocated annually for reconstruction projects in the latter region.

In the fall of 1943, after almost a month of conferences between Sheng Shih-ts'ai and Chiang Kai-shek at Chungking, a great pilgrimage toward Chinese Central Asia began. By October 23, fifteen hundred Chinese settlers, refugees from the famine area of Honan, had arrived at Tihwa to engage in land reclamation, over four thousand more had reached the town of Ch'i-t'ai and many additional thousands were expected to migrate to such Sinkiang cities as Tihwa and Kashgar. It was reported that the Sinkiang provincial government was to make a loan of $5,000 Chinese currency available to the settlers, and each family was to receive over fifteen acres of land. "Provisions, seeds, cows, farmhouses and all necessary farm implements," together with an outright subsidy of $2,500 CNC for "each family" were also to be theirs. Is it any wonder that the hard-pushed Chinese peasant, weak from the barest of sustenance, has straightened up with new hope at the promise of land, tools, and capital in Sinkiang!

"Sinkiang today," a Chinese writer has stated, "is like California before 1849 and Altai is like Alaska before 1867." Not only can the land be made to produce more food, but the mineral wealth is relatively untouched. It has been said that wars make nations, and it may well be that the Chinese in days to come will feel positively indebted for the restlessness of necessity which Japan's aggression has aroused in the melting pot of Asia. For thousands of picked men out of the fifty millions who fled from Eastern China to Szechwan and Yünnan in 1938 and 1939, once more have picked up possessions and have poured across the mountains and plains—this time north and westward into Sinkiang. Over the gravel-mud roads of Shensi and Kansu, across the turbid Yellow River, west of the River, and then through the Jade Gate to Central Asia they went, taking their bedding, their baskets, treasured family heirlooms, needed household utensils, their wives and sons and hopes. The man on foot, the riksha, the rubber-tired cart, a camel of the Gobi, a General Motors or a Russian Ziss truck—all these have been China's "covered wagon." The throng of people has been jolly, too; jammed in with youth, and gasoline drums, and the *ch'i-lai* of the Chinese marching song. Behind this push into China's vast Northwest has been largely a determination to build a land hard with metal and tough with industrial sinew. But there has been also the lure of adventure, good living, age-old lore, and rich cultural promise.

Into the land of the Wei-wu-erh to which Sheng Shih-ts'ai has brought his Six Great Policies and the understanding and justifiable pride among races that they have taught, the Chinese today once again has come. This time he has come not merely as in antiquity but also as a producer—a farmer, a laborer, a technician, a leader united with the leaders of many other races. As a Chinese he has been among the first to perceive that superlative amounts of ideas, energy, men, and machinery are needed in a hurry in Sinkiang and that part of all this may come from any one or more of a number of neighboring areas—India, Afghanistan, Soviet Turkestan, Siberia, and Mongolia—as well as from China proper. Ultimately the matériel and technical initiative for much of it, he knows, must flow from the United States and Britain, as in the past decade much has come from Soviet Russia. Pioneers of American and English, as well as of Asiatic, background may be expected to hear this call of the Chinese Far West. Through them, and others, Sinkiang promises to be transformed into a grand new frontier area of progress.

That there has been serious American interest in these Sinkiang developments was revealed on April 19, 1943, with the temporary appointment of Mr. Oliver Edmund Clubb as United States Consul to Tihwa. Mr. Clubb's assignment, the later arrival in the Sinkiang capital of a British colleague, and reports from usually reliable sources in October, 1943, that "Russians" have been "leaving Sinkiang Province in large numbers" and "dismantling and removing Russian-built plants," that the roads of the province have been "dotted" with "cars hauling out Russian equipment" and that a "Russian garrison" was leaving "by truck, in small units"—these suggest that Chinese aid and influence in the province may already be replacing that which the Soviets have apparently decided not to continue. Should such a change in Sinkiang affairs be in the process of accomplishment with friendly understanding on the part of the four great powers of China, Soviet Russia, the United States, and the United Kingdom, it might prove to be an important diplomatic achievement in Sino-Russian relations.

XI

GATEWAY TO ASIA

IT IS WELL, indeed, for the United Nations that Generalissimo Chiang Kai-shek and General Sheng Shih-ts'ai have been able to arrange the reopening of Sinkiang. For Japan's blockade of China extends in an arc from the northernmost tip of Manchuria southward around the coast and up into Burma and western Yünnan Province. Except for the northern tip of Burma, the remaining land gaps, the terrain not yet caught in the Japanese blockade pincers, are on the Chinese inland frontier of Tibet, Sinkiang, and Mongolia.

The physical difficulties of sending matériel into China across upper Burma are not at all insurmountable, and this is now being demonstrated by the Assam-China air transport service, which is now the main source of foreign supply and carrying more than the Burma Road used to. Construction of the Ledo Road, too, indicates the belief that land supply can be pushed along mountain trails of Indian Assam and over the Burma-Yünnan ranges—some of the loftiest in the world. But traffic run across this terrain meets exceptional difficulties. It passes on the edges of bristling war fronts, confronts danger from Japanese guns, can carry only a limited volume of goods, and must defy day-to-day uncertainty. When a successful military campaign reopens the Burma Road, it may again become one of China's "lifelines." But too much should not be immediately hoped for from even that direction in view of adjacent Japanese armies and of the uncertainties of the sup-

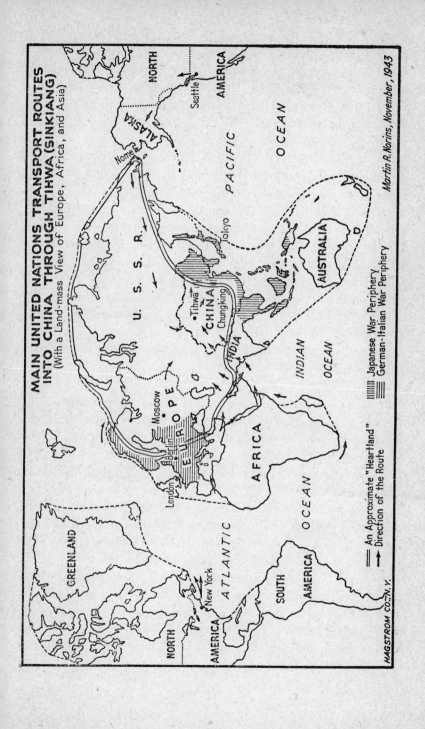

MAIN UNITED NATIONS TRANSPORT ROUTES
INTO CHINA THROUGH TIHWA (SINKIANG)
(With a Land-mass View of Europe, Africa, and Asia)

Martin R. Norins, November, 1943

||||| Japanese War Periphery,
≡≡≡≡ German-Italian War Periphery

══ An Approximate "Heartland"
→ Direction of the Route

HAGSTROM CO., N.Y.

ply problem. Until a large part of Southeast Asia is cleared of danger from Japan, reopening of the Burma Road probably not only is not imminent but even loses a great deal of its value. It is well to look elsewhere at present for the route along which large-scale supply to China may be maintained.

The Siberia-Outer Mongolia-Ningsia Route

The shortest and most direct potential route through still peaceful United Nations zones from North America to China is that via Canada, Alaska, and Siberia to Chinese Ningsia. Some 6,500 miles long, it extends from Seattle to Alaska, then across the narrow Bering Strait, and along the Trans-Siberian Railway as far as Verkhneudinsk (Ulan Ude). At Verkhneudinsk, in Siberia, it branches southward through Ulan Bator, capital of the "Mongolian People's Republic," to Ningsia. The Ulan Bator (Urga) to Ningsia part of this route, according to available information, before Pearl Harbor was still little more than a desert camel trail. It has been, besides, vulnerable at the Ningsia end, since 1937, to an ever-threatening Japanese push through Suiyüan Province.

The Sinkiang Routes

Remaining routes now geographically practicable enter China through Sinkiang. One such, an extension of the above-mentioned Siberian route, runs along or on the Trans-Siberian Railway beyond Verkhneudinsk and, utilizing the Turksib Railway, reaches Alma-Ata, in Soviet Kazakhstan. From there it crosses back eastward into Sinkiang via Sui-ting or T'a Ch'eng, and passes on the modern Sinkiang-Kansu motor road toward Chungking and the Chinese war fronts. This route, probably under 9,000 miles in all, deserves primary attention. It utilizes already existing modern transport facilities and, with the exception of possible political obstacles, might become a very useful supplementary avenue for United Nations supplies into the China area.

American goods can also obtain entrance into Sinkiang from the Middle East and India. Delivery requires a long ocean journey—one which runs from the eastern coast of the United States to the Persian Gulf or the Arabian Sea. But once the long maritime part of the trip is complete, shipments into China are quite feasible. Two routes have gained special public attention, one through Persia (Iran) and the other through India. The first begins at the Persian Gulf port of Bushire, in Iran, and runs by road and rail to Bandar Shah on the Caspian Sea. Once the Caspian is crossed by boat, the goods can be loaded on freight cars and carried by rail from Krasnovodsk to Alma-Ata, but a short distance by good highway from Sinkiang. The other route starts at Karachi, Indian port on the Arabian Sea, and runs by rail to Peshawar, then by road from Peshawar to Kabul in Afghanistan and north through Termez to Samarkand in Soviet Uzbekistan. From Samarkand the goods, again, can be shipped by rail to Alma-Ata and then by highway into Sinkiang.

Further major possibilities for United Nations transport into Sinkiang include the well-tested pack trails into Kashgaria (South Sinkiang) from Kashmir (Northwest India) and from Afghanistan. One of the most desirable of these routes, that passing through Kashmir, utilizes the cities of Karachi and Srinagar and covers some 4,500 miles of India-China terrain. Crossing 18,000-foot passes, these trails are not yet feasible for motorized transport, though they have long been used for caravan trade. There is, however, no serious physical obstacle (other than possibly the altitude limits of airplane flight) to air transport from Srinagar, for instance, (or from Kabul), over the Karakorum Mountains (or Pamirs) to Kashgaria. From Kashgaria there is already available roadbed for motor travel on the old Sinkiang South Road to Tihwa or to other parts of Sinkiang, and from there into China Proper.

With the Nazis now boxed up in Europe and with the Mediterranean open, sea shipments to the Middle East now need not (though they still can) take the long haul by way of the Cape of Good Hope; they are able, instead, to go directly—say, New York-Port Said and then across Syria and Iraq to Iran. But up to only recently adequate preparations for passage of goods to China through Iran and Soviet Russia may not have been completed. An Associated Press dispatch from Chungking dated July 5, 1943, cited Chinese Minister of Communications Tseng Yang-fu as declaring that "at last" arrangements had been concluded for use of this supply line. Yet Tseng even then qualified his statement by saying that "heavy military supplies cannot be brought in." There is reason to believe that shipments into Sinkiang via Iran and Russian Turkestan still may not be unrestricted. Since peculiar political problems have existed in regard to China's diplomatic position *vis-à-vis* Afghanistan, it may also still be politically inconvenient to send goods to China through that country. Yet air transport into Sinkiang from Northwest India in any case ought to be practicable under current conditions, as a supplement to the Assam-Yünnan route now being used.

Indian and Siberian Routes to Sinkiang

Passage (by air or by land) through Northwest India has both political and physical difficulties but those difficulties are not insurmountable. American use of the routes appears to be subject to the political approval of the British, Indian, and local governments concerned. But in this case political obstacles ought not to be too serious, for India (as part of the British Empire) is allied with the United States in war against Japan as well as against the European part of the Axis.

The chief Indian seaport for entry of goods bound for Sinkiang via the Northwest Frontier Province is Karachi, in peacetime a city of some 260,000 persons, a port on the Arabian Sea, and a station on the Indian Northwest Railway. It is a total distance of 1,133 miles, by railway and then road, from Karachi to the Kashmir metropolis of Srinagar farther north. Railway shipped, Sinkiang-bound goods would probably need to be unloaded from trains at Jammu and transshipped by truck on the motor road which leads sixty miles beyond Srinagar to the town of Baltal. Beyond that point a land traveler would probably pack in.

Nowadays the airplane may well help nullify mountain hazards of Northwest India, and replace old Karakorum trade routes for war and post-war purposes. Air transport from Srinagar to Kashgar, roughly 375 miles as a plane might fly, would present a difficult task, but one for which veteran American airmen are now in all probability sufficiently trained. In comparison with the now regularly negotiated Upper Burma (Assam-China) ferry farther east, Srinagar-Kashgar flights might even seem simple. A force of 100 American transport planes of even the current Douglas C-47 type with a capacity of two tons (crew and equipment already accounted for) ought to be able to deliver some 9,000 tons of air cargo a month between the Indian and Sinkiang termini. With the newer type transports (some reported capable of carrying seven tons each) or with increased planes of the first indicated type, the tonnage potential of this route would be correspondingly raised.

There would be serious but not insuperable problems of personnel, fuel, and food. Probably 1,400 men would be required—including plane and ground crews—to deliver those 9,000 tons. Quarters, suitable new and enlarged hangars, administrative establishments, barracks, and storage facilities would probably have to be erected, particularly on the China side. Fuel would be a problem, but Iranian and Iraq oil would be obtainable. Aviation gasoline would, however, probably have to be ferried into Kashgar in order that return trips to Srinagar might be practicable. Part of the food for such a force of this small size would be obtainable in the Kashgar area.

Enthusiasm over United Nations possession of such an Indian "back door" to Sinkiang is warranted, for it can be of substantial importance. But one should not be blinded to its limitations. The American road to Chungking via the Atlantic Ocean, India and Sinkiang is still terrifically long, even now that it is possible to cut out the intermediate ocean trek around Africa and go through the Mediterranean. And on the lap into South Sinkiang from India, the lofty, jagged, mountainous terrain is a great hardship to man and his carrier—whether it be foot, horse, motor car, railway, or plane. Last, these maritime and mountain hazards place limitations on the tonnage that may be transported within a given time. Such a journey requires a tremendous expenditure of human energy, time, and materials, and much of this can and should be saved. Transit into Sinkiang through India and the Middle East can be helpful to the United Nations. It is a welcome change in the war outlook that it is daily becoming more practicable. But there might be much more value in a supply route to Sinkiang through Alaska and Soviet Asia.

Since the Siberian route passes through Soviet Russian territory before actual access to Sinkiang is gained, however, its use by Americans for United Nations war purposes poses an extremely delicate problem in international relations. The Soviet Union, though allied with the United States and others of the United Nations against the European Axis, is at "peace" with Japan. So long as that Russo-Japanese "peace" is maintained, Russia may not feel free, or be able, to permit sizable shipments of American war materials to pass through her Siberian terrain. For that reason use of the Siberian-Turkestan-Sinkiang route may, perhaps, not be realized.

United Nations Opportunity

Supply routes from India and Iran would provide more than half the groundwork for effective use of Sinkiang in the Chinese war theater; but "half" is written advisedly, for unequivocal United Nations strategy would have a supply line extend from Seattle through Alaska, Eurasia, and Africa to eastern North America. This would mean untrammeled intercommunications all the way, in both directions, for all the United Nations. Well protected, it could be a continuous United Nations highway passing through the core of the Sino-Russian Rear and there meeting central crossroads which traverse Soviet Asia and Chinese Sinkiang—a global, north-south transport way to United Nations mastery of what Mackinder called the "World-Island" and its "Heartland." This could be one of the answers to the supply problem which meets and then utilizes Axis west-east geopolitics. American entree to the Sino-Russian Rear through India, the Middle East, and Siberia, offers rare opportunity to the United Nations today.

XII

A FRONTIER FOR THE WAR AND AFTER

IF ONE PREMISES that Han Chinese in large numbers by the thousands will continue to migrate westward into Turkestan and that Sinkiang will take her rightful place in the new China, what might some of the characteristic wartime and post-war developments in the province be?

Readjustments will naturally be called for, but the 1933-1943 program of the New Sinkiang has already provided an introduction to the modern, machine-type economy and to some of the equipment and products associated with it, and has given the native population the opportunity to work on a cooperative basis with both Han Chinese and other outsiders. The new problem, then, need not require the breaking of ground; it can be, instead, largely one of amplifying the cooperation, good-will, and training built up in the past decade through the program of the Six Great Policies. Sympathetic appreciation of this point of view by incoming Han Chinese settlers, as well as by non-Chinese, may prove especially valuable. Since Han Chinese probably will settle permanently in Sinkiang, the relations between them and the native inhabitants will be of special significance. Third party nationals will probably stay in the province only as long as they are needed to help perform the groundwork of a particular United Nations project or see that it gets well under way; yet the way in which they are able to get along among themselves and with the local population in Sinkiang can be a practicable test for—and guide to future—international cooperation of a broader scope.

Large-scale wartime activities in Sinkiang Province may, nevertheless, involve many other "ticklish" and complicated questions. The importation of considerable capital equipment and technical personnel will be the number one problem. Nor will the shipment of a particular item from, perhaps, the United States to a stipulated city in Sinkiang be solely a matter of selecting the most advantageous route or routes. Since Sinkiang is surrounded on all four sides by land, on two sides of which there is foreign terrain, and since China is under blockade, permission must be obtained to send the item across non-Chinese and non-American territory. Once it arrives in Sinkiang, it must be transported within the province or through it and into China Proper. All this involves adequate personnel and facilities. Then the problems of installation and of operation will have to be solved. When the traffic mounts, as it must to be effective, the questions of personnel, equipment, fuel, and food will become correspondingly more pressing.

Transport into China Proper

As already explained the truck roads, say, from T'a Ch'eng in the north or from Kashgar in the south to Tihwa and, further, across the Sinkiang-Kansu border to Lan-chou and then to Chungking, already have seen use. From the latter two points the highway network, though rough, is extensive. In addition, Sinkiang transport facilities from Kashgar through South Sinkiang are extendable to and across Ch'inghai while those from Tihwa in North Sinkiang have practicable caravan links with Mongolia. By means of these basic traffic arteries eventually even the furthest of the Chinese war fronts may be reached. The problem of oil supply is admittedly far from simple but—with adequate backing from appropriate United Nations quarters—it can be solved.

A Sinkiang Development Commission

Whatever the international transport base for matériel and capital equipment to enter China via Sinkiang, United Nations administrative machinery will be needed to handle the development and utilization of Sinkiang communications. Such a mechanism could conceivably be at least a four power commission, with the Republic of China, the United Kingdom, the Soviet Union, and the United States represented. But should the Siberia route not be used and should the Soviet government possibly continue its "peaceful" relationship with Japan, it might be embarrassed by formal involvement in such a commission. Consequently membership might need to include only three national interests directly —the Republic of China, the United Kingdom, and the United States. Other interested United Nations powers (such as the Soviet Union) might be invited to send non-voting auditors to the commission meetings or might merely be apprised informally of commission activities.

On the other hand, China (and through her, Sinkiang) might with no little cause contend that Sinkiang development is solely a Chinese concern, and that membership in the commission should be solely at Chinese invitation and on Chinese sufferance; in that case it would be vital that the other United Nations make known their positions to the Chinese Government in advance in order to ensure that outside aid in the development of Sinkiang would be used with the interests of the other United Nations as firmly considered, for the duration of the war, as the interests of China herself. Such a stand on the part of China, far from being a cause for abandoning the commission scheme, ought to be considered sympathetically as but one more possible means of its inception. For, once administrative machinery were established and a flow of materials well under way, economic and military developments on a vast scale would be opened up. The effect upon the war and upon the future development of Sinkiang and all China would be immeasurable. Not only would such a move be timely and far-sighted, but it might well be a valuable contribution toward postwar peace and stability in Central Asia.

Wartime Development Needs

If China and/or the United Nations as a whole act on these premises and give sizable attention to development of Sinkiang, this development will doubtless take two forms: one to expedite victory, the other to further permanent construction in Sinkiang and China.

The primary wartime needs of Sinkiang are further improvement of her truck road facilities, airplane landing fields, petroleum potential, communications, agricultural and animal husbandry, and her cultural sympathies with the United Nations cause. As far as the Sinkiang road system is concerned, most good can be done by improvement and care of existing facilities and by development of the South Sinkiang-Ch'ing-hai and the North Sinkiang-Mongolia routes. There is not yet need for finished, American-style paved roads; what is needed is maintenance and repair of gravel roads along which military trucking and heavy tanks can move. Second in priority is the improvement and/or establishment of adequate airfields, hangars, barracks, and storage facilities to facilitate airplane transport between such outlying cities as T'a Ch'eng (in the north) and Kashgar (in the south) (1) to other points in the province and (2) to neighboring Chinese areas. For some time it will probably be necessary to import airplane fuels, but intensified extraction and more modern cracking of Sinkiang mineral oil promise to provide an expanding source of gasoline and oil for both automobile and airplane transport. The skeleton of radio and wireless communications already exists in the province, but this will require extension and modernization. With the influx of new foreign and Chinese technical and military personnel there will be an added drain on existing food resources, which will call for a broadened irrigation, farm, and animal husbandry improvement program. Last, it would be well for information services of the other United Nations together with China to take more active measures to acquaint the people of Sinkiang with all favorable phases of the United Nations war effort.

Both wartime and post-war Sinkiang will benefit by these innovations, and the ground will be laid for long-range international development of the province.

Long Range Development of Sinkiang

Early pioneering in proposals for such long-range international development of Sinkiang as might be considered here was undertaken by Dr. Sun Yat-sen, the "father" of modern China. According to the preface of his book *The International Development of China,* he wanted:

> . . . the vast resources of China . . . developed internationally . . . for the good of the world in general and the Chinese people in particular. . . . Thus the root of war will be forever exterminated so far as China is concerned.

Strikingly enough, the construction of a Northwestern Railway System to end in Sinkiang and the colonization of that province and Mongolia were among Dr. Sun's foremost proposals. The Northwestern Railway System as he foresaw it, was to start at a port on the Northeast China Coast and to pass westwards via Dolon Nor some 1,600 miles to

Tihwa, in Sinkiang. It was to have a number of branch lines, among them a veritable Sinkiang network. He suggested that the state should launch colonization in Sinkiang by buying up land and then in turn leasing it to colonists "on perpetual terms"; he further proposed that the state furnish the colonists with initial capital, implements, and houses at cost for cash or on the installment plan. Some ten million people, Dr. Sun anticipated, could be settled in Mongolia and Sinkiang within ten years by these methods. It appears that the Chinese Nationalist Government has already started in 1943 to carry out part of Dr. Sun's colonization proposals.

Dr. Sun's far-sighted emphasis upon railway construction to link Sinkiang more effectively with the Chinese interior and to link together outlying settlements within Sinkiang was long considered visionary. It is not practicable even now to carry out his scheme in its entirety for the war needs of 1944. Emphasis on Sinkiang truck roads and airports is for the time being more practicable than emphasis on railways; for the war, a stepped-up colonization by Chinese seems less pressing than the passage of vital war materials and Occidental technical and military help to interior China. Yet both programs place positive emphasis on the type of modernization Sinkiang now needs. Today extraction of Sinkiang minerals, expanded food production, scientific animal husbandry, furtherance of education, and widespread modernization of various kinds, all deserve a prominent place in any plan for practicable wartime use of the area. True, the difficulties to be confronted are not few. Mineral resources, for example, are in the main unsurveyed. Sizable expansion in food production, too, will probably depend on attempts at extensive land reclamation which, in turn, faces restrictions due to the limitations of available water supply. But serious as these and other problems are, they are not so serious that they cannot be solved.

In the post-war world the opening of Sinkiang communications—road, air, river, and railway (both provincial and extra-provincial) as well as wireless, radio, newspaper, and motion picture—promise a tremendous and needed outlet for Western as well as Eastern energies. The expansion of irrigation together with the resultant extension of agricultural production; the modernization and broadening of provincial "industry"; the development of almost untouched mineral resources; the transfer of Chinese colonists from crowded coastal and interior cities to the relatively open northwestern frontier; the revitalization of the indigenous culture through improved educational methods; and the influx of modern ideas and implements of all kinds—all these can turn this now so little appreciated Central Asian region into a throbbing, pulsing artery of a new Eurasia. There is need to supplement the guide-points already laid down by such as Dr. Sun Yat-sen and to draw up an even more specific prospectus for the post-war world. No matter how or when such a prospectus may evolve, the modernization of the New Sinkiang is predestined and will help to bring to complete fruition the New China. For best fulfillment of both wartime and post-war needs, such modernization requires foreign goods and technical personnel. But the development, notwithstanding, cannot much longer be restrained. Part of the inevitable drive toward modernization of the Sino-Russian Rear, the development of the New Sinkiang should have a noteworthy influence on the course of Chinese and Asiatic affairs.

APPENDIX

A Selection of Paraphrases from the Book

Sheng Shih-ts'ai yü Hsin Hsin-chiang

1. The Racial Question of Sinkiang

The races of Sinkiang are very mixed, as past academic investigation has disclosed. What stock there was in the province originally is not clear, but since the introduction of the policies of Sheng Tu-pan, fourteen racial types have been recognized. They are: *Han, Man, Meng, Hui, Wei-wu-erh, Ha-sa-k'o, T'a-chi-k'o, T'a-lan-chi, T'a-t'a-erh, Ko-erh-k'o-tzu, Wu-tzu-pieh-k'o, Hsi-po, So-lun,* and *Kuei-hua.*

There are no accurate statistics in regard to the total population of the province. South Sinkiang adjoins India and the customs of its people are more or less like those of the inhabitants there. Therefore, since there is free intercourse east and west between both places, they get a sort of dual national classification. On their entering India they are called Chinese, but if they enter China they are called Indians! As it happens, some of these nomads have been taking advantage of the situation and carry on business in both places.

But when inhabitants of Sinkiang talk about this question, in general they say there are fourteen races and four million people. It would be useful to get an idea of the differing types which make up those four million. They say that the *Wei-wu-erh* people (or *Ch'an Hui*) are most numerous, comprising about eighty per cent of the total; of the remainder about ten per cent are *Han* and ten per cent other races.

The *Han* who have come to Sinkiang are divided into four groups: (1) One group includes the criminal exiles of the type which, they say, were sent to Yünnan and Sinkiang before the Tso Tsung-t'ang era. (2) Hunanese comprise the second group. These came as military or political workers during the Tso Tsung-t'ang period and became Sinkiang farmers or officials. (Not a few Yünnanese came in the time of Yang Tseng-hsin, and not an inconsiderable number of Kansu men came when Chin Shu-jen got political control. This brings us up to the present day, when Sheng Shih-ts'ai governs. During his control not a few men from Northeast China have been added, for that is the way of modern Chinese politics.) (3) When there were merchant transactions or when annual salaries were paid, all exchange from Ch'ing Dynasty currency to Sinkiang currency went through the hands of Shansi money brokers. The latter obtained command of Sinkiang economics for a while, though by now their control has lessened. When Tso Tsung-t'ang was subjugating Sinkiang, Pei-p'ing and Tientsin men organized a merchant corps. Whenever a great army was sent out, they furnished the army with its military supplies, and they in turn possessed great military authority. Afterwards there came a time in which not only Pei-p'ing and Tientsin peoples traded with Sinkiang, but in which Hunan and Hupeh men even came there to deal in tea bricks. All these are included in the third group. (4) Agriculturists of Kansu and Shensi, farmers who were poor and bitter, are reported to have fled as refugees to Sinkiang. These refugees are a fourth *Han* type. But there have not been very many of these; escape from their bitter livelihood has not been easy for the farming people of Kansu and Shensi. It is said that officials have decreed joint responsibility, and that one cannot of his own free will cross the boundary. For if one family escapes, then ten other families are held responsible.

The *Man* [Manchu] people began coming to Sinkiang at the beginning of Ch'ing times, and a great group migrated there during the reign of Ch'ien Lung. After Ch'ien Lung had pacified Sinkiang, I-li was selected as the administrative center and officers were established there to command the Manchu soldiers stationed throughout the province. At the time the expressions Old *Man* Fort, New *Man* Fort, *Hsi-po* Fort, and *So-lun* Fort were in use. (*Hsi-po* and *So-lun* are tribal language characters also referring to the Manchu people.) In the time of the Ch'ing Dynasty, when the Manchus took over governmental power in China and became imperious and wealthy, the orders they "sent down" brought enmity among many races.

The Mongol people originally were to be found along the Road North of the Heavenly Mountains. In the beginning of the Ch'ing times they were named *Chun-ko-erh Pu* [Jungars] and their soldiers were of four kinds: (1) *E-lu-t'e Pu,* which herded cattle in the neighborhood of Urumchi; (2) *Chun-ko-erh Pu,* which herded cattle in the I-li area; (3) *Tu-erh-po-t'e Pu,* which herded cattle along the banks of the E-erh-ch'i-ssu River; and (4) *Tu-erh-hu-t'e Pu,* which herded in the neighborhood of Tarbagatai.

Now many of the Mongol people dwell in the Altai of North Sinkiang. Mongols herd cattle as their livelihood and, because they haven't any other homes, travel from oasis to oasis. In the winter they dwell on the south slope of those mountains and, to escape the cold weather take to what they call winter nests [*tung-wo*]; in the summer they dwell on the high plateaus in order to get cool and take to what they call summer nests [*hsia-wo*]. They believe in Buddhism and consider milk and lamb great delicacies, although they also eat other food made of flour.

The *Hui* [Moslems] are divided into two types, the *Han Hui* [Chinese

Han Moslems] and the *Ch'an Hui* [Turban Moslems] or *Wei-wu-erh*. The *Ch'an Hui* or *Wei-wu-erh* [Uighurs] were called *Ch'an Hui* from the white turbans they wear. But after Sheng Tu-pan gained government control, they became known as the *Wei-wu-erh* people. Originally the *Ch'an Hui's* own name was *Wei-wu-erh*. Sheng Tu-pan, in line with his aim to attain real racial peace, saw that the two characters *wei* and *wu* had a very exalted meaning for the people themselves, and so he reverted to use of that name. As for the *Han Hui* they are Moslems who have emigrated from Kansu or Shensi. These Mohammedan people are, in speech and customs, for the most part like the *Han* Chinese. But they believe in Mohammedanism, are forbidden to eat pork, and are forbidden to smoke opium or to drink intoxicants. A great part dwell in such places as Yen-ch'i and Ha-mi, and not a few dwell in I-li, Tihwa, and Ch'i-t'ai along the North Road.

The *Wei-wu-erh* are the original settlers of Sinkiang. They are in all of South and in many places of North Sinkiang. More specifically they are in four groups: Ha-mi, Kucha, Kashgar, and Khotan. The Ha-mi group includes those of Turfan and Shan-shan counties. These places originally were strong forts of the Mongols. The people all believed in Buddhism but afterwards, as Mohammedanism replaced the Mongol faith, they were converted to Mohammedanism. This place always was characterized by warfare, but the people were not always powerful. The Kucha group includes the three hsien of Yen-ch'i, Kucha, and Aqsu. The people of these places are peaceful, and besides engaging in agriculture, have handicraft trades. The Kashgar group includes all the counties of K'o-shih Ch'ü. This is the principal center of the *Ch'an Hui,* who are Mohammedan merchants and farmers. The people of this group and of that at Khotan are very patient and so are excellent at handicraft work. In Tihwa one can see many famous and precious types of rugs from these two places. The deep eyes and high noses of the *Wei-wu-erh* are similar to those of the Turks. It would, in fact, not be far wrong if these two were classified as types of one race, for the areas in which they dwell are not far from each other.

The girls' eyelashes are sharp and distinct and are inclined upwards slightly in order to attract men. The men and women mature early, and a girl is eligible for marriage before she is fifteen. The marriage ceremony is closed to outsiders and is very meaningful. The girl goes out of doors veiled. Otherwise if the *A-hung* (the ruling priest) happens to come along, he can interfere. In Southern Sinkiang this is enforced very much but in Tihwa there is more leniency. Girls in the home avoid a stranger, for they dare not be seen. The males have more than one wife and, according to the faith, they are allowed four. Betrothal is pledged by the father and mother, after which the *A-hung* is invited to perform a ceremony. At the time she is wed, the new bride covers her head with a veil, there is piping and drumming, and she is taken on a donkey to the husband's household. Then the *A-hung* completes the ritual. If the husband and wife are not compatible, they are free to divorce. In case the husband separates from his wife, the household goods are entrusted to the wife; if the wife separates from her husband, she does not get to take the household goods. A son is the property of his father; a girl, the property of the mother. After a half year's separation, it is not improper to remarry. The general idea at such a time is that "the broken mirror has become round again."

According to the system of funerals, if a man dies the corpse is wrapped in a white cloth, is carried into a cave, and the *A-hung* is called on to perform a ceremony. At this time members of the family wear a white cap and sash for forty to a hundred days in the home. The head of the corpse is not shaved, Chinese clothes are not worn, and the body is buried in a grave—in a ceremony not unlike that of Chinese. It is because there are very many *Wei-wu-erh* people in Sinkiang that these particulars concerning their marriage and funeral ceremonies are cited.

The *Ha-sa-k'o* [Kazakh] people, classified racially between the *Hui* and the *Meng* [Mongol], are also nomadic and so their life habits are wont to be like the Mongols. But many also respect the Mohammedan faith, and their marriage and burial ceremonies are in general similar to those of the Moslems. It is reported that the *Ha-sa-k'o* originally were a united tribal group. During the reigns of T'ung Chih and Kuang Hsü of the Ch'ing times, however, China and Russia twice demarcated their national boundaries. As a result one branch was said to have been put under Russian and another under Chinese sovereignty.

This people excels at horsemanship, and children five and six years old have been known for their riding ability. There are none at the age of ten who do not have unusual talent such as enables them to tell the sickness of a horse, to control the animal, to stand on its back, to bend from the horse to pick up things, to straighten up quickly, and above all to ride as though glued on the animal. Such feats as these are performed by *Ha-sa-k'o* soldiers in Soviet motion pictures. The *Ha-sa-k'o* people are very strong but also very lazy, and outside of tending cattle, often do not have any occupation. So some, when winter season comes, take to the life of a lancer. A few steal cattle and horses, and many kill men and take their goods. For this is only an outgrowth of their military talent, and they lack any other way in which to use it. Wouldn't one think that if these excellent warriors were persuaded to attack the enemy in this time of resistance, each would do the work of a hundred?

The *T'a-t'a-erh* [Tatars] people are originally from the *T'a-t'a* stock of the Mongols. They migrated to the border woods among the Lamas, then they absorbed some Moslem culture. Later, when they had moved to the Russian border, they mixed with the white people. Some of their offspring are even white in color. Over one half of this race are merchants while others are engaged in animal husbandry. Few have very well-to-do-homes.

There are, besides, the *T'a-chi-k'o* [Tajiks], *T'a-lan-chi* [Taranchi], *K'o-erh-k'o-tzu* [Khalkha], *Wu-tzu-pieh-k'o* [Uzbeks], and many smaller racial divisions which cannot be given much discussion here. As for the so-called *Kuei-hua* people, their speech indicates they are related to the White Russians. During the Great Soviet Revolution a few capitalists could not stand the bitterness of the times and escaped to Sinkiang and China. Therefore they have been called *Kuei-hua* [naturalized] people. Recently, as Soviet Russia has become a strong nation and as the livelihood of the Soviet people has improved, the *Kuei-hua* have gradually been attracted once again to the culture of their homeland.

2. The Importance of Sinkiang in Chinese National Defense

On the occasion of the Moslem rebellion during the Ch'ing Dynasty, Tso Tsung-t'ang epitomized Sinkiang's importance as follows: "Great weight should be given to Sinkiang as a protection for Mongolia. For as it protects Mongolia, it ensures that the power of the capital and the forearm of the Northwest work in unison. It also ensures that there is no break in the country's topographical defenses. But if Sinkiang is not strong, then Mongolia will not be at peace. Moreover, then bandits might outflank the whole Kansu, Shensi, and Shansi frontier. In such an emergency those places might be defended, but not victoriously. In such a case, Sinkiang would be a direct north gate to the mountains, and there would not be a day of rest or sleep."

If Sinkiang is protected, the savages won't dare to graze their horses in the southeast (as was proved in the Han times, when Chang Ch'ien was sent into the Western Regions, and in T'ang times, when Kuo Tzu-i was sent to pacify the Moslems [Uighurs?]). If Sinkiang is lost, the savages can spread far into the interior (as was proved when the Sung Dynasty was forced to migrate to the south and when the Ming Dynasty was not able to protect the province). But the present is by no means the same as the past. The so-called savages of today are not people of a mere tribe; they do not stop with merely bows and arrows. They have airplanes and cannon, scientific learning of the most advanced type, gold, strategists, and even secret traitors in their employ. The position of Sinkiang in the national defense of today is as different from that of the Han, T'ang, Sung, and Ming times, as heaven is different from earth. Enemies do not stop with merely attempting to disturb relations between Sinkiang and the interior. We have learned that several years ago the enemy established espionage agents in Ch'inghai and Ningsia with instructions to see that unrest in Sinkiang did not stop. Recently the enemy attempted to send Tientsin traitors overland to Sinkiang with $3,000,000 Chinese money in sabotage funds. The enemy knew that Sino-Soviet cooperation is at the core of the Chinese resistance and that if China and Russia want to further their mutual unity they must protect Sinkiang; but the enemy also knew that if there is disturbance in Sinkiang and if Sino-Russian relations are harmed there, then the Chinese resistance will show a great change. So money was spent in an attempt to buy off merchants and officials in Tihwa and even a Vice-Chairman of Sinkiang Province. But the plot was smashed.

3. The Eight Point Proclamation and the Six Great Policies

As soon as Sheng Tu-pan began his rule, on the one hand he ordered his soldiers to pacify the rebellion and on the other he issued an Eight Point Proclamation. The eight points of this proclamation as originally issued are as follows: (1) Establishment of Racial Equality; (2) Guarantee of Religious Freedom; (3) Equitable Distribution of Agricultural and Rural Relief; (4) Reform of Government Finance; (5) The Cleaning Up of Government Administration; (6) The Expansion of Education; (7) The Promotion of Self-Government; (8) The Improvement of the Judiciary.

But the Eight Point Proclamation served only as a guide to the type of government toward which the Sinkiang revolution was to lead. If the principles of the Eight Point Proclamation were to be carried out for long, they needed a new guarantee. Therefore, once he had eliminated internal rebellion, unified Sinkiang, and firmly established government authority, Sheng Tu-pan invoked his Six Great Policies. What were they? They were: (1) Anti-imperialism; (2) Kinship to Sovietism; (3) Racial Equality; (4) Clean Government; (5) Peace; and (6) Reconstruction. By means of the Six Great Policies the Eight Point Proclamation could be guaranteed. With the Eight Point Proclamation a beginning could be made along the political road of the Six Great Policies. The Eight Point Proclamation and the Six Great Policies dovetailed.

Number 1. If we want to know about Sinkiang we first want to talk about Anti-imperialism. Behind the facade of the racial and cultural complex of the province every imperialist force has sought to cause dissension and division. A certain imperialist force, for instance, has increasingly fostered independence for South Sinkiang, and Japanese imperialism has helped the *Ch'an Hui* promote a Mussulman state. If this matter is not put

146

foremost, if it is not struck a decisive blow, if all the people of the province are not cautioned about it, then all Sinkiang government will share a like fate.

Number 2. If we want to know about Sinkiang we want to talk also about Kinship to Sovietism. The Soviet Russia of today is not the same as the old Russian Tsar, and she does not have aggressive designs. This lack of aggressive intent is not merely a kind of slogan; it has its base in economics. In the past aggression has come from the imperialist king first and second from the capitalist. These two phenomena are impossible in Soviet Russia. If the system of man destroying man has been eliminated what reason can there be for aggression? The testament of Dr. Sun Yat-sen has told us that in order to get the world to unite for peace it is necessary for the people to join in the common struggle. The kind of state which he indicated would be required is clear to all.

Number 3. The border speaks of Racial Equality very much. In what manner is Racial Equality to come? First, a political equality is wanted; second, educational equality. Formerly the people were permitted to read only *Han* books and not the works of their own races; and even if they did study the *Han* books they were not permitted to hold office, but could only serve as half-slave translators. Therefore none of the races wanted to read the *Han* books. In the Yang-Chin period force was used to make some do it. But (since a wealthy *Ch'an Hui* could not be forced to do it) just as soldiers had to be hired in the interior, so only poor persons could be hired to do the reading. Now it is not the same. Since Sheng Tu-pan issued his Eight Point Proclamation each race and every educational institution has received help from the government; and, though reading of Han books is required, each race can also read its own literature. Since this has happened readers have multiplied like the spread of mist. Government positions have since been opened to all the educated, and the self-respect of each race has been restored.

Number 4. Why should one have to mention Clean Government? The Yang-Chin period was lengthy and greedy. The politician did not believe in working but only in officiating; even when he was officiating he aimed only at making money. This arose from the fact that Yang and Chin were basically that type. In general if a person were to come to Sinkiang from the interior it was not asked whether he had qualifications or not, whether he was talented or not. All that was necessary instead was that he be of an "experienced" temperament or perhaps that he had served in an office of a military governor or of a provincial government for eight to ten years so that it could be seen he had been reared in the atmosphere of slavery. . . . Or, again, if he were appointed, say as a county magistrate or as a tax collector, it was only desired that he collect eighty to one hundred thousand dollars in a year's work. Can one ask that a man's talents be developed in this type of government atmosphere? Since the culture of other peoples of Sinkiang had been submerged so much, the *Han* official became like a god, and if a magistrate were appointed for a county in South Sinkiang he need not have been especially greedy to receive fifty to sixty thousand from the Moslems on one visit. Therefore all people coming to Sinkiang from the interior had such hopes. But now it is not possible! Since the administration of Sheng Tu-pan was instituted there is a provincial accounting commission that operates everywhere. If a sum of money goes through a public office not the smallest bit of it may be used before it is entered on the accounts of the office of the Tu-pan and is checked. Sheng himself gets a monthly salary of 200,000 taels in Sinkiang paper currency. This does not amount to over 100 dollars of Nationalist currency. (Due to the past years of war confusion in Sinkiang metal currency has been difficult to get.) Mrs. Sheng, who administers a girls' middle school, gets a salary of not more than 10 dollars each month. With this spirit of honesty and self-control they truly set an example. Can one not see that they are not troubled with all the difficulties of the former Yang-Chin times, that there is no distrust of Sheng Tu-pan's persistence or of his ability to endure hardship?

Number 5. Now consider Peace. How is Peace included among the Six Great Policies? Peace is that which is the opposite of war. Because of the bitter internal struggle in Sinkiang in recent years, and because the people have experienced great difficulties and bitterness as a result of the recent civil wars in the province, the word "peace" is like an anguished cry from the masses. In putting out this slogan the government has expressed the feelings of the people. Since ancient times the people have wanted administrators who know the people's mind. If you give a man water to drink when he wants food or if you give him food when he wants water, you will never reach his heart. When Imperialist Russia entered war, the common people were displeased. But Lenin, when he offered the slogan of "Bread and Peace," was able to start thousands upon thousands and myriads on myriads of people along the revolutionary road. It is that type of slogan.

Number 6. In discussing the question of Reconstruction we must recall that in the more than twenty years of the Yang-Chin administrations . . . there was not a penny's reconstruction for the masses of Sinkiang. Yet, when Sheng Tu-pan had administered the province for less than four years, I visited the Tihwa hospital and pharmacy and saw the ill all treated alike . . . by physicians and nurses, many of whom have come from Soviet Russia. It is reported that this is the practice in every executive district and is not restricted to Tihwa alone. Attendance at the Boys and Girls Middle School, the Normal School, and the Sinkiang Academy is paid for by the government, and this is something other provinces do not have. Attendance at some primary schools is also provided for. Again, the changes for the better in the types of sheep, cattle, horses, and chickens under the guidance of Soviet advisers have been very good. All races have been welcomed. Such things as improvement of the streets, the relief of rural agriculture, the establishment of electric light plants, are not these all real proof that this slogan has been able to feel the pulse of the people?

All the reconstruction of Sinkiang has been according to plan. A Reconstruction Commission, composed of all the highest officials, decided to undertake the work in three year periods and requested Soviet advisers to come and to help.

4. Relations with Soviet Russia

With the military movements in Sinkiang in recent years, its people have not had a healthy life, and the monetary system there has been upset. Even now the equilibrium of the province has not been completely recovered. How then can one say that there has been any reconstruction in Sinkiang?

This point cannot be discussed unless one speaks of diplomatic relations with Soviet Russia. After Sheng Tu-pan had become well established politically, he was anxious for reconstruction for he knew that by it he could resurrect Sinkiang; that if there were reconstruction, he could protect all the races. But reconstruction requires man-power and financial backing and cannot be accomplished by an empty cry. Where was the way out of this difficulty? He began diplomatic relations with Soviet Russia, and then thought of a method. As a result he asked that much of the technique and talent which had brought about the five-year plans in Soviet Russia be sent to assist Sinkiang in its three-year plan of reconstruction.

According to Sheng Tu-pan himself, every person in any of the number of Sinkiang households who was asked about the matter requested education for his kin . . . For instance, such measures and weights as a foot, an inch, an ounce, a catty, all are used in China; but they have different names in Sinkiang. Education up to Sheng's time had been mainly a question of what could be done in the home alone, and most people could not do business with people from outside of their own community . . . These were only temporary expedients, anyway; moreover, the government could only control them at the beginning and could not actually watch what was being done. Moreover, any progress that way would be slow. How, under such circumstances, could reconstruction be completed? From where could the money for it come? Sheng Tu-pan borrowed 5,000,000 rubles from Soviet Russia, it is reported, with an interest rate of only four per cent and no strings attached.

Having written this much, I wish to mention that I know that the people of the nation have had many rumors in regard to Sinkiang. There has been talk that Sinkiang has gone Red; or it has been said that, although Sinkiang may not be Red, the great military and administrative power of the province is in the hands of Soviet Russia. I never seriously believed this talk. Yet, before I had come to Sinkiang and had seen Sheng Tu-pan, I had no way to dispel it. But this much I have seen with my own eyes! Reconstruction in Sinkiang is only being aided by Soviet resources and talent, and there is no political side to it. As for the so-called great military and administrative power of Soviet Russia in Sinkiang, etc., etc., and as for the words of fear expressed in regard to Soviet specialists and educational officials, one must believe what I have seen. Soviet people are the specialists in animal husbandry, the doctors in the hospitals, the pharmacists in the provincial pharmacy, and the educators in the Military Officers Academy and in the Air Force. All the specialists of the three-year plan are Soviet people. But is this enough to show that the military and administrative authority of Sinkiang are not in the hands of China?

If Sinkiang has already become a Soviet Russian puppet state, why then are several tens of thousands of White Russian soldiers there? It is a fact that even many of the truck drivers of Sheng Tu-pan's office are White Russians. Can Soviet Russia tolerate this? Did not Soviet Russia, at the beginning of her national reconstruction, request assistance from thousands upon tens of thousands of capitalist experts? Yet, wouldn't it be difficult to say Soviet Russia is White?

According to what I have seen of Sinkiang, all the primary schools are reading the Three People's Principles textbooks. Moreover, these texts are not special texts, and one book bought is like all others bought. In Sinkiang not only is the *Han* language used for printing, but there are also translations into several other languages. In every public office and every school of the province homage is paid to the blue heaven and white sun of the Chinese national flag and to the honorable picture of the Tsung-li [Sun Yat-sen]. It is a pity that the Tsung-li passed away a generation too early. If he could have come to Sinkiang today, he certainly would smile and say: "Ah! One can see my honorable descendants in Sinkiang have talent and righteousness." This is not only my view. Before I went to Sinkiang, Mr. Ch'en Li-fu [Chinese Minister of Education] also was there and saw these things. I believe that he also received the same impression.

If we are to classify a country as either an "enemy country" or a "friendly country" we must take the broad view in passing judgment, not just a narrow view or one man's view. Japan, for example, is our enemy. Yet are there not also many good friends dwelling in Japan? Can they stop their capitalism from its ravages? Can they stop their midget army from its barbarism? Yet, on the other hand, what kind of a country is Soviet Russia? From the beginning there has been no oppression in Soviet Russia, nor do they have people there who oppress other people. Can one get aggression from this?

GLOSSARIES

Some Chinese terms, place names, and proper names from the text have been collated in the following glossaries. These are arranged with brief explanatory notes and, often, with helpful cross references to other spellings for a particular transliteration or translation. The general system of transliteration for the Chinese is a modified form of that found in Herbert A. Giles, *A Chinese-English Dictionary* (one volume, second edition, revised and enlarged, Shanghai, 1912). The modification follows for the most part the system suggested by Peter A. Boodberg and Woodbridge Bingham in the work by Robert J. Kerner, *Northeastern Asia, A Selected Bibliography* . . . (University of California Press, Berkeley, 1939), I, p. xiii. Hyphenated forms are used for compound terms and in the case of proper names are capitalized only on the first syllable (i.e., Sui-ting; An-chiu-an-ch'ia; Su-pa-yi; T'a-la-k'o). In translation and spelling of Chinese words, however, common geographical names (Nanking for Nan-ching, Tihwa for Ti-hua) and personal names current in English literature (Chiang Kai-shek for Chiang Chieh-shih) have been employed. It is additionally to be noted that the circumflex over the "e" and the short mark over the "u" (found in Giles) are eliminated for typographical reasons. In certain cases, moreover, where a place name includes (usually as the last word or words of the name) an especially common generic term, the romanization for that term is set off from the rest of the place name, its respective first letter capitalized, and the hyphen before it omitted (Pai Ch'eng; not Pai-ch'eng, Paich'eng, Paicheng, or Pai-Ch'eng). In some cases it has, on the other hand, been found advisable to link all the component romanizations for a place name with hyphens even if such common generic terms are included (T'ien-shan-nan-lu; not T'ien Shan Nan-lu or T'ien-shan-nan Lu). Names of Chinese provinces follow the *China Postal Atlas* (Inspectorate General of

Customs, Nanking, 1936) with the exception of the names Tsinghai, Chahar, and Sikang, which are herein spelled respectively Ch'inghai, Ch'ahar, and Sik'ang. A brief chronology of some Chinese dates has also been included to assist the lay reader. Pagination is as follows:

A SELECTED LIST OF TERMS

A-hung: a priest of the Wei-wu-erh people

Agrico: a British firm doing business in Sinkiang during the 1920's

Aqsaqal: a native headman of South Sinkiang

"Bannermen": Manchu soldiers, some of whom were sent to fortify and then settled down in Sinkiang

Bato Setkhiltu League: a branch of the Mongols found in Sinkiang

Catty: a Chinese pound weighing approximately 1 and 1/3 pounds avoirdupois; a chin

Central News: the official news agency in Nationalist China

Ch'ang: a workshop

Ch'ahar Mongols: a branch of the Mongols found in Sinkiang

Ch'an Hui ("Turban Moslems"): a Chinese name for the Wei-wu-erh people of Sinkiang

Ch'an-t'ou ("Turban Heads"): a Chinese name for the Wei-wu-erh people of Sinkiang

Chen: a trading town

Ch'eng: a city

Ch'eng-pao: a petty military station or rampart used in Sinkiang defenses

Chi-mi chou: a "restrained" Department; another name for chün fu

Chien-kuo ("Reconstruction"): a basic element in the wartime program of China

Ch'ien: before

Ch'ien Ti Tsung Chih-hui: Commander in Chief at the Front

Ch'ien-fang (the "Front"): the "War front"

Chin: a Chinese pound; a catty

Ching Setkhiltu League: a branch of the Mongols found in Sinkiang

Chou (a Department): a political division

Chun-ko-erh Pu (the Jön Gar): a branch of the Mongols found in Sinkiang

Ch'ü (a Region): a political division

Chün (a Prefecture): a political division

Chün fu: a Military-political division

"Clean Government": one of the Six Great Policies

"Comfort": a Chinese technique for frontier pacification

Commander in Chief at the Front (Ch'ien Ti Tsung Chih-hui): a high military title peculiar to Sinkiang

Cultural Progress Society (Wen-hua-tzu-chin Hui): an educational institution of Sinkiang Province

Dulanis: a people found in Sinkiang

E-lu-t'e Pu (the Eleuths or Ölöts): Western Mongols; found in Sinkiang

Eight Point Proclamation: the early theoretical keynote to Sheng Shih-ts'ai's rule

Elder Brother Society (Ko-lao Hui): a Chinese secret organization

Eleuths: see Ölöt Mongols

"Four-Twelve" Affair: the Sinkiang uprising of April 12, 1933

Fourteen racial types: the fourteen racial types assertedly recognized by the people of Sinkiang as dwelling in the province

Habdals: a people found in Sinkiang

Hai: an expanse of water

Han: in general recognized as a so-called "superior" clan of people dwelling in interior China as opposed to the so-called "barbarian" peoples dwelling on or beyond the Chinese frontiers; the name of a Chinese dynasty

Han Hui: Han Moslems

Ha-sa-k'o (the Kasakhs): a people of Sinkiang

Hoshots: a type of Mongol found in Sinkiang

Hou: behind

Hou-fang (the "Rear"): the "War rear"

Hsi: west

Hsi-po (Sibos): a Tungusic people from Manchuria who in modern times have also been living in Sinkiang

Hsia: down; a pass; summer

Hsia-wo: "summer nest" of the Altai Mongols

Hsiao: small; little

Hsiao P'ai Chang: a Second Lieutenant

Hsien: a county

Hsin: new

Hsiung-nu: a nomadic dweller of Mongolia and Siberia; identified by some as the ancient "Hun"

Hui: Moslems; a meeting; a society

Hunanese: Chinese from the province of Hunan; some were brought into Sinkiang by Tso Tsung-t'ang

Hung: red

Jön Gar: Jungars

Jungars (Jön Gar; Dzungars; Zungars): a branch of the Mongols who dwell in Sinkiang

Kan Hui: "Mohammedans of Kansu"

K'ang-chan Chien-kuo ("Resistance and Reconstruction"): the basic program of wartime China

K'ang-chü (Sogdiana): an ancient state of the Chinese Western Regions

Kara-Kasakh: a people found in Sinkiang

Kara-Khitai: a Khitan kingdom set up in the area of Sinkiang about the twelfth century

Kazakhs: nomadic Moslems dwelling in North Sinkiang

Khalkha: so-called Northern Mongols, some of whom dwell in Sinkiang

Khitan: a people whose prince once established the kingdom of Kara-Khitai

"Kinship to Sovietism": one of the Six Great Policies of Sheng Shih-ts'ai

Kirei: said to have been the "purest Turks of all . . ."

Kirgiz: a people known to live in the Pamirs and the T'ien Shan; the legendary Prester John is said to have ruled them in the Middle Ages

Kirgiz-Kazakh: a little-known nomad of Turkestan

Kirkrai: a Soviet institution which gained control of Semipalatinsk trade in 1922

Kirvneshtorg: a Soviet foreign trade agency on the Kirgizia frontier

Ko-erh-k'o-tzu: Khalkha

Ko-lao Hui: Elder Brother Society

Kou: a ditch

Ku: ancient

Kuei-hua: naturalized White Russians dwelling in Sinkiang

Kung: workshop

Kuomintang: the Chinese Nationalist Party, the pre-eminent political organization of modern China

Lao: old

Liang: a tael or Sinkiang dollar

Ling: a mountain range

Lin-shih Pien-fang Tu-pan: Provisional Border Defense Commander, a high military post in Sinkiang held by Sheng Shih-ts'ai

Man: Manchurians, representatives of whom dwell in Sinkiang

Manichaeists: those who believe in the doctrines of Manes and who stress the conflict of Light and Darkness

Meng (Meng-ku): the Mongols

Min-tsu ("race"): a clan of people; a tribe; a nation

Mukden Incident of 1931: the incident of September 18, 1931, when Japanese forces "protecting" the South Manchuria Railway attacked a Chinese garrison near Mukden and mastered the city; this may be termed at least one of the opening incidents, if not the opening incident, of World War II

Nan: south

Nestorian Christianity: the dogma of Nestorius, patriarch of Constantinople in the fifth century

New Fourth Army: Chinese Communist troops famed as late as 1941 for semi-autonomy in the Anhwei-Kiangsu region of China

Northeast Resist Japan Army from Manchuria: an army from Northeast China, refugee troops of which have played an important role in the New Sinkiang

Northwest Epidemic Prevention Bureau, Chinese: an institution noted as a medical and veterinary pioneer in Northwest China

Northwest Highway Administration, Chinese: the transportation agency which maintains highway control in Northwest China from Szechwan through Kansu

Ölöt Mongols: the so-called Western Mongols who once ruled Turkestan

Orianggai Mongols: a people found in Sinkiang but who mainly dwell in the small nearby territory of Tanu Tuva

Panthay: a Moslem of Yünnan Province in China

"Peace": one of the Six Great Policies of Sheng Shih-ts'ai

Pei: north

Provisional Border Defense Commander of Sinkiang: Lin-shih Pien-fang Tu-pan of Sinkiang

Pu: a league

Pu-lo: a barbarian horde

"Racial Equality": one of the Six Great Policies

Resistance and Reconstruction: K'ang-chan Chien-kuo

San: three

San Min Chu-i: the Three People's Principles—Nationalism, Democracy, and the People's Livelihood—the theoretical foundation of the Chinese National Revolution

Shan: mountain; range

Shang: up

Shih: a municipality

Sibsel'soius: a Russian trade organization at Novo-Nikolaevsk in the 1920's

Sibo: Hsi-po

Sinkiang Daily News: the official newspaper of the Sheng Shih-ts'ai administration

Sino-Soviet Aviation Company: a Chinese and Russian aviation combine to facilitate Chungking-Moscow air travel

Six Great Policies: these, with the Eight Point Proclamation, have been the theoretical basis of the New Sinkiang

Solon: So-lun

So-lun: Solon

Ta: great; big

Ta Hsia Kuo: Bactria: an ancient state of the Chinese Western Regions

Ta Kung Pao: a semi-independent and authoritative Chinese newspaper

Ta Tu-tu Fu: a political division; important in T'ang times

Ta Yüan: an ancient state of the Chinese Western Regions

Tael: a Sinkiang dollar; a liang

T'a-chi-k'o: the Tajiks

Tajiks: a people dwelling in the Pamirs bordering Sinkiang

T'a-lan-ch'i: the Taranchi

Taranchi: a little-known people of Sinkiang

Tatars (T'a-t'a-erh): a people of mixed Mongol and white blood, now found in Sinkiang and other parts of Central Asia

T'a-t'a-erh: Tatars

T'ai-p'ing Rebellion: a religiously inspired Chinese uprising of the nineteenth century

Three People's Principles: San Min Chu-i

Three-year Plan of Reconstruction: modeled in great measure on the Soviet Five-year Plans, this was instituted in 1937 with Soviet help by Sheng Shih-ts'ai's Sinkiang administration

Torgot Mongols: a type of Mongols found in Sinkiang

Tsung-li: reverent Chinese reference to Dr. Sun Yat-sen, "Father" of the Chinese Republic

Tu-tu: a Chinese colonial military governor

T'u-chüeh: a people, possibly of Turkish stock, once inhabiting the Chinese Western Regions

Tu-erh-hu-t'e Pu: a type of Mongol dwelling in Sinkiang

Tu-erh-po-t'e Pu: a type of Mongol dwelling in Sinkiang

Tung: east; winter

Tung-hu: a people of the ancient Chinese frontier

Tung-kan (Chinese Moslems): predominantly of Shensi and Kansu but also to be found in Sinkiang; to be distinguished from the Wei-wu-erh Moslems

Tung-wo: "Winter nest" of the Altai Mongols

Tungusic: of or related to the Tungus peoples of Siberia and Manchuria

"Turban Heads": Ch'an-t'ou; a Chinese name for the Wei-wu-erh

Turki: the language, especially Eastern Turki, spoken by the majority of Sinkiang natives

Turkic-Tatar: of or related to the Turks and Tatars

Turks: an Asiatic people who speak Turki or Turkic languages and who dwell predominantly in an area ranging between the Adriatic and the Okhotsk seas

Uighur: a Turkic people powerful in Mongolia and Sinkiang between the third century B.C. and the twelfth century A.D.; possibly the "original" Turks and the "original" dwellers of Sinkiang

Unen Susuktu League: a branch of the Mongols found in Sinkiang

Ural-Altaic: a family of languages with a range from Turki and Mongol to Finno-Ugrian

Uzbek: a people predominantly found in Sinkiang and Russian Turkestan; Wu-tzu-pieh-k'o

Wei-wu-erh: possibly the original inhabitants of Sinkiang and about an 80 per cent majority of the modern population of the province; the Ch'an Hui; Ch'an-t'ou; and possibly the Uighurs

Wen-hua-tzu-chin Hui: Cultural Progress Societies

Wu-sun: an ancient state of the Chinese Western Regions

Wu-tzu-pieh-k'o: the Uzbeks

Ying: an encampment; a fort; a battalion

Ying Chang: a battalion commander

Yu-pu piao: oilcloth notes; a kind of Sinkiang currency

Yüan: a dollar of the Chinese Nationalist Government

Yüeh-chih, Ta: an ancient state of the Chinese Western Regions

Yünnanese: people of the Chinese province of Yünnan

Zungars: the Jungars

A SELECTED LIST OF PLACE NAMES

With estimates of longitude and latitude based on Ting, V. K., Wong, Wen-hao, and Tseng, Shih-ying, *Chung-kuo Fen Sheng Hsin T'u* (Shen Pao, Shanghai, 1936)

A Shan: the Altai Mountains of North Sinkiang; A Shan Ch'ü; Altaiskii okrug

A Shan Ch'ü: the A Shan Region of Sinkiang; Altaiskii okrug; one of the nine major administrative divisions of Sinkiang

A-erh-t'ai: the Altai Mountains

A-ha-mai-ti Mountain: site of an iron vein near Yangi Hissar

A-ha-t'a-k'o Shan: site of a gold mine in the Keriya area

A-k'o-su: Aqsu

Altai, the: a mountain range in North Sinkiang

An-chi Hai, Lake: about 80 miles from Manas and site of a large oil field

An-chiu-an-chia: one of the termini for a copper deposit northwest of Kashgar

An-hsi: a principal city of Northwest Kansu; longitude 96°, latitude 40° 30′

Anhwei: a province in Eastern China

Aqsu: A-k'o-su: a principal city of Sinkiang; longitude 80°, latitude 41°

Aqsu Ch'ü: the Aqsu Region of Sinkiang; the Aksuiskii okrug; one of the nine major administrative divisions of Sinkiang

Baboon Pass: Hsing-hsing Hsia

Bai: Pai Ch'eng

Barkol (Chen-hsi): a principal city of North Sinkiang; longitude 93°, latitude 43° 30′

Big Yellow Mountain: site of a coal mine near Fou-k'ang

Bishbalik: an ancient Uighur capital near, or in, present-day Tihwa

Black Oil Mountain: near T'a Ch'eng; site of nine "oil springs"

Bogdo-ola: a mountain region near Turfan

Borotala Valley: between Tihwa and I-ning

Burma Road: the rail and road communications line from Rangoon through Lashio and K'unming to Chungking

Canton: a prominent city of Kwangtung Province

Ch'a Kung: site of a gold mine near T'a Ch'eng

Ch'a-han-a-t'eng: site of a gold mine near T'a Ch'eng

Ch'a-han-wu-su: site of a coal mine in Ch'ang-chi county

Ch'ahar: a province in Northeast China

Chai-o-pao: site of six copper deposits east of Tihwa

Ch'ang-chi: a principal city of North Sinkiang; longitude 87° 30′, latitude 44° 5′

Ch'e-lu Kou: site of a gold mine near T'a Ch'eng

Chen-hsi: Barkol

Ch'eng-tu: capital of the province of Szechwan

Ch'eng-hua (Sharasume): a principal city of North Sinkiang; longitude 88°, latitude 47° 58′

Cherchen (Ch'ieh-mo): a principal city of Southeast Sinkiang; longitude 86°, latitude 38°

Ch'i-chio-ching: a city on the Sinkiang North Road; longitude 91° 58′, latitude 43° 56′

Ch'i-erh Shan: one of the termini for a some 130 mile iron vein in the vicinity of T'a Ch'eng

Ch'i-t'ai: Kitai; Ku Ch'eng-tzu; a city in North Sinkiang; longitude 89° 50′, latitude 44° 3′

Ch'ia-pa Shan: site of a gold mine in the Keriya area

Ch'ia-tzu Wan: site of an oil deposit in the Sui-lai (Manas) region

Ch'iao-li-k'o River: location of a gold mine near Sui-ting

Ch'ieh-mo: Cherchen

Ch'ien Kou: a gold mine in the Altai Mountains

Chinese Turkestan: Sinkiang; perhaps more precisely, South Sinkiang

Ching-ho: a town in North Sinkiang; longitude 83° 20′, latitude 44° 40′

Ch'inghai: Kokonor, a province of the Chinese Far West

Chuguchak: T'a Ch'eng; Tarbagatai

Chung Kou: a gold mine in the Altai Mountains

Chungking: the wartime capital of Nationalist China

Ch'ü-chiang: Shao-kuan; Shaokwan; Shao-chou; Shuichow; a prominent city in Kwangtung Province still held by Nationalist China

Clear Rock Gorge: not far from T'a Ch'eng

Dolon Nor: a prominent city of Inner Mongolia; longitude 116° 30′, latitude 42° 10′

Dzungaria: Jungaria

E-erh-ch'i-ssu River: a river of North Sinkiang

Feng-t'ien: Mukden

Fou-k'ang: a town in North Sinkiang; longitude 88° 5′, latitude 44° 10′

Fu-yüan: a town in North Sinkiang; longitude 88° 30′, latitude 44°

Ha-erh-han-t'u Shan: site of copper deposits near I-ning

Ha-hsiung Kou: a gold mine in the Altai Mountains

Ha-man Kou; a coal mine near Karashahr

Ha-mi (Qomul): a prominent city of Eastern Sinkiang; longitude 93° 50′, latitude 42° 40′

Ha-mi Ch'ü: the Ha-mi Region; Komul'skii okrug (Khami); one of the nine major administrative divisions of Sinkiang

Ha-t'u Shan: near the site of a major Sinkiang gold deposit which is to be found between the T'a-erh-ta-mu-t'u and the Su-erh-t'u rivers

Han-k'ou: Hankow

Hankow (Han-k'ou): a prominent city in Central China

Heavenly Mountains: the T'ien Shan

Heilungkiang: a province of Northeast China; part of Manchuria

Ho-se-erh T'ung Ch'ang: site of a copper works in the Pai Ch'eng area

Ho-t'ien: Khotan

Hou Kou: a gold mine in the Altai Mountains

Hsi Hsin Yüeh Kung: site of a gold mine near T'a Ch'eng

Hsi Kou: a gold mine in the Altai Mountains

Hsi Yü: the Western Regions; the ancient Chinese name for an area that included the territory in which modern Sinkiang is found

Hsi-k'ang: Sik'ang

Hsi-ning: Sining

Hsia T'ung Ch'ang: a copper works in the Yen-ti Kou area of Pai Ch'eng

Hsiao Lan-chou Wan: a gold mine site near T'a Ch'eng

Hsiao Liu Kou: a bituminous coal deposit near Barkol

Hsin-chiang: a transliteration of the Chinese name for Sinkiang

Hsin T'ung Ch'ang: a copper works in the mountains of Kucha

Hsing-hsing Hsia: a prominent border terminal point on the Sinkiang-Kansu highway

Hui-yüan: a city in the I-li Ch'ü of Sinkiang

Hunan: a province of Central China

Hung Miao-ssu: the Red Temple; another Chinese name for Tihwa

Hupeh: a province of Central China

I-ho: one of three Sinkiang counties formed from the old Moslem principality of Qomul

I-ko-jih-ya-yen Mountain: near Yangi Hissar and site of an iron vein

I-li: Sui-ting; Kuldja; a chief city in North Sinkiang; longitude 81°, latitude 44° 5′

I-li Ch'ü: the I-li Region; Iliskii okrug (Ili); one of the nine major administrative divisions of Sinkiang

I-ning: Ning-yüan; a city of North Sinkiang; longitude 81° 30′, latitude 43° 57′

Inner Mongolia: roughly the provinces of Ch'ahar, Suiyüan, and Ningsia in the Chinese Northwest

I-wu: one of three Sinkiang counties formed from the old Moslem principality of Qomul

Jehol: a province of Northeast China

Jungaria: Dzungaria or Zungaria; named for the Mongol Jön Gars; the part of Sinkiang which lies between the T'ien Shan and the Altai Mountains, i.e., North Sinkiang

K'a-la-pa-erh-ka-hsün Mountain: Kara Balgasun Mountain

K'ai-yüan: in Liaoning, Manchuria; birthplace of Sheng Shih-ts'ai

Kan-chu-t'e: an old principality claimed by China; the site of the present Gilgit Agency and Hunza Valley of modern Northwest India

"Kanjut": Kan-chu-t'e

Kansu: a province in Northwest China

K'an-chi-kang: a coal mine in the vicinity of Kashgar

K'an-chü-t'i: Kan-chu-t'e

K'ang-shan: site of a Sinkiang copper deposit

Kara Balgasun Mountain: near Turfan; site of an iron vein

Kara Shar: Karashahr

Karashahr: Kara Shar; Yen-ch'i; Yenki; a city of Southwest Sinkiang; longitude 87°, latitude 42°

Karghalik: Yeh Ch'eng; a city of Southwest Sinkiang; longitude 77° 40', latitude 38°

Kashgar: Su-fu; in Southwest Sinkiang; the largest oasis of Chinese Turkestan; longitude 76°, latitude 39° 45'

Kashgaria: a general term, possibly approximating the present K'o-shih Ch'ü

Keriya (Yü-t'ien): a city in Southwest Sinkiang; longitude 81° 50', latitude 37°

Khotan (Ho-t'ien): a prominent oasis of Southwest Sinkiang; longitude 79° 59', latitude 37° 4'

Khotan Ch'ü (the Khotan Region; Khotanskii okrug; Khetian): one of the nine major administrative divisions of Sinkiang

Kiangsu: a coastal province of Eastern China

Kirin: a province of Northeast China; part of Manchuria

Kitai: Ch'i-t'ai; Ku Ch'eng-tzu

K'o-pu-to: Kobdo

Kobdo: a chief city of a Mongolian region of the same name

Kokonor: Ch'inghai

Ko-ko-ya Mountain: a coal site in Shan-shan county

Korla (K'u-erh-lo; Kurla): a city in South Sinkiang; longitude 86° 57', latitude 41° 50'

K'o-kan-ch'ia: a coal and iron site north of Aqsu

K'o-la-t'a-fu-pan: one of the termini of a some 130-mile iron vein in the vicinity of T'a Ch'eng

K'o-la-ya-lun field: an oil field north of Kucha

K'o-p'ing: site of a coal mine near Pai Ch'eng

K'o-shih: Kashgar; Su-fu

K'o-shih Ch'ü (K'o-shih Region): possibly approximating Kashgaria; Kashgarskii okrug (Kashi); the region of Southwesternmost Sinkiang; one of the nine major administrative divisions of Sinkiang

K'o-shih-k'o-k'o-pa-shih Shan: site of an iron deposit northeast of Pai Ch'eng

K'o-t'a T'ung Ch'ang: a copper works in the Pai Ch'eng area

Ku Ch'eng-tzu: Ch'i-t'ai

Kuan-t'an-yao: site of a bituminous coal mine of the Barkol area

Kucha (K'u-ch'e): a city of South Sinkiang

Kuei-sui: a prominent city in the Chinese province of Suiyüan

Kuldja: Sui-ting; I-li

Kung Po T'ung Ch'ang: a copper deposit in the Pai Ch'eng area

Kurla: Korla

K'u-ch'e: Kucha

K'u-erh-lo: Korla

K'u-erh-tai Shan: site of a thin copper vein near Karashahr

K'u-k'o-ts'ang Mountain: anthracite coal is found here in the Tarbagatai Range near T'a Ch'eng

K'unlun Mountains: a range dividing Sinkiang and Tibet

K'unming: capital of Yünnan Province in Southwest China

Kwangtung: a province in South China

La-sa: Lhasa

Ladakh (Ladok): a British outpost for Northwest India-South Sinkiang trade

Ladok: Ladakh

Lan-chou: capital of the province of Kansu in Northwest China

Lao Nan Kung: site of a gold mine near T'a Ch'eng

Lao Tung Kung: site of another gold mine near T'a Ch'eng

Lao T'ung Ch'ang: a copper mine in the mountains of Kucha

Lhasa (La-sa): chief city of Tibet

Liaoning: a province in Northeast China; part of Manchuria

Little Yellow Mountain: location of a coal mine near Fou-k'ang

Ma-la-shui: location of a gold mine near T'a Ch'eng

Ma-li-li-k'o Shan: site of an oil field south of Wen-hsü

Manas (Sui-lai): a city in North Sinkiang; longitude 86° 50', latitude 44° 15'

"Manchoukuo": the Japanese puppet state in Manchuria

Manchuria: the Chinese Three Eastern Provinces—Heilungkiang, Kirin, and Liaoning

Maralbashi (Pa-ch'u): a city in Southwest Sinkiang; longitude 78° 20′, latitude 39° 50′

Meng-k'o-t'u Ling: site of an iron vein in Ch'ang-chi county

Middle Kingdom: China

Ming-pu-la-k'o Shan: location of an iron deposit northeast of Pai Ch'eng

Mongolia: the Meng-ku Ti-fang of North China; the land of the Mongols; roughly comprising Inner Mongolia, Outer Mongolia, and Tanu Tuva

Mukden (Shen-yang; Feng-t'ien): a chief city of Liaoning Province in Northeast China

Nanking: former capital of the Chinese National Government; now held by the Japanese and administered ostensibly by the puppet government of Wang Ching-wei

Neng-li-ha-t'a Shan: location of an iron deposit northeast of Pai Ch'eng

"New Dominion, The": Hsin-chiang; Sinkiang

Ningsia: a province in Northwest China

Ning-yüan: I-ning

Outer Mongolia: roughly that part of Mongolia which is now administered as the "Outer Mongolian People's Republic" and which has historically been the home of the Khalkha Mongols

"Outer Mongolian People's Republic": the present Russian sponsored soviet state in Outer Mongolia

Pa-ch'u: Maralbashi

Pai Ch'eng; Bai: a city in Southwest Sinkiang; longitude 81° 58′, latitude 41° 50′

Pan-tang Kou: a gold mine in the Altai Mountains

Pei-p'ing: Peking

Peking (Pei-p'ing): a city of Hopei Province; a former capital of China

Po-lo-t'ung-ko: a Manas oil field

Pu-erh-ching: a city in North Sinkiang; longitude 87°, latitude 47° 40′

Qara Shahr: Karashahr

Qomul: Ha-mi

Sa-pa-t'i-k'o: a coal mine in the mountains north of Yangi Hissar

San-chio Shan: site of rich Sinkiang copper findings northeast of Ta-pan Ch'eng

San-t'ang Hu: site of a bituminous coal mine in the Barkol area

San-tao Mountains: location of coal mines near Ha-mi

San-tao Pa: a region in North Sinkiang near Tihwa

Sariquol: in Southwest Sinkiang; home of the Tajiks

Shan-shan: in South Sinkiang; longitude 90° 30′, latitude 43°

Shang T'ung Ch'ang: a Pai Ch'eng copper deposit

Shang-wo-p'u Oil Shaft: an oil site southwest of So-ch'e

Shansi: a province in North China

Shao-chou: Ch'ü-chiang

Shao-kuan: Ch'ü-chiang

Shaokwan: Ch'ü-chiang

Sharasume: Ch'eng-hua

Shen-yang: Mukden

Shensi: a province of North China

Shih-yü Yen: a Manas oil field

Shui-hsi Kou: site of an iron vein about 65 miles from Fu-yüan

Shui-mo Kou: a coal mine in the Tihwa area

Shuichow: Ch'ü-chiang

Sik'ang: a province in the Chinese Far West

Sining: the capital of Ch'inghai Province

Sinkiang: Hsin-chiang; the "New Dominion"; Chinese Turkestan; Zapadnyi Kitai; Chinese Central Asia; the Northwesternmost province of China

So-ch'e: Yarkand

Ssu-pen Kou: an oil field about 13 miles west of Tihwa

Su-erh-ko Ling: site of an iron vein southeast of Sui-ting

Su-erh-t'u River: one of the termini for placer gold findings near T'a Ch'eng

Su-fu: Kashgar

Su-hun Shan: site of a copper deposit west of Kashgar

Su-lo: a town in Southwest Sinkiang near Kashgar; longitude 76° 5', latitude 39° 40'

Su-pa-yi: a coal mine in the mountains north of Kucha

Su-pa-shih T'ung Ch'ang: a copper mine in the mountains north of Kucha

Su-ta-chang: an oil field some 17 miles east of Tihwa

Suchow: a town in Northwest Kansu; longitude 98° 30', latitude 39° 40'

Sui-lai: Manas

Sui-ting: I-li; Kuldja

Sui-tung: site of a Sinkiang gold mine (Sui-ting?)

Suiyüan: a province in Northwest China

Szechwan: a province in Western China

Ta Lan-chou Wan: a gold mine near T'a Ch'eng

T'a Ch'eng (Tarbagatai; Chuguchak): a prominent Chinese city near the Sinkiang-Soviet border; longitude 83° 10', latitude 46° 30'

T'a Ch'eng Ch'ü (T'a Ch'eng Region; Tarbagataiskii okrug): one of the nine major administrative divisions of Sinkiang

T'a-erh-ch'i Shan: site of an iron deposit northeast of Pai Ch'eng

T'a-erh-pa-ka-t'ai: Tarbagatai

T'a-erh-ta-mu-t'u River: one of the termini for placer gold findings near T'a Ch'eng

T'a-la-k'o: a coal mine near Pai Ch'eng

T'a-na-k'o: an oil field northeast of Wen-hsü

T'a-pan Ch'eng: the site of an iron vein in North Sinkiang

Takla Makan: the Takla Makan Desert of South Sinkiang

Tarbagatai: T'a Ch'eng; Chuguchak

Tarim: the Tarim River and the Tarim Basin of South Sinkiang

Tihwa (Urumchi; Wu-lu-mu-ch'i; Hung Miao-ssu): the capital city of Sinkiang Province; longitude 87° 53', latitude 43° 56'

Tihwa Ch'ü: the Tihwa Region; one of the nine major administrative divisions of Sinkiang

T'i-li-k'o Shan: site of a coal mine near Pai Ch'eng

Tibet (Hsi-ts'ang): a frontier territory in the Chinese Far West over which China asserts suzerainty

T'ieh-pen-erh-k'o-la-pu-la-k'o: site for coal and iron deposits north of Aqsu

Tientsin: a city of Hopei Province in Northeast China

T'ien Shan Mountains (the Heavenly Mountains): a range bisecting Sinkiang from west to east

T'ien-shan-nan-lu: the so-called Road South of the Heavenly Mountains or South Sinkiang

T'ien-shan-pei-lu: the so-called Road North of the Heavenly Mountains or North Sinkiang

T'o-k'o-hsün: Toqsun

Toksun: Toqsun

Toqsun (T'o-k'o-hsün; Toksun): a city on the Sinkiang South Road; longitude 89° 30', latitude 42° 48'

T'ou-t'un Ch'ang: a coal mine near Tihwa

T'ou-t'un Ho: site of a coal mine in Ch'ang-chi county

Tsaidam: the wastelands of Western Ch'inghai

Ts'ang-huang Kou: a coal mine near Tihwa

Tsao-li-ya-k'o: a gold mine near Keriya

Tu-lan: a city in Ch'inghai; longitude 98° 15', latitude 36° 59'

T'u-lu-fan: Turfan

Tu-tzu Shan: site of an oil field southeast of Wu-su county

Tun-huang: a town in Northwest Kansu; longitude 94° 55', latitude 40° 5'

Tung Hsin Yüeh Kung: a gold mine near T'a Ch'eng

Tung Kou: a gold mine in the Altai Mountains

T'ung-ku P'o: a Manas oil field

Turfan; T'u-lu-fan: a town in South Sinkiang; longitude 89°, latitude 43°

Ulan Bator (Urga): capital of the "Outer Mongolian People's Republic"

Uliasutai (Wu-li-ya-su-t'ai): a city in Outer Mongolia

Urumchi: Tihwa

Wen-hsü: a city in Southwest Sinkiang; longitude 79° 58', latitude 41° 20'

"Western China": Zapadnyi Kitai

Western Regions: Hsi Yü

Wu-erh-t'eng: an outpost of Western Ch'inghai; longitude 91°, latitude 37° 53'

Wu-la-k'o Shan: one of the termini for a copper vein northwest of Kashgar

Wu-lan-wu-su River: a copper vein is found along its course northwest of Kashgar

Wu-li-ya-su-t'ai: Uliasutai

Wu-lu-mu-ch'i: Urumchi; Tihwa

Wu-su: a town in North Sinkiang; longitude 85°, latitude 44° 30'

Wu-ts'ung-tao Shan: site of copper findings near Sui-ting

Ya-ha-a-li-tu-ko-erh Mountain: location of the Shang T'ung Ch'ang copper deposit

Ya-hsiang-pa: a coal mine near Pai Ch'eng

Ya-se-li-min Shan: site of an iron deposit northeast of Pai Ch'eng

Yangi Hissar (Ying-chi-sha): a city in Southwest Sinkiang; longitude 76° 3', latitude 39°

Yarkand (So-ch'e): a city in Southwest Sinkiang; longitude 77° 40', latitude 38° 50'

Yeh Ch'eng: Karghalik

Yen-ch'i: Karashahr

Yen-ch'i Ch'ü (Yen-ch'i Region): one of the nine major administrative divisions of Sinkiang

Yen-ti Kou: site of the Hsia T'ung Ch'ang copper deposit of Pai Ch'eng

Yenki: Yen-ch'i; Karashahr

Ying-chi-sha: Yangi Hissar

Yu-mo-chiang Shan: site of a gold mine near Keriya

Yü-t'ien: Keriya

Yünnan: a province of Southwest China

Zapadnyi Kitai ("Western China"): a Russian name for Sinkiang

Zungaria: Jungaria

A SELECTED LIST OF PERSONS MENTIONED IN THE TEXT

Chang Chi-luan: the late editor of the *Ta Kung Pao*

Chang Ch'ien: Han Dynasty emissary to the Hsi Yü

Chao Lieh: Chinese authority on the New Sinkiang

Chao, Samuel: Chinese journalist who has traveled widely in the northwestern provinces of his country

Ch'en Chi-jung: Ta Kung Pao correspondent who has recently had extensive travel experience in Sinkiang

Ch'en Chung: elected as a member of the Sinkiang Provincial Maintenance Committee at the time of the "Four-Twelve" Affair

Ch'en Li-fu: Chinese Minister of Education

Cheng Jun-ch'eng: leader of Manchurian refugee troops who were instrumental in putting down the Sinkiang Moslem insurrection of the 1930's

Ch'eng Shao-chung: Chinese authority on animal husbandry matters

Chiang Chün-chang: author of a comprehensive Chinese study concerning Sinkiang

Chiang Kai-shek: Generalissimo and President of China

Chin Shu-hsin: son of Chin Shu-jen, former Sinkiang Military Governor; Chin Shu-hsin was shot as a consequence of the "Four-Twelve" Affair

Chin Shu-jen: former Sinkiang Military Governor; sentenced to imprisonment by Nanking for unlawful conduct while in office

Fan Yao-nan: assassin of Yang Tseng-hsin, July 7, 1928

Gabitov: a Soviet authority on Sinkiang

Galdan: Khan of the Ölöts when they ruled Sinkiang

Genghis Khan: Mongol leader of the twelfth and thirteenth centuries

Haushofer, Dr. Karl: leader of the German school of geopolitics

Hedin, Sven: noted explorer and writer

Jagatai: second son of Genghis Khan

Kao Hsien-chih: led a Chinese army through Sinkiang as far as Gilgit in 747

Khoja Niaz: a prominent military leader during the Sinkiang Moslem uprising of the 1930's

Kuo Sung-ling: a prominent war lord of Northeast China who befriended Sheng Shih-ts'ai

Li Ken-yüan: an old time Yünnan militarist-revolutionary who had charge of a famous military academy in Kwangtung Province

Li Kuang-t'ing: a Chinese authority who has prepared a map of the Hsi Yü of Han times

Liu Mien-t'ang: a nineteenth century Chinese colonist of Sinkiang

Liu Sheng-shi: Director of the Chinese Northwest Epidemic Prevention Bureau

Liu Wen-lung: Sinkiang Commissioner of Education in 1933

Lo Chia-lun: former Chancellor of the Chinese National Central University and more recently Special Commissioner of the Chinese Control Yüan for Sinkiang Province

Lu Chan-pin: Chinese Consul-General at Semipalatinsk in 1927

Lu Hsüeh-tsu: Sinkiang Province General Secretary in the 1930's

Ma Chung-ying: leader of the Moslem uprising in Sinkiang, 1931-1934

Ma Pu-ch'ing: Moslem leader in Northwest China; appointed Pacification Commissioner of the Tsaidam Marches in July, 1942

Ma Shih-ming: a leader of the Sinkiang Moslem uprising of the 1930's

Nazaroff: a White refugee from Soviet Central Asia who has recorded his impressions concerning the closing of the Sinkiang frontier in the 1920's

Pai Yü-hsiu: a Sinkiang notable of the 1930's

Pan Ch'ao: a general who extended Han Dynasty rule widely in Central Asia

Prester John: a legendary, perhaps actual, ruler of the Kirgiz people in the Middle Ages

Qutaiba: a Turkish military leader of the eighth century

Rabdan: the leader of the Jön Gar; a nephew of Galdan, Khan of the Olöts

Shen Hung-lieh: Chinese Minister of Agriculture and Forestry

Sheng Shih-chi: brother of Sheng Shih-ts'ai and Sinkiang representative on the National Political Council of China

Sheng Shih-ts'ai: Concurrent Chairman and Provisional Border Defense Commander of Sinkiang

Sheng Shih-ts'ai, Mrs.: the wife of the Sinkiang Chairman; administrator of a girls' middle school in Sinkiang

Sun Yat-sen: the "Father" of the Chinese Republic

Sung Yün: a Manchu Dynasty general who furthered irrigation developments around present Sui-ting

T'ao Ming-yüeh: a Sinkiang notable of the 1930's

Tien Shen-chi: a Secretary of the Semipalatinsk Consulate in 1928

Tseng Yang-fu: Chinese Minister of Communications

Tso Tsung-t'ang: Manchu military leader who put down the Sinkiang rebellion of Yakub Beg in the 1870's

Ts'ui Chao-chi, Commander: a Sinkiang military leader in the 1930's

Tu Chung-yüan: a one-time Chancellor of Education of the New Sinkiang and a biographer of Sheng Shih-ts'ai

Wang Ching-wei: puppet ruler of Japanese Occupied Central China

Wong Wen-hao: Chinese Minister of Economic Affairs
Wu, Aitchen K.: one-time official of Sinkiang and author of a study of the New Sinkiang
Wu Chai-hsing: Chaucer H. Wu
Wu, Chaucer H.: a British educated Chinese; appointed Sinkiang Commissioner for Foreign Affairs in 1942
Yakub Beg: leader of a Moslem revolt in Sinkiang in the late nineteenth century
Yang Hsüeh-yüan: a Sinkiang notable of the 1930's
Yang Tseng-hsin: Military Governor of Sinkiang, 1912-1928
Yang Tsuan-hsü: a Hupeh revolutionary once prominent in the Sui-ting area
Yulbaz: a Moslem prominent in the Sinkiang revolt of the 1930's

A BRIEF CHRONOLOGY OF SOME CHINESE DATES

(By dynastic, period, and reign dates)

Han Dynasty B.C. 206-220 A.D.
Sui Dynasty 589-618
    Wen Ti 589-604
T'ang Dynasty 618-907
    Hsüan Tsung 713-756
Sung Dynasty 960-1280
Ming Dynasty 1368-1644
Ta Ch'ing or Manchu Dynasty 1644-1912
    K'ang Hsi 1662-1722
    Yung Cheng 1723-1735
    Ch'ien Lung 1736-1795
    Chia Ch'ing 1796-1820
    Tao Kuang 1821-1850
    Hsien Feng 1851-1861
    T'ung Chih 1862-1874
    Kuang Hsü 1875-1907
    Hsüan T'ung 1908-1912
The Republic 1912-

WORKING BIBLIOGRAPHY

The following is but a brief working bibliography. The reader will find herein some of the best general references to the subject of Sinkiang. Should he be interested, he will find extended and technical bibliographies also attached to M. A. Czaplicka, *The Turks of Central Asia . . .*, Robert J. Kerner, *Northeastern Asia, a selected bibliography . . .*, and Owen Lattimore, *Inner Asian Frontiers of China.*

Carruthers, Douglas, *Unknown Mongolia* (2 v., London: Hutchinson and Company, 1914).

Castagné, Joseph, "Le probleme du Turkestan Chinois (Sin-Kiang)," *Revue des études islamiques* (1933, II), pp. 153-84.

Chao Lieh, "Hsin-chiang Chin Ching-lu," *Kuei-lin Ta Kung Pao* (September 8, 1941).

Chao, Samuel Ming-chiu, *China's Northwest* (unpublished manuscript dated Chungking, September 15, 1940, made available through Mr. William L. Holland, Institute of Pacific Relations, New York City).

———, "China's Northwest Revitalized," *China at War*, XI, 2 (August, 1943).

Chavannes, Edouard, *Documents sur les Tou-kiue (Turcs) occidentaux* Sbornik' trud'ov orkhonskoi ekspeditsii, VI (St. Petersburg, 1903).

Ch'en Chi-jung, "A-la-mu-t'u Jih Tsa-chi," *Ta Kung Pao,* February 10, 1941.

———, "Hsin Hsin-chiang Ti Ts'ai-cheng," article obtained by the author in Lan-chou, China, January 4, 1940.

———, "T'ien-shan San-tu Wu Ts'ao," *Ta Kung Pao,* November 15-16, 1942.

Ch'en Fu-kuang, *Wai-chiao Shih* (Chungking: Ch'ing-nien Shu-tien, 1939).

Cherbakoff, Doctor, "In Kashgar, December, 1927, to October, 1931," *Journal of the Royal Central Asian Society,* XX (1933), IV, pp. 541-42.

Chiang Chün-chang, *Hsin-chiang Ching-ying Lun* (third edition. China: Cheng Chung Book Company, 1939).

Ch'ien Mu, *Kuo Shih Ta Kang* (2 v., Changsha, China: Commercial Press, 1940).

Ch'ien Shih-fu, *Chung-kuo Ti Shih Ti* (Nanning: Min-t'uan Chou-k'an She, 1939).

China, Inspectorate General of Customs, *China Postal Atlas* (Nanking, 1936).

————, *Treaties, Conventions, Etc., Between China and Foreign States* (2 v., second edition. Shanghai, 1917).

China, Ministry of Communications. Road map of the Northwest Highway Administration.

China, Ministry of Information of the Republic of, *China After Five Years of War* (New York: Chinese News Service, 1942).

————, *China Handbook 1937-1943. A Comprehensive Survey of Major Developments in China in Six Years of War* (New York: The Mac-Millan Company, 1943).

Conolly, Violet, *Soviet Economic Policy in the East: Turkey, Persia, Afghanistan, Mongolia, and Tana Tuva, Sinkiang* (London: Oxford University Press, 1933).

Czaplicka, M. A., *The Turks of Central Asia in History and at the Present Day. An Ethnological Inquiry into the Pan-Turanian Problem, and Bibliographical Material Relating to the Early Turks and the Present Turks of Central Asia* (Oxford: Clarendon Press, 1918).

Edelstein, Julius C., *Alaska Comes of Age* (American Council, Institute of Pacific Relations, Far Eastern Pamphlets No. 8, New York [etc.], 1942).

Engstrand, Warren Maxfield, *The Kuldja Affair and Its Significance in Sino-Russian Relations* (Unpublished Master's thesis in History, Deposited at the University of California. Berkeley, 1933).

Etherton, Lieutenant Colonel P. T., *In the Heart of Asia* (Boston and New York: Houghton Mifflin Company, 1926).

"Faces and Fashions of Asia's Changeless Tribes," *The National Geographic Magazine*, LXIX, I (January, 1936).

Fleming, Peter, *News From Tartary A Journey from Peking to Kashmir* (New York: Charles Scribner's Sons, 1936).

Gabitov, I. E., "La Situation Economique du Turquestan Chinois," *Novyi Vostok (Nouvel Orient)*, No. 8-9 (1925), pp. 26-39.

Giles, Herbert A., *A Chinese-English Dictionary* (second edition, revised and enlarged. Shanghai: Kelly and Walsh, Limited, 1912).

Goldman, Bosworth, *Red Road Through Asia* (London, 1934).

Grajdanzev, A. J., "The Trans-Siberian Railway and the Problem of Soviet Supply," *Pacific Affairs* (December, 1941), pp. 389-415.

Grenard, Joseph Fernand, *Gengis-Khan* (Paris: Librairie Armand Colin, 1935).

————, *Mission scientifique dans la Haute Asie 1890-1895* (3 v., Paris: Ernest Leroux, 1897-1898).

Hawks-Pott, F. L., *A Sketch of Chinese History* (Shanghai: Kelly and Walsh, Limited, 1915).

Hedin, Sven, *The Flight of "Big Horse" The Trail of War in Central Asia* (translated by F. H. Lyon. New York: E. P. Dutton and Company, Inc., 1936).

———, *Riddles of the Gobi Desert* (translated by Elizabeth Sprigge and Claude Napier. New York: E. P. Dutton and Company, Inc., 1933).

"Hsi-pei K'ai-fa Sheng Chung Chih Hsin-chiang Ts'ai-cheng Ching-chi," *Ts'ai-cheng P'ing-lun,* VIII, 5 (Research staff, November, 1942).

"Hsin-chiang Feng-ching Hsien," *Hsin Shu Pao,* September 12, 1943.

"Hsin-chiang Ti-san-tz'u Ch'üan Sheng Tai-piao Ta-hui," *Meng-Ts'ang Yüeh-k'an,* IX, No. 2 (October 31, 1938).

Hu, Charles Y., *The Historical Occupancy and Economic Prospect of the Tarim Basin* (Master's Thesis in Geography, Deposited at the University of California. Berkeley, February, 1936).

Huang, Fen-sheng (ed.), *Meng-Ts'ang Hsin Chih* (2 v., Canton: Chung Hua Book Company, 1938).

Hung, Ti-ch'en, *Hsi-ts'ang Shih Ti Ta Kang* (Nanking: Cheng Chung Book Company, 1936).

Kerner, Robert Joseph, *Northeastern Asia, a selected bibliography; contributions to the bibliography of the relations of China, Russia, and Japan, with special reference to Korea, Manchuria, Mongolia, and Eastern Siberia, in Oriental and European languages* . . . (2 v., Berkeley: University of California Press, 1939).

Lattimore, Owen, "China's Turkistan-Siberian Supply Road," *Pacific Affairs* (December, 1940).

———, "Chinese Turkestan," *The Open Court,* XLVII (March, 1933).

———, "Chinese Turkestan or Sinkiang (Hsinchiang)," *The China Year Book, 1934.*

———, *High Tartary* (Boston: Little, Brown, and Company, 1930).

———, *Inner Asian Frontiers of China* (American Geographical Society, Research Series No. 21. London, New York: Oxford University Press, 1940).

———, "Mongolia," *The China Year Book, 1934.*

———, *The Desert Road to Turkestan* (Boston: Little, Brown, and Company, 1929).

Le Coq, Albert von, *Buried Treasures of Chinese Turkestan An Account of the Activities and Adventures of the Second and Third German Turfan Expeditions* (translated by Anna Barwell. London: George Allen and Unwin, Limited [1928]).

Li Yao-san, "K'en-min Tao Hsin-chiang Ch'ü-liao," *I-shih Pao,* September 22 (?), 1943.

Lu Ko, "Hsin Hsin-chiang Ti Chang-ch'eng; Sheng Shih-chi Hsien-sheng Fang-wen Chi," *Shang-wu Jih-pao,* November 10, 1942.

Mackinder, Right Honourable Sir Halford J., *Democratic Ideals and Reality A Study in the Politics of Reconstruction* (New York: Henry Holt and Company, 1942 reissue).

Maillart, Ella K., *Forbidden Journey—From Peking to Kashmir*—(translated from the French by Thomas McGreevy. New York: Henry Holt and Company, 1937).

Malaia Sovetskaia Entsiklopediia (second edition, tom IX, State Institute for the "Soviet Encyclopedia," Moscow, 1941; consulted through the courtesy of Mr. William Mandel, American Russian Institute, New York City).

Morden, William J., "By Coolie and Caravan across Central Asia," *The National Geographic Magazine,* LII, 4 (October, 1927).

Murray, Edward, "With the Nomads of Central Asia," *The National Geographic Magazine,* LXIX, I (January, 1936).

Murray, John, *A Handbook for Travellers in India Burma and Ceylon* (London, 1938).

Nazaroff, P. S., *Hunted Through Central Asia* (Edinburgh, London, 1932).

Norins, Martin R., "The New Sinkiang—China's Link with the Middle East," *Pacific Affairs* (December, 1942).

Perry-Ayscough, H. G. C., and Otter-Barry, Captain R. B., *With the Russians in Mongolia* (London, 1914).

"Report from Turkestan," *Time Magazine* (October 25, 1943), pp. 27-28.

Rocher, Emile, *La Province du Yün-nan* (2 v., Paris, 1879).

R.S.F.S.R., *Glavnoe Tamozhennoe Upravlenie Statistika Vneshnei Torgovli SSSR.,* 1936, XII (December), p. 7 and 1937, XII (December), p. 7.

Scott, John, *Behind the Urals* (Cambridge, Massachusetts, 1942).

Skrine, C. P., *Chinese Central Asia* (Boston and New York: Houghton Mifflin Company, 1926).

Soffner, Heinz, "The Axis and the Moslem World A New Problem for America," *Amerasia* (April 25, 1943, Spring Issue).

Stein, M. Aurel, *Ancient Khotan* (2 v., Oxford: Clarendon Press, 1907).

Sun Yat-sen, *The International Development of China* (reprinted from the 1928 edition. Chungking, Hong Kong: China Publishing Company, 1941).

Sykes, Ella and Brigadier General Sir Percy, *Through Deserts and Oases of Central Asia* (London: Macmillan and Company, Limited, 1920).

Sykes, Sir Percy, *Sir Mortimer Durand* (London: Cassell and Company, Limited, 1926).

Teichman, Sir Eric, *Journey to Turkistan* (London: Hodder and Stoughton, Limited, 1937).

———, "Chinese Turkestan," *Journal of the Royal Central Asian Society,* XXIII (1936), IV, p. 571.

"Ti-hua T'ung-hsün," *Sao Tang Pao,* September 16, 1943.

Ting, V. K., Wong, Wen-hao, and Tseng, Shih-ying, *Chung-kuo Fen Sheng Hsin T'u* (Shanghai: Shen Pao, 1936).

Treanor, Tom, "The Home Front," *Los Angeles Times,* June 16, 1943.

Tsang, O. Z., *A Complete Chinese-English Dictionary* (revised edition. Shanghai: The Republican Press, 1937).

Tu Chung-yüan, *Sheng Shih-ts'ai Yü Hsin Hsin-chiang* (fourth edition. Chungking [etc.]: Life Book Company, 1939).

Tung Ching-kua, "Hsi-pei chih Sheng: Wu Sheng Ts'an-cheng-yüan T'an-hua; Chien-she Wan Tuan Chiao-t'ung Ti-i," *I-shih Pao,* October 22, 1942.

United States, Department of Commerce, Bureau of Foreign and Domestic Commerce, "Troubles of the Turkestan-Siberian Railway," *Russian Economic Notes,* No. 88 (September 19, 1930).

United States, Department of State, *Foreign Service List* (Washington, D. C., May, 1943).

Vostokov, P., "L.'U.R.S.S., la Mongolie exterieure et le Sin Kiang," *Le Monde Slave,* 1936, II (June).

Wang, Tso-cheng, *Chung-kuo Fen Sheng Hsiang-t'u* (Shanghai: Ya-Kuang Geographical Society, 1939).

Wechsberg, Joseph, "Alaska, Springboard of Attack," *Canadian Geographical Journal,* XXVI, No. 4 (April, 1943), pp. 185-87.

Wiegert, H. W., "German Geopolitics," *Harper's Magazine* (November, 1941), pp. 586-97.

Williams, Maynard Owen, "From the Mediterranean to the Yellow Sea by Motor," *The National Geographic Magazine,* LXII, 5 (November, 1932).

Willkie, Wendell L., *One World* (Paper edition, New York: Simon and Schuster, 1943).

Wong, W. H., "Chapter XXVI—Minerals and Mines in China," *The China Year Book, 1934.*

Woodbury, Major Murray C., "Cargo and Transport," *Flying and Popular Aviation* (September, 1941).

Wu, Aitchen K., *Turkistan Tumult* (London: Methuen and Co., Limited, 1940).

———, "Will China Save Its Far West?" *Asia* (December, 1939).

Zashchuk, G., "La situation économique de Sindsian," *Novyi Vostok (Nouvel Orient)*, No. 26-27 (1929), pp. 105-24.

The author has also consulted editions of the *China Year Book* which were issued from 1931 to 1939 as well as editions of the *Chinese Year Book* issued in the period, 1935 to 1941. Newspapers and periodicals not otherwise mentioned which have proved especially helpful include: the *China Daily News, Chinese News Service, Chinese Times, Contemporary China, Far Eastern Survey, Hsin Hua Jih-pao, Hsin-chiang Jih-pao (Sinkiang Daily News), Izvestiia, Kuo Min Wai Chiao, Life, New York Times,* and *PM.*

REFERENCE NOTES

(Listed by page number according to occurrence in the text)

30. *Chinese News Service,* October 5, 23, November 27, 1943; January 10, 19, February 3, 4, 16, 1944; *Kuo Min Wai Chiao,* I, 1 (January, 1943), p. 43; Samuel Chao, "China's Northwest Revitalized," *China at War,* XI, 2 (August, 1943); Li Yao-san, "K'en-min Tao Hsin-chiang Ch'ü-liao," *I-shih Pao,* September 22 (?), 1943. The author is indebted to William L. Holland, Institute of Pacific Relations, New York City, for use of this last-named source. The author here wishes to acknowledge his indebtedness to Holland also for the use of certain other materials. These include: Ch'en Chi-jung, "T'ien-shan San-tu Wu Ts'ao," *Ta Kung Pao,* November 15-16, 1942; "Hsi-pei K'ai-fa Sheng Chung Chih Hsin-chiang Ts'ai-cheng Ching-chi," *Ts'ai-cheng P'ing-lun,* VIII, 5 (November, 1942); Lu Ko, "Hsin Hsin-chiang ti Chang-ch'eng: Sheng Shih-chi Hsiensheng Fang-wen Chi," *Shang-wu Jih-pao,* November 10, 1942; and Tung Ching-kua, "Hsi-pei chih Sheng; Wu Sheng Ts'an-cheng-yüan T'an-hua; Chien-she Wan Tuan Chiao-t'ung Ti-i," *I-shih Pao,* October 22, 1942. Y. Y. Hsu, also of the Institute of Pacific Relations, has made a rough abstract of material from the four last named clippings, and the author has consulted that abstract as well as the original material. Holland has also made available two additional clippings: "Hsin-chiang Feng-ching Hsien," *Hsin Shu Pao,* September 12, 1943; and "Ti-hua T'ung-hsün," *Sao Tang Pao,* September 16, 1943; and he has permitted the author to consult Samuel Ming-chiu Chao's unpublished manuscript entitled, *China's Northwest* (dated Chungking, September 15, 1940).

32. There are apparently no definitive figures on the area of Sinkiang Province, and the various estimates have ranged from 400,000 to well over 700,000 square miles. Similarly, estimates of the Sinkiang population have differed—running from as low as one to as high as six million persons. The *China Handbook 1937-1943 A Comprehensive Survey of Major Developments in China in Six Years of War* (Ministry of Information of the Republic of China, compilers, New York, The MacMillan Company, 1943, pp. 1 and 2) offers a 1938 figure of 1,828,418 square kilometers (which converts roughly into

705,953 square miles) for the area, and a 1933 figure of 4,360,020 for the population of the province. In 1939 Owen Lattimore judged the Sinkiang area to be *"of the order of"* 600,000 square miles and the Sinkiang population *"of the order of"* 3,500,000 persons. *Vide: Inner Asian Frontiers of China* (American Geographical Society, Research Series No. 21, London, New York, Oxford University Press, 1940), pp. 10-11.

Since the Sheng Shih-ts'ai administration came to power, however, the Sinkiang people speak locally of their population as "four million persons." Cf. Tu Chung-yüan, *Sheng Shih-ts'ai yü Hsin Hsin-chiang,* fourth edition, Chungking [etc.], Life Book Company, 1939, p. 54; and Chao Lieh, "Hsin-chiang chin Ching-lu," *Kuei-lin Ta Kung Pao,* September 8, 1941. The present writer accepts the figure from the latter two sources as a rough, but probably sound estimate for today. So far as area is concerned, moreover, he is inclined to agree with the figure of 550,579 square miles offered for Chinese Turkestan by *The China Year Book, 1934* (H. G. W. Woodhead, editor, Shanghai, The North China Daily News & Herald, Ltd.), p. 2.

The China Year Book, 1934 gives 38,610 square miles as the area and 896 as the population per square mile of Kiangsu Province. In contrast, the population density of Sinkiang (on the basis of a 4,000,000 provincial total) would be slightly less than some eight persons per square mile. If one accepted figures of the *China Handbook 1937-1943,* the Sinkiang population density could even be calculated at a smaller amount, some six persons per square mile!

For other useful information on this general subject, cf. especially Council of International Affairs, *The Chinese Year Book 1938-39 Issue* (Commercial Press, Chungking), p. 121; Chiang Chün-chang, *Hsin-chiang Ching-ying Lun* (third edition, China, Cheng Chung Book Company, 1939), p. 51; and Owen Lattimore, "Chinese Turkestan or Sinkiang (Hsinchiang)," *The China Year Book, 1934,* pp. 80-81. The author wishes to remark at this point that he is indebted considerably to the last article for its concisely summarized facts regarding the land, people, and early history of Sinkiang.

32. For information on the terrain of Sinkiang and concerning the designations which Chinese have formerly used for the area, *vide* Chiang Chün-chang, *op. cit.,* pp. 2, 5, and 9; Owen Lattimore *High Tartary* (Little, Brown, and Company, Boston, 1930), pp. 34-35; Tu Chung-yüan, *op. cit.,* especially his "Outline Map of Sinkiang;" *vide* also V. K. Ting, Wong Wen-hao, and Tseng Shih-ying, *Chung-kuo Fen Sheng Hsin T'u* (Shen Pao, Shanghai, 1936), pp. 54-55.

33. Cf. Owen Lattimore, *Inner Asian Frontiers of China,* especially pp. 172-173; and *vide* Lieut.-Colonel P. T. Etherton, *In the Heart of Asia* (Houghton-Mifflin Company, Boston and New York, 1926), pp. 57-59, 79-83, 105, 108, 109, 145, 196, and 245.

34. The iron bridge, witnessed by the author while he was in Lan-chou, 1939-1940, bears a sign reading: "1909 Telce & Schroeter Tientsin 1909 American Bridge Co., New York U.S.A. 1908 1907."

It has been the fashion for writers on this subject to refer to the Chinese characters for Sinkiang (*Hsin-chiang*) in English as "The New Dominion." *Vide,* for example, Peter Fleming, *News From Tartary: A Journey from Peking to Kashmir* (New York, Charles Scribner's Sons, 1936), p. 29, note 1. However, a literal translation of the characters involved can furnish material for lively academic debate. The character *hsin,* ordinarily translated as "new," is made up of the following component parts: *li* (a man standing erect over the earth), *mu* (a tree), and *chin* (an ax with a splinter underneath). The character *chiang,* ordinarily referred to in this case as "dominion," is made up of the following parts: *t'u* (earth), *kung* (a bow), and *chiang* (a character which in itself can be substituted for the *chiang* in question, and one which depicts two partitioned fields and which may be roughly interpreted as a boundary). On the basis of this information the author hazards the guess that the character *hsin* designates "a man cutting wood" and that it has extensions such as "to get fuel," "to get wood," "to repair," "to renew," "to make new," and finally "new." So far as the character *chiang* is concerned, it would seem to represent the idea of "boundary." On this groundwork, there is some justification for translating *Hsin-chiang* as the "New Boundary" or, perhaps, the "New Frontier." However, these translations need not by any means be considered definitive, for the subject has been given only fragmentary attention here and is deserving of a much more detailed analysis.

The author has tasted the Ha-mi melon in dried form at Lan-chou. Tu Chung-yüan mentions the large size rice kernel and the excellent Turfan grapes. *Op. cit.*, p. 47.

34-36. Chiang Chün-chang, *op. cit.*, pp. 100-108; Lattimore, "Chinese Turkestan or Sinkiang (Hsinchiang)," *loc. cit.*, p. 81; *Ts'ai-cheng P'ing-lun, loc. cit.*; Tu Chung-yüan, *op. cit.*, pp. 48-51. In regard to the figure on the Tihwa population, cf. *Chinese News Service*, November 10, 1943, and Lattimore, "Chinese Turkestan or Sinkiang (Hsin-chiang)," *loc. cit.*, p. 81. For the Kashgar data, *vide* Lattimore, *Inner Asian Frontiers of China*, p. 157, note 12 citing Fernand Grenard, *Haute Asie*, Geographie Universelle, vol. VIII (Paris, 1929), pp. 319, 321; also *vide The China Year Book, 1931*, p. 42; and Etherton, *op. cit.*, pp. 66-67.

36-37. Etherton, *loc. cit.* Edward Murray, "With the Nomads of Central Asia," *The National Geographic Magazine*, LXIX, 1 (January, 1936), p. 3; Albert von Le Coq, *Buried Treasures of Chinese Turkestan An Account of the Activities and Adventures of the Second and Third German Turfan Expeditions* (translated by Anna Barwell, London, George Allen and Unwin Limited), p. 42.

38-40. The biographical information is from Tu Chung-yüan, *op. cit.*, pp. 31-38.

40-43. Chiang Chün-chang, *op. cit.*, p. 45; Tu Chung-yüan, *op. cit.*, pp. 65-71. Cf. Sven Hedin, *The Flight of "Big Horse" the Trail of War in Central Asia* (translated by F. H. Lyon, New York, E. P. Dutton and Company, Inc., 1936), pp. 2-6, 240-247; and Ella K. Maillart, *Forbidden Journey—From Peking to Kashmir*—(translated from the French by Thomas McGreevy, New York, Henry Holt and Company, 1937), pp. 196, 214-219. The quotation on page 43 is from Tu Chung-yüan, *op. cit.*, pp. 70-71. Cf. also *ibid.*, pp. 37-38.

44-45. Hedin, *The Flight of "Big Horse,"* pp. 12-15, 17, 25, 40, 46-47, 55, 58, 110, 148, 149, 158-160, 170, 180, 213, 240-243, 245-247.

45-46. *Vide infra*, pp. 103-122.

46. The quotation is from Tu Chung-yüan, *op. cit.*, pp. 71-72. *Vide ibid.*, p. 72, for the Eight Point Proclamation.

47. The Six Great Policies are named in Tu Chung-yüan, *op. cit.*, p. 73; the quotation is from the same page reference.

48. The quotation is from Tu Chung-yüan, *op. cit.*, pp. 73-74.

48-49. This, admittedly, touches on the fringe of the so-called "extreme" or "romantic;" and when sophisticates have related these tales, eyes have twinkled all too knowingly. *Vide* Peter Fleming, *News From Tartary*, p. 261; Maillart, *Forbidden Journey*, pp. 218-223; and cf. Chiang Chün-chang, *op. cit.*, pp. 76-78.

49. For references in regard to the ancient *Hsi Yü* or Western Regions, *vide* Chiang Chün-chang, *op. cit.*, pp. 10-18. Cf. also Charles Y. Hu, *The Historical Occupany and Economic Prospect of the Tarim Basin* (Master's thesis in Geography, Deposited at the University of California, Berkeley, February, 1936), especially "A List of Ancient King-

doms in the Western Regions and their Corresponding localities at the present, as found in the Han Annals," pp. 67-68.

49. The quotation is from Lattimore, *Inner Asian Frontiers of China*, pp. 170-171. *Vide* also Chiang Chün-chang, *op. cit.,* pp. 9-10, 18, 25.

49-50. Chiang Chün-chang, *op. cit.,* pp. 26-27, 32-37, 41-45; Douglas Carruthers, *Unknown Mongolia* (two vols., Hutchinson and Company, London, 1914), II, pp. 356-357, 383, 384, 386-387; Edouard Chavannes, *Documents sur les Tou-kiue (Tures) occidentaux.* Sbornik trud'ov orkhonskoi ekspeditsii, VI (St. Petersburg), p. 151; F. L. Hawks-Pott, *A Sketch of Chinese History* (Kelly & Walsh, Limited, Shanghai, 1915), p. 107; Sven Hedin, *Riddles of the Gobi Desert* (translated from the Swedish by Elizabeth Sprigge and Claude Napier, E. P. Dutton and Company, New York, 1933), pp. 65-69; Lattimore, *High Tartary*, pp. 38, 225-226; *idem,* "Chinese Turkestan or Sinkiang (Hsinchiang)," *loc. cit.,* pp. 85-87; C. P. Skrine, *Chinese Central Asia* (Boston and New York, Houghton Mifflin Company, 1926), p. 59.

51-53. Tsarist advances: *Vide* Warren Maxfeld Engstrand, *The Kuldja Affair and Its Significance in Sino-Russian Relations* (Unpublished Master's Thesis, Deposited, University of California, Berkeley, 1933), for the story of this period. Cf. Lattimore, *High Tartary,* pp. 225-226. British activities: The Forsyth Mission of 1873-1874 "bore a letter and presents from Queen Victoria herself to the 'Amir' Yakub Beg, Bedaulat of Kashgar," Skrine, *op. cit.,* pp. 59, 62, 65. *Vide* also *ibid.,* pp. 4, 19-21. Cf. Chiang Chün-chang, *op. cit.,* pp. 74-75. *K'an-chü-t'i* is identified by another Chinese writer as a feudatory and as having become part of China ("attached to the interior") in 1764. He, curiously enough, nevertheless classifies it as a feudatory of both England and China. Ch'ien Shih-fu, *Chung-kuo Ti Shih Ti* (Min-t'uan Chou-k'an She, Nanning, 1939), pp. 5, 6, 7. For one of the clearest of modern statements from a British official in regard to his country's policy toward Sinkiang *vide* Sir Eric Teichman, *Journey to Turkistan* (London, Hodder and Stoughton Limited, 1937), pp. 191-192. Last Manchu efforts: Lattimore, *High Tartary*, pp. 69-70; I. E. Gabitov, "La situation économique du Turquestan Chinois," *Novyi Vostok (Nouvel Orient)*, 8-9 (1925), pp. 30-31.

53-54. The convenience factor: Joseph Castagné, "Le problème du Turkestan chinois (Sin-Kiang)," *Revue des études islamiques*, 1933, II, pp. 164-165. It is worthwhile to note that the distances Ch'en Chi-jung gives for more recently constructed truck roads passing between some of the same termini mentioned by M. Castagné seem considerably longer. *Vide,* in passing, the chapter on "Reconstruction" *infra* under "Road transportation." Note also the mention by Skrine in 1926 that the highest pass on "the Indo-Central Asian trade" route is 18,550 feet above sea level. *Loc. cit.,* p. 4. Fleming says the Chichiklik is the "biggest" of the Pamir passes and "some" 15,000 feet high. The Mintaka Pass, "the Pass of a Thousand Ibex," at the "extremest boundary of China," writes Fleming, is 15,600 feet above sea level; *loc. cit.,* pp. 339, 352.

54-55. Skrine, *op. cit.,* p. 66; Gabitov, *loc. cit.,* pp. 27-29, 30-31, 35; and United States, Department of Commerce, Bureau of Foreign and Domestic Commerce, "Troubles of the Turkestan-Siberian Railway," *Russian Economic Notes*, No. 88 (September 19, 1930), p. 3. It was decided to construct the line on December 3, 1926. The length of the line, as cited in 1931, was 926 miles (1,481 kilometers). *The China Year Book 1931*, p. 42. *Vide* also P. Vostokov, "L'U.R.S.S., la Mongolie extérieure et le Sin Kiang," *Le Monde Slave*, 1936, II (June), pp. 448 and 457, for the Sinkiang-Soviet trade position in 1930. Various testimony as to signature of the 1931 Sinkiang-Soviet agreement is available in Chiang Chün-chang, *op. cit.,* pp. 45, 69; Doctor Cherbakoff,

"In Kashgar, December, 1927, to October, 1931," *Journal of the Royal Central Asian Society*, XX (1933), IV, pp. 541-542; Sir Eric Teichman, "Chinese Turkestan," *ibid.*, XXIII (1936), IV, p. 571; and Castagné, *loc. cit.*, p. 173 *inter alia*.

55. Chiang Chün-chang, *op. cit.*, pp. 69, 73, and 74, as well as 83 note 16 (citing a text from the *Shen Pao Year Book*, 1934). Cf. Lattimore, *Inner Asian Frontiers of China*, p. 195 and note 73, who indicates "the Chinese" obtained arms from the British in India.

56. *Vide infra*, pp. 71-72.

56-57. Tu Chung-yüan, *op. cit.*, pp. 73-74; Chiang Chün-chang, *op. cit.*, pp. 75-79; Heinz Soffner, "The Axis and the Moslem World A New Problem for America," *Amerasia* (April 25, 1943, Spring Issue), pp. 80-89.

57-58. The quotation is from Tu Chung-yüan, *op. cit.*, p. 61. An English language text of the Sino-Russian Pact of Non-Aggression is to be found in the *New York Times*, August 30, 1937.

58. For pledges of the All-Sinkiang Congress *vide* "Hsin-chiang Ti-san-tz'u Ch'üan Sheng Tai-piao Ta-hui," *Meng-Ts'ang Yüeh-k'an*, IX, No. 2 (October 31, 1938), pp. 1-4. Pertinent reference to the "Anglo-Americans" is to be found in the *Sinkiang Daily News*, December 17, 1939, and October 4, 1940.

59. The quotation is from Tu Chung-yüan, *op. cit.*, p. 74; cf. Chao Lieh, "Hsin-chiang Chin Ching-lu," *loc. cit.* This two-part feature is dated Kao-lan, August 20, 1941.

60-62. Early Soviet-Sinkiang trade (1918-1920): Gabitov, *loc. cit.*, pp. 27, 35. The closing of the Chinese frontier: P. S. Nazaroff, *Hunted Through Central Asia* (Edinburgh, London, 1932), especially pp. 228-262; cf. Skrine, *op. cit.*, p. 66. The 1920 agreement: Castagné, *loc. cit.*, pp. 156-157.

62-63. Gabitov, *loc. cit.*, pp. 28, 32-33, 35-36, 37; cf. Skrine, *op. cit.*, p. 66. But Skrine adds that "a Russian consul (without escort) has been in residence at Kashgar since July 1925." *Ibid.*, n. 1.

63-65. Gabitov, *loc. cit.*, p. 38.

65. Ch'en Fu-kuang, *Wai-chiao Shih* (Ch'ing-nien Shu-tien, Chungking, 1939), pp. 71-72; *Izvestiia*, December 31, 1924; October 31, November 15, 1925; January 8, 1928; Skrine, *op. cit.*, p. 61, n. 1.

65-67. *Izvestiia*, January 8, 1928. The underscoring is the author's. Russians traditionally have reserved the term *Zapadnyi Kitai* ("Western China") especially for Sinkiang.

67. Chiang Chün-chang, *op. cit.*, p. 45; cf. Hedin, *Riddles of the Gobi Desert*, pp. 65-69.

67-68. Sven Hedin, *The Flight of "Big Horse" The Trail of War in Central Asia* (Translated by F. H. Lyon, E. P. Dutton and Company, Inc., New York, 1936), p. 3; Tu Chung-yüan, *op. cit.*, pp. 65-67; and Chiang Chün-chang, *op. cit.*, pp. 45, 69. For reference to the 1931 agreement, *vide* notes to page 55 *supra*.

68-69. Tu Chung-yüan, *op. cit.*, pp. 69-71; Chiang Chün-chang, *op. cit.*, p. 46; Hedin, *The Flight of "Big Horse"* especially pp. 16-17; cf. Bosworth Goldman, *Red Road Through Asia* (London, 1934). The quotation is from Lattimore, *High Tartary*, pp. 73-74. *Vide* also *supra*, pp. 41-44 and notes to pp. 54-55.

69. Lattimore, "Chinese Turkestan or Sinkiang (Hsinchiang)," *loc. cit.*, pp. 83-84. *Vide infra*, pp. 105-106.

69. The following is a statement of Sinkiang-Soviet trade from the economic year 1923/24 to 1937 inclusive:

Date	Exports From Sinkiang To the U.S.S.R.		Imports Into Sinkiang From the U.S.S.R.		Total Trade	
	Th. Rubles	Tons	Th. Rubles	Tons	Th. Rubles	Tons
1923/24	3,015	12,215	418	839	3,433	13,054
1924/25	4,535	18,321	2,611	2,912	7,146	21,233
1925/26	10,331	27,925	6,092	4,659	16,423	32,584
1926/27	11,754	21,788	10,232	7,302	21,986	29,090
1927/28	13,528	24,575	10,647	7,800	24,175	32,375
1929	16,435	20,440	16,396	12,502	32,831	32,942
1930	16,033	27,232	16,027	10,957	32,060	38,189
1931	10,212	23,936	13,954	7,148	24,166	31,084
1932	12,305	21,838	15,698	8,006	28,003	29,844
1933	18,822	35,899	10,856	7,412	29,678	43,311
1934	5,945	22,630	4,730	18,894	10,675	41,524
1935	6,049	26,665	4,550	20,113	10,599	46,778
1936	25,671	28,498	26,145	22,786	61,816	51,284
1937	25,774	28,990	34,753	25,733	60,527	54,723

Figures to and including 1927/28 are from C. Zashchuk, "La situation économique de Sindsian," *Novyi Vostok*, No. 26-27 (1929), pp. 120-121; figures from and including 1929 to and including 1935 are from P. Vostokov, "L'U.R.S.S., la Mongolie extérieure et le Sin Kiang," *Le Monde Slave*, 1936, II (June), pp. 448 and 457; figures for 1936 and 1937 are from R. S. F. S. R., *Glavnoe Tamazhennoe Upravlenie Statistika Vneshnei Torgovli SSSR*, 1936, XII (December), p. 7; and 1937, XII (December), p. 7. From October of one year to September 30 of the next constituted an "economic year" up to 1929 for the Russian Customs. The statistics for 1930-1933 are particularly subject to question due to the existence of conflicting official Russian data. *Vide* Vostokov, *loc. cit.*, p. 456, n. (2). A 1941 Soviet source adds that the "annual trade turnover" of Sinkiang is "nearly 62,000,000 rubles." *Malaia Sovetskaia Entsiklopediia* (Second edition, *tom* IX, State Institute for the "Soviet Encyclopedia," Moscow, 1941), column 716.

An idea of the type of commodities exchanged between Soviet Russia and Sinkiang is seen in 1931 trade figures offered in the *Ts'ai-cheng P'ing-lun* for November, 1942:

Important Items of 1931 Soviet-Sinkiang Trade (Rubles)

Imports to Sinkiang from Soviet Russia		Imports to Soviet Russia from Sinkiang	
Textile goods	11,361,000	Sheep wool	4,896,000
Petroleum products	144,000	Leather	2,009,000
Sugar	978,000	Livestock	2,891,000
Electrical products	850,000	Cotton	767,000

The same publication, for purposes of rough comparison, gives statements of commodity exchange between Sinkiang on the one hand and China Proper, India, and

Afghanistan respectively on the other. The pertinent figures are assertedly based upon a 1927 British Consulate report but, since the citations are offered by the Chinese source with certain internal inconsistencies, they ought not to be considered here as valuable for more than rough approximations of an actual situation. The figures, given below, make available a crude and very limited commodity yardstick for comparison of former Sinkiang trade relations with neighboring areas. Due to the above-mentioned inconsistencies, the Sinkiang-Indian import and export trade totals and the Sinkiang-Afghanistan import trade totals here are the author's own computation of the available *Ts'ai*-

Sinkiang Trade with China Proper (Rubles)

Imports to Sinkiang		Exports from Sinkiang	
Red tea	770,000	Gold	475,000
Pearls	600,000	Cotton cloth	200,000
Japanese silk	256,000	Canvas	36,000
Cotton yarn	76,000	"High quality" cotton cloth...	26,250
Coins and gold	69,750	Total	737,250
Total	1,771,750		

Sinkiang Trade with India (Rubles)

Imports to Sinkiang		Exports from Sinkiang	
European cotton cloth	276,848	Horses and ponies	101,235
Drugs	29,426	Cotton cloth	35,698
Skins (not including sheep and goat skins)	61,663	Copper	742,654
Leather goods	41,448	Raw and waste silk	47,331
Paints and dyes	226,254	Woolen goods	358,451
Pearls (European)	71,335	Felt carpets	25,524
Down of the wild swan	115,334	Coins	26,789
Silk goods (Indian)	24,876	Gold, silver, and silver "shoes"	233,759
Spices	36,562	Leather goods	16,339
Red tea (Indian)	27,386	Sheep wool	17,288
Red tea (not including Indian)	23,098	Donkeys and horses	7,508
European woolen goods	42,000	Hard jade	8,272
Total	976,230	Total	1,620,848

Sinkiang Trade with Afghanistan (Rubles)

Imports to Sinkiang		Exports from Sinkiang	
Opium	675,000	Cotton cloth	167,500
Mountain goat gut	600,000	Sheep wool felt goods (carpets and blankets?)	80,000
Horses	45,000	Silk floss	75,000
No-tun (?) skin	10,000	Ceramics	21,200
Fox skin	24,000	Horse blankets	16,800
Mountain cat skin	4,350	Mules and horses	13,000
Foreign almonds	3,600	Khotan silk	12,500
Total	1,361,950	Total	386,000

cheng P'ing-lun commodity data. *Vide* Violet Conolly, *Soviet Economic Policy in the East: Turkey, Persia, Afghanistan, Mongolia, and Tana Tuva, Sinkiang* (Oxford University Press, London, 1933) for additional basic discussion concerning related economic problems in the period previous to inception of the New Sinkiang.

71. "Unity" in 1936: Ch'en Chi-jung, "Hsin Hsin-chiang Ti Ts'ai-cheng," article obtained by the author in Lan-chou, China, January 4, 1940. Sheng's desire to "revive" Sinkiang: Tu Chung-yüan, *op. cit.,* p. 92.

71-72. *Ibid.,* pp. 93-94.

72. The fact (1) that there are today varying interpretations within China of the Three People's Principles and of the direction which the Chinese National Revolution should take and (2) that China has been constantly revising her program of action to meet dire wartime necessities, indicates that Resistance and Reconstruction may have, for the immediate practicable purposes of prosecution of war against Japan, taken precedence over the Three People's Principles.

73. Lattimore, "Chinese Turkestan or Sinkiang (Hsinchiang)," *loc. cit.,* p. 88; *idem, Inner Asian Frontiers of China,* p. 201; Hedin, *The Flight of "Big Horse,"* pp. 13, 246; Peter Fleming, *op. cit.,* pp. 30, 253.

73-74. For the text of the Sino-Russian treaty see notes to pages 57-58 *supra.* For resolutions of the All-Sinkiang Congress *vide* "Hsin-chiang Ti-san-tz'u Ch'üan Sheng Tai-piao Ta-hui," *loc. cit.* Reference to the June 16, 1939 trade agreement is to be found in the *New York Times,* June 25, 1939.

74. An English language text of the Russo-German Pact of August, 1939, is to be found in the *New York Times,* August 24, 1939. The Chinese defensive measures were personally witnessed by the author. Final ratification of the Sino-Russian trade pact was announced as taking place January 5, 1940.

74-75. *Sinkiang Daily News,* December 17, 1939, and October 4, 1940; *Hsin Hua Jih-pao,* December 12, 1940; and *Ta Kung Pao,* January 28, 1941. An English language text of the Soviet-Japanese Non-Aggression agreement is to be found in the *New York Times,* April 14, 1941.

76. Wendell L. Willkie wrote in early 1943 that Sheng Shih-ts'ai had "shifted his allegiance to the Generalissimo." This might have been worded more fortunately, but it was nevertheless indicative even then of a subtle shift in Sinkiang affairs and is pertinent to some other comments in Willkie's book, *One World.* According to the latter, "the legends which pass as news in Asia have it that Russians were accused of complicity in" the "murder" of Sheng Shih-ts'ai's "brother" in June, 1942. In his book Willkie has emphasized the overt appearance of "cordial friendship between Russia and China" yet has spoken of Sheng Shih-ts'ai as having "once" been "sympathetic with the Communists." This would suggest that the switch in Sinkiang affairs away from "Kinship to Sovietism" was becoming noticeable even as early as 1942 when Willkie was traveling through the province en route to Chungking. The recently published information concerning Russian "withdrawal" from Sinkiang, as well as the press dispatches mentioning the alleged Soviet-Chinese border incidents on the Sinkiang-Mongolian frontier, has exposed the shift even more. *Vide* Wendell L. Willkie, *One World* (Paper edition, New York, Simon and Schuster, 1943), p. 47; "Report from Turkestan," *Time Magazine* (October 25, 1943), pp. 27-28; *New York Times,* October 16, 1943, April 3, 4, and 5, 1944.

77-78. For remarks in regard to the Sinkiang population, *vide* also the reference notes for page 32 *supra.* Tu Chung-yüan states that approximately eighty per cent of the

Sinkiang population are Ch'an-t'ou or Wei-wu-erh. *Op. cit.*, pp. 54-58. Owen Lattimore identifies the Ch'an-t'ou as "predominantly Turki" but connects with them a "strong basic stock of the race called by anthropolgists, 'Alpine' . . ." "Chinese Turkestan or Sinkiang (Hsinchiang)," *loc. cit.*, p. 82. *Vide* also Tu Chung-yüan, *op. cit.*, pp. 54-60; Chiang Chün-chang, *op. cit.*, pp. 50-56; and Etherton, *op. cit.*, pp. 73-74 *et seq.*, for general statements on the racial components of Sinkiang. Tu Chung-yüan clarifies the meaning of "Racial Equality" on pages 71 and 74-75 of his above mentioned book.

78-79. Cf. Samuel Chao, *China's Northwest;* and *vide* also Joseph Fernand Grenard, *Mission scientifique dans la Haute Asie 1890-1895,* II, p. 10. Carruthers suggests that the Uighurs, "a wandering people" with a "problematic" origin, emerged into prominence from somewhere "far south of Mongolia" "about the third century B.C." The greatest power of the Uighurs, he intimates in citing A. B. Adrianoff of Minusinsk, extended from the fourth to the eighth century in the Yenisei regions and ultimately "over the whole of Northern Mongolia from Lake Kossogol to the Black Irtish." But he extends their geographical range when he associates them—as of the same family—with the Kirgiz and, in turn, the Kirei whose "birthplace" he says, was "the Altai ranges and the Kemchik pastures." He does it again when he intimates that the Uighurs came from "the far south of Mongolia, perhaps from the borders of China—from the present-day provinces of Shensi and Kansu . . ." Carruthers, *op. cit.*, I, pp. 51, 53; II, 351-353. The present writer is inclined to agree that Carruthers may have been justified in suggesting such an hypothetical extension of origin for the Uighurs, but fears that he did not go far enough. The present writer, in fact, is inclined to look for an even further extension of the Uighur origin; one that leads ultimately to the Kashgarian fringe of that rugged backbone of Asia, the Tibetan uplands. It is worth while to point out, however, that Sir Percy Sykes feels the Uighurs "originally lived in north-west Mongolia." Ella Sykes and Brigadier General Sir Percy Sykes, *Through Deserts and Oases of Central Asia* (London, MacMillan and Company, Limited, 1920), p. 258. Also *vide, ibid.,* pp. 257, 259, and 260-261; Lattimore, "Chinese Turkestan or Sinkiang (Hsinchiang)," *loc. cit.*, p. 85; and M. Aurel Stein, *Ancient Khotan* (two vols., Clarendon Press, Oxford, 1907), I, pp. 4-17.

"It would be presumption for me to attempt even the briefest survey of the immense field covered by the archaeological discoveries of Sir Aurel Stein in the sands of the Takla Makan and elsewhere in Chinese Turkistan and Kansu." Skrine, *Chinese Central Asia,* p. 189. In the face of such words from one so well qualified the present writer feels that he is justified in not attempting to treat of the subject here and in referring the reader instead to abundant materials and commentary in works such as Stein, *Ancient Khotan;* Sykes, *Through Deserts and Oases of Central Asia;* Chavannes, *op. cit.;* Fernand Grenard, *op. cit.;* and Le Coq, *op. cit.*

79. Tu Chung-yüan, *op. cit.*, pp. 54-55, 57-59; cf. Samuel Chao, *China's Northwest;* Etherton, *op. cit.*, pp. 74, 76. Chiang Chün-chang cites a fellow countryman, Ch'en Yüan-an, who claims that in the *Yüan-Shih* (an ancient Chinese chronicle) the term, Wei-wu-erh, was used to refer to a Chinese Moslem group, possibly the Uighurs of the Middle Ages. *Op. cit.*, p. 66. Tu Chung-yüan indicates that Sheng Shih-ts'ai's administration has purposely kept the sound of a similar old term in naming the Wei-wu-erh (or Ch'an-t'ou) of present day Sinkiang. *Op. cit.*, p. 57.

79. Islam: Etherton, *op. cit.*, pp. 14, 15, 74.

79-81. Wei-wu-erh characteristics: Tu Chung-yüan, *op. cit.*, pp. 57-58; Etherton, *op. cit.*, pp. 80-82, 84-89, 112; Maynard Owen Williams, "From the Mediterranean to the Yellow Sea by Motor," *The National Geographic Magazine,* LXII, 5 (November, 1932), p. 520.

81-83. "Han" Chinese: Tu Chung-yüan, *op. cit.*, pp. 54-56; Lattimore, "Chinese Turkestan or Sinkiang (Hsinchiang)," *loc. cit.*, pp. 81, 83. *Vide* also p. 126 *infra*.

83-84. Tung-kan Moslems: Chiang Chün-chang, *op. cit.*, pp. 52-53; Tu Chung-yüan, *op. cit.*, p. 57; Lattimore, "Chinese Turkestan or Sinkiang (Hsinchiang)," *loc. cit.*, p. 83; Carruthers, *op. cit.*, II, p. 618; Fleming, *op. cit.*, pp. 30, 253; Maillart, *op. cit.*, pp. 196, 214-219; Hedin, *The Flight of "Big Horse,"* pp. 4-6, 240-247; *China Daily News* (New York), July 20, 1942.

84-85. Manchus and Manchurians: Chiang Chün-chang, *op. cit.*, pp. 38, 55; Tu Chung-yüan, *op. cit.*, pp. 54, 56; Lattimore, "Chinese Turkestan or Sinkiang (Hsinchiang)," *loc. cit.*, p. 85; *idem*, *High Tartary*, pp. 67-68, 210; Hedin, *The Flight of "Big Horse,"* p. 12; and Carruthers, *op. cit.*, II, p. 387.

85-86. Mongol characteristics: Chiang Chün-chang, *op. cit.*, p. 52; Murray, *loc. cit.*, pp. 48, 56-57; Etherton, *op. cit.*, pp. 200-209.

86. Mongol history: Carruthers, *op. cit.*, II, pp. 356-357; 384-386; Chiang Chün-chang, *op. cit.*, p. 33; Lattimore, "Chinese Turkestan or Sinkiang (Hsinchiang)," *loc. cit.*, p. 85; *idem*, *Inner Asian Frontiers of China*, p. 180. Carruthers states, however, that "Dzungaria fell to the lot of . . . Oktai, or Ogodai . . ." after the death of Genghis Khan. He adds that "it seems, however, to have been a bone of contention between Oktai and his brother Chagatai . . ." *Op. cit.*, II, pp. 384-385.

87. Mongol leagues and location: Huang Fen-sheng (ed.), *Meng-Ts'ang Hsin Chih* (two vols., Chung Hua Book Company, Canton, 1938), I, pp. 18-19, 109, 110. Lattimore, "Mongolia," *The China Year Book 1934*, p. 76; Murray, *loc. cit.*, pp. 46-57.

87-88. Mongol characteristics: Etherton, *op. cit.*, p. 205; Murray, *loc. cit.*, pp. 46-57; "Faces and Fashions of Asia's Changeless Tribes," *The National Geographic Magazine*, LXIX, No. 1 (January, 1936), p. xv; Williams, *loc. cit.*, pp. 534-536.

88-90. Kirgiz: Carruthers, *op. cit.*, II, 351-369; Etherton, *op. cit.*, pp. 26-42; Murray, *loc. cit.*, pp. 19-45; Lattimore, *High Tartary*, pp. 257-259. Cf. John Scott, *Behind the Urals* (Cambridge, Massachusetts, 1942), pp. 59-60 and Appendix 1.

90-91. Kazakhs: Lattimore, *High Tartary*, pp. 41, 54, 243-244, 257-258; Tu Chung-yüan, *op. cit.*, pp. 59-60; Skrine, *op. cit.*, p. 41; and Carruthers, *op. cit.*, II, pp. 351-352.

91. Tajiks or Sarikolis: Skrine, *op. cit.*, pp. 41, 167; Lattimore, "Chinese Turkestan or Sinkiang (Hsinchiang)," *loc. cit.*, p. 82; Etherton, *op. cit.*, pp. 29-32. Habdals and Dulanis: Lattimore, "Chinese Turkestan or Sinkiang (Hsinchiang)," *loc. cit.*, p. 82; Etherton, *op. cit.*, p. 145. Taranchis: Lattimore, *High Tartary*, p. 223. Uzbeks: Tu Chung-yüan, *op. cit.*, p. 60.

91-92. The "fourteen" races: Tu Chung-yüan, *op. cit.*, p. 54.

92-93. The quotations are from Tu Chung-yüan, *op. cit.*, p. 75. *Vide* also "Hsinchiang Ti-san-tz'u Chüan Sheng Tai-piao Ta-hui," *loc. cit.*, pp. 1-4, and related dispatches in the same journal.

94. Chiang Chün-chang emphasizes the Chinese administration in Sinkiang during the Han, T'ang, Manchu, and Republican periods (*op. cit.*, pp. 4, 1-40), and it is mainly on his authority that they have been singled out here for special consideration. However, within these same periods China has achieved a kind of exceptional strength so far as her own political unity, her frontiers, and her international relations in general are concerned. This makes such a restricted treatment additionally warranted. Ch'ien Mu says that China "began to deal with the problem of foreign relations" in early years of the Ch'in-Han reigns, a period when "China became unified, established her territorial outposts, and became racially mature." *Kuo Shih Ta Kang* (two vols., Commercial Press, Changsha, China, 1940), I, p. 137. He reminds his readers also that "it was not until after a four hundred year long period of chaos that, under the Sui and T'ang reigns, once again a

unified government emerged for China." *Ibid.,* p. 276. In turn the Manchu accession to power, according to his view, was a "regeneration of racial sovereignty," though "in a narrow sense." *Ibid.,* II, p. 571.

95. ". . . the important duties of the *Tu-tu* were to watch the Wu-sun and K'ang-chu [ancient principalities in the Chinese Western Regions] and all their activities with foreign states. If practicable these matters were to be handled peaceably; if necessary by force." Chiang Chün-chang, *op. cit.,* p. 23.

95. T'ang: *Ibid.,* pp. 30-31.

96. *Ibid.,* pp. 32-35; cf. Hung Ti-ch'en, *Hsi-ts'ang Shih Ti Ta Kang* (Cheng Chung Book Company, Nanking, 1936), pp. 148-58.

96-97. Chiang Chün-chang, *op. cit.,* pp. 36-40.

97-98. The quotation is from Tu Chung-yüan, *op. cit.,* p. 76; cf. Lattimore, "Chinese Turkestan," *The Open Court,* XLVII (Chicago, March, 1933), p. 99.

98. "Clean Government" is a free translation of the Chinese term, *Ch'ing-lien;* the Chinese is also translatable more literally as "clean-handedness" or "honesty." Tu Chung-yüan, *op. cit.,* pp. 76-77.

99. Administrative Divisions: *Ibid.,* pp. 42-43. Chao Lieh wrote in 1941 that there are twelve administrative districts with a total of seventy-five hsien in Sinkiang. *Loc. cit.,* Wang Tso-cheng, *Chung-kuo fen sheng Hsiang-t'u* (Ya-Kuang Geographical Society, Shanghai, 1939), states instead under "Sinkiang Province" that there are fifty-nine counties and six Provisional Administrative Offices in the province. The Soviet accounts seem, however, to corroborate or to have accepted Tu Chung-yüan's account. *Vide* the *Malaia Sovetskaia Entsiklopedia, tom* IX, column 715, which lists nine *okrug* ("district" or "circuit") on its map of "Sinkiang (Western China)," as follows: Kashgarskii okrug (Kashi), Khotanskii okrug (Khetian), Karasharskii okrug (Yanshzi), Aksuiskii okrug, Illiskii okrug (Ili), Urumchinskii okrug (Dikhua), Komul'skii okrug (Khami), Tarbagataiskii okrug, and Altaiskii okrug (Ashan'). *Vide* also Lattimore, "Chinese Turkestan or Sinkiang (Hsinchiang)," *loc. cit.,* pp. 82-83.

100. *Vide supra,* p. 55. *Vide* also, for example, the *New York Times,* June 26, 1937, which cites a Pei-p'ing dispatch stating *inter alia,* that "Russia . . . is keenly interested in maintaining paramountcy in Northern Chinese Turkestan, a territory held strategically vital as a cushion against infiltration of Japanese influence along the Siberian frontiers." The same article refers to the "provincial governor who is considered a Russian puppet . . ." *Vide* also dispatches dated October 22, 1937, and October 10, 1938. The latter states "Russian influence, politically and militarily, is extensive in Sinkiang . . ." Such items from the well considered *New York Times* are mild compared to others that have appeared in less discriminating newspapers.

102. Hedin, *Flight of "Big Horse,"* pp. 156-157. Kara-Khitai: In 1123 a Khitan prince, who swept into Turkestan at the head of a considerable mercenary following, set up the kingdom of Kara-Khitai. Cf. Carruthers, *op. cit.,* II, pp. 356-357; 384; Lattimore, "Chinese Turkestan or Sinkiang (Hsinchiang)," *loc. cit.,* p. 85.

103. Tu Chung-yüan, *op. cit.,* p. 77.

103-104. Chao Lieh, *loc. cit.;* Ch'en Chi-jung, "Hsin Hsin-chiang Ti Ts'ai-cheng," *loc. cit.* Chao Lieh reports (*loc. cit.*): "The first three-year plan began in 1937 . . ." Ch'en Chi-jung says ("Hsin Hsin-chiang Ti Ts'ai-cheng," *loc. cit.*): "After the middle of 1936 the whole province gradually became united . . . and it was possible to institute the three-year plan of reconstruction." Ch'en Chi-jung claims that in addition to the Sinkiang Commercial Bank, the Central Bank of China established a Tihwa office in 1938 to facilitate financial transactions between Sinkiang and the interior, and that the Farmers Bank of China has also opened an office there. *Loc. cit.*

104-105. Education: Tu Chung-yüan, *op. cit.,* pp. 74-75, 80-83. According to the statistics of Chiang Chün-chang, of the fifty-nine counties in the province during 1931 less than a half had any (or at best not over one or two) primary schools. In contrast to Tu, Chiang states that there were not over 7,380 students in the whole province; and of those 7,162 were attending primary school. *Op. cit.,* p. 139. Cf. Ch'en Chi-jung, "Hsin Hsin-chiang Ti Ts'ai-cheng," *loc. cit.* Figures on Sinkiang education are largely derived from the following sources: *The Chinese Year Book 1937 Issue* (Nanking), p. 1225; Ch'en Chi-jung, "Hsin Hsin-chiang Ti Ts'ai-cheng," *loc. cit.;* Samuel Chao, *China's Northwest;* Tu Chung-yüan, *op. cit.;* and Chao Lieh, *loc. cit.* Ch'en Chi-jung mentions a *Hsin-chiang Hsüeh-yüan* (i.e., a Sinkiang Academy) but Samuel Chao calls this Sinkiang institution of higher learning the Sinkiang College. Tu Chung-yüan speaks of "ten institutions including middle schools and an academy;" *The Chinese Year Book 1937 Issue* mentions three middle schools; Samuel Chao lists nine; and Chao Lieh says there are fifteen. Tu Chung-yüan names fifty so-called people's schools, *The Chinese Year Book 1937 Issue* mentions "15 popular and vocational schools," Samuel Chao, "203 people's schools," and Chao Lieh, "122 mass education academies." Tu Chung-yüan names "1,291 local and private academies," Samuel Chao 1,291 "private schools," and Chao Lieh 2,000 "private schools." "Cultural Progress Societies" is a translation of the original term, *Wen-hua-tzu-chin Hui.* The figures on the number of Cultural Progress Societies are from, and therefore ought to be dated in accordance with, Tu Chung-yüan's statistics. *Op. cit.,* pp. 81-83. Samuel Chao's are only slightly different figures, while Chao Lieh merely says there are "cultural societies everywhere." The reference to "pocket money" is from Ch'en Chi-jung, "Hsin Hsin-chiang Ti Ts'ai-cheng," *loc. cit.*

105-107. Currency and finance: Chao Lieh, *loc. cit.; Ts'ai-cheng P'ing-lun, loc. cit.;* Ch'en Chi-jung, "Hsin Hsin-chiang Ti Ts'ai-cheng," *loc. cit.*

107-108. Cultivated acreage: Chiang Chün-chang, *op. cit.,* pp. 98-99. *Vide* also Samuel Chao, *China's Northwest.*

108. *Ibid.;* Chao Lieh, *loc. cit.; Ts'ai-cheng P'ing-lun, loc. cit.;* Tu Chung-yüan, *op. cit.,* pp. 46-48. There is, however, considerable uncertainty about the exact amount of land that has been under cultivation in Sinkiang, and there are great variances in available estimates. For example, Chao Lieh, *loc. cit.,* gives a figure which indicates that traditionally there have only been slightly over 30,000 acres of land suitable for cultivation ("land that can be cultivated," *k'o-keng-chih-ti"*). Chiang Chün-chang, *op. cit.,* pp. 96-97, however, cites a table from the *Hsi-yü T'u-chih,* the total of which indicates that "reclaimed land" (*ken-ti*) alone in Sinkiang during Ch'ien Lung times (1736-1795) amounted to over 48,000 acres. Further, English language estimates for 1932 (*vide* the *China Year Book, 1934,* pp. 39, 41) have given the cultivated acreage for rice and wheat in Sinkiang alone respectively at the equivalent of approximately 279,334 and 785,000 acres. The question deserves extended study.

108-109. Agricultural products: Chiang Chün-chang, *op. cit.,* p. 98; Tu Chung-yüan, *op. cit.,* pp. 47-48; *Ts'ai-cheng P'ing-lun, loc. cit.*

109-112. Animal husbandry: *Ts'ai-cheng P'ing-lun, loc. cit.;* Ch'en Chi-jung, "T'ienshan San-tu Wu Ts'ao," *loc. cit.;* Samuel Chao, *China's Northwest;* Tu Chung-yüan, *op. cit.,* pp. 89-91.

112. Mineral resources: *Ts'ai-cheng P'ing-lun, loc. cit.; The Chinese Year Book, 1938-39,* p. 124; Tu Chung-yüan, *op. cit.,* pp. 48-50.

112-113. Petroleum: *The China Year Book 1931,* p. 42; Tu Chung-yüan, *op. cit.,* pp. 51-52; *The Chinese Year Book 1938-39,* p. 124; Samuel Chao, *op. cit.; Ts'ai-cheng P'ing-lun, loc. cit.*

113-114. Iron: Tu Chung-yüan, *op. cit.,* pp. 49-50; Chiang Chün-chang, *op. cit.,* pp. 102-103; *Ts'ai-cheng P'ing-lun, loc. cit.*

114-115. Coal: Samuel Chao, *China's Northwest;* W. H. Wong, "Chapter XXVI— Minerals and Mines in China," *The China Year Book 1934,* p. 734; Tu Chung-yüan, *op. cit.,* pp. 49-51; *Ts'ai-cheng P'ing-lun, loc. cit.*

114-117. Gold: Tu Chung-yüan, *op. cit.,* p. 49; *Ts'ai-cheng P'ing-lun, loc. cit.;* Chiang Chün-chang, *op. cit.,* pp. 100-101; Samuel Chao, *China's Northwest.*

117. Copper and other minerals: Samuel Chao, *China's Northwest;* Tu Chung-yüan, *op. cit.,* pp. 50-53; Chiang Chün-chang, *op. cit.,* pp. 108-109; *Ts'ai-cheng P'ing-lun, loc. cit.* The Wu-lan-wu-su River deposit runs from An-chiu-an-ch'ia to the lower Wu-la-k'o Mountains.

117-118. Industry: Lattimore, "Chinese Turkestan or Sinkiang (Hsinchiang)," *loc. cit.,* p. 83; Skrine, *op. cit.,* p. 5; Tu Chung-yüan, *op. cit.,* pp. 85-87; Chao Lieh, *loc. cit.;* cf. Etherton, *op. cit.,* pp. 284-290, for a far-sighted view in the 1920's of Sinkiang's industrial potential; *Ts'ai-cheng P'ing-lun, loc. cit.*

118. Communications: *The Chinese Year Book 1938-39,* p. 126. According to comment by Owen Lattimore, the experiments of 1921 were made at Tihwa as well as at Kashgar. Chao Lieh, *loc. cit.; vide* also the *Sinkiang Daily News.*

119. Aviation: Samuel Chao, *op. cit.;* Ch'en Chi-jung, "A-la-mu-t'u Jih Tsa-chi," *Ta Kung Pao,* February 10, 1941 (a first hand report by one who has flown the route). Samuel Chao, *China's Northwest,* puts the distance from Chungking to Ha-mi at about 1,700 miles. Ch'en Chi-jung, "A-la-mu-t'u Jih Tsa-chi," *loc. cit.,* gives 884 miles (1,415 kilometers) as the distance from Ha-mi to Alma-Ata via Tihwa and I-ning. Samuel Chao, who had not flown in Sinkiang at the time he wrote this manuscript, says the distance from Ha-mi to Alma-Ata via Tihwa and T'a Ch'eng is only "about 700 miles making the total distance 2,400 miles."

119-120. Road transportation: Ch'en Chi-jung, "Hsin Hsin-chiang Ti Ts'ai-cheng," *loc. cit.;* the kilometers of his original statistics have been converted to miles. Note, however, that a map of the Northwest Highway Administration of the Chinese Ministry of Communications gives the distance from Tihwa to Hsing-hsing Hsia at 928 kilometers (580 miles). Cf. Chao Lieh, *loc. cit. Vide* also *Far Eastern Survey,* XI, No. 20 (October 5, 1942), p. 204. The figure of 800 miles as the distance from Lan-chou to Hsing-hsing Hsia is from a Chinese Northwest Highway Administration map. Samuel Chao (*China's Northwest*) gives 728 miles. The Sinkiang-Ch'inghai and Sinkiang-Mongolia routes are shown clearly in Ting et al, *Chung-kuo Fen Sheng Hsin T'u,* p. 54. Cf. Martin R. Norins, "The New Sinkiang—China's Link with the Middle East," *Pacific Affairs,* XV, No. 4 (December, 1942), pp. 457-459, 470.

120-122. Some recent developments: Ch'en Chi-jung, "T'ien-shan San-tu Wu Ts'ao," *loc. cit.; Chinese News Service,* May 28, October 23, November 10 and 27, 1943. Tung Ching-kua, *loc. cit.;* cf. Lu Ko, *loc. cit.,* who points out that at the time Sheng Shih-chi was only 31 years old. He is a younger brother of Sheng Shih-ts'ai. *Vide* also "Report from Turkestan," *loc. cit.*

124. Ch'en Chi-jung, "A-la-mu-t'u Jih Tsa-chi," *loc. cit. Vide,* as examples of trespass penalties, the notices of the Sinkiang Border Defense Air Corps in the issues of the *Hsin-chiang Jih-pao (Sinkiang Daily News).* One, that appearing December 17, 1939, warns *inter alia* that under certain circumstances guards for Sinkiang air fields are authorized to shoot to kill in the case of trespass.

125-126. Generalissimo Chiang's visit to India: *New York Times,* February 14, 1942. The Chu-Sheng conversations: "Report from Turkestan," *loc. cit.,* p. 28. Dr. Wu's appointment: cf. *Chinese News Service,* September 16, 1942; and *Far Eastern Survey, loc.*

cit., p. 204. The Lan-chou conference: Norins, "The New Sinkiang—China's Link with the Middle East," *loc. cit.,* p. 458. Ma's appointment: *China Daily News* (New York), July 20, 1942. Madame Chiang's trip: "Report from Turkestan," *loc. cit.,* p. 28. Dr. Wong's trip: *Vide* Norins, *loc. cit.,* p. 458. Generalissimo Chiang's trip to Northwest China and announcement of the development program: *Kuo Min Wai Chiao,* I, 1 (January, 1943), p. 43. The Chinese migration: *Chinese News Service,* October 5, 23, and November 27, 1943; Li Yao-san, "K'en-min Tao Hsin-chiang Ch'ü-liao," *loc. cit.*

126-127. The quotation is from Aitchen K. Wu, "Will China Save Its Far West?" *Asia* (December, 1939), p. 677. The description of the Chinese migration is meant to be a composite one. It is based not only on the dispatches consulted by the author but also on his own observations in the Chinese Northwest in 1939 and 1940.

127. In the Department of State, *Foreign Service List* (May 1, 1943), p. 10, there is mention of the appointment on April 19, 1943, of Mr. Oliver Edmund Clubb as United States Consul at Tihwa. This appointment is qualified as "Temporary. Functions under the general supervision of the Embassy at Chungking." Cf. also *Chinese News Service,* June 17, 1943; "Report from Turkestan," *loc. cit.,* p. 28, which mentions arrival of a British colleague in September, 1943; and the *New York Times* of October 16, 1943. *Vide* "Sinkiang, Heart of Asia," *Life* (December 6, 1943), pp. 27-35, and "Sinkiang Land at the Back of Nowhere," *ibid.* (December 13, 1943), pp. 94-103, for rare first hand documentation concerning the New Sinkiang and Russian "withdrawal." The reports were made available by the magazine's correspondent, Theodore H. White, and photographer, William Vandivert.

128. In January, 1943, over a year ago, President Franklin D. Roosevelt revealed that we were "flying as much lend-lease material into China as ever traversed the Burma Road," and press dispatches of March 26, 1944, have testified that "the Chinese now are receiving more supplies monthly" by planes flying the "hump" route into China "than during an average month over the old Burma Road." "China's Slender Skyline," *Far Eastern Survey,* XII, No. 3 (February 8, 1943), p. 25; and *Los Angeles Times,* March 26, 1944.

Developments concerning the new "Ledo Road" by now have become historic. As early as September 25, 1943, a delayed Associated Press report announced that United States Engineers had "hacked" the new route toward China. It appears that intensive work on the avenue began December 15, 1941, but ("for security reasons," it is explained) the military authorities allowed "no" announcement about it until September, 1943. *Vide* the *New York Times,* September 28, 1943; and cf. also *PM,* March 23, 1942. At this writing it appears quite possible that United Nations forces may be able to push the Ledo Road through to a juncture with Chinese transport routes of Western Yünnan Province.

130. The distance over Russian and Chinese terrain for this Alaska-Siberia-Turkestan-Sinkiang route may be estimated to be something around 7,000 miles. It is of interest here to refer readers to Joseph Wechsberg ("Alaska, Springboard of Attack," *Canadian Geographical Journal,* April, 1943, XXVI, 4, p. 187) on this general subject of Alaska-Siberian transport even though he puts stress on contact between "the railway frontiers of Canada" and "Irkutsk" (a chief office of the Trans-Siberian Railway further west than Verkhneudinsk).

130-131. As for the Iran-India-Afghanistan routes, *vide Far Eastern Survey,* XI, 20 (October 5, 1942), p. 204; Skrine, *op. cit.;* Sykes, *Through Deserts and Oases of Central Asia;* especially the map, "Persia and Afghanistan," attached to Sir Percy Sykes, *Sir Mortimer Durand* (Cassell and Company, Limited, London, 1926); and *Chinese News Service,* January 19, 1944. Figure the distance from the Russian border, say, ·via Sui-ting or

T'a Ch'eng through Tihwa, Ha-mi, and Hsing-hsing Hsia, to Lan-chou, at an estimated 2,000 miles, gasoline (or fuel alcohol or charcoal) as available, and the distance from Lan-chou to the Shensi-Shansi war front (via Sian) at about 450 miles. This is rough calculation. Cf. Owen Lattimore, "China's Turkestan-Siberian Supply Road," *Pacific Affairs* (December, 1940), pp. 393-412, for more detailed discussion of the route.

131-132. Citation of the statement by the Chinese Minister of Communications: *Los Angeles Times,* July 6, 1943. Of related interest is the Chinese announcement of March 27, 1944, that a recent agreement has been reached between Chinese and Soviet postal authorities on the transmission of parcels not exceeding five kilograms in weight between China and Soviet Russia through Sinkiang. "Owing to war conditions in China," the announcement states, "parcel post is limited to these two countries only, and no parcels for transit to other countries are accepted." *Chinese News Service,* March 27, 1944.

132. Reported signature of a new treaty of amity between China and Afghanistan on March 2, 1944, has made it more practicable than at any time since the bombing of Pearl Harbor to anticipate dispatch of goods between the two countries. For in the new treaty the two governments reportedly have agreed "to enter into negotiation as soon as possible for the purpose of concluding a commercial treaty." This is a considerable step forward in Sino-Afghan relations which have not always been at their best. Afghanistan benefited, and China lost, territorially by the terms of a Russian-British agreement signed in 1895, to which the Chinese have never previously appeared willing to acquiesce. A principal dispute has been that over the Sino-Afghan boundary, especially questions concerning the general area of the Wakhan Pamir. The Wakhan, which the British and the Russians awarded to Afghanistan in 1895, has since been considered by them as a narrow, insulating strip of territory between Russian Turkestan and British India. But Chinese maps still designate national boundaries in that general area as undelimited. *Vide* the map, "Persia and Afghanistan," *loc. cit.;* Etherton, *op. cit.,* pp. 25-29; *New York Times,* March 5, 1944; *Chinese News Service,* March 6, 1944; and "Map of China," attached to *China Handbook 1937-1943* as well as Ting et al, *op. cit.,* pp. 54-55.

132. Data on transport in India: John Murray, *A Handbook for Travellers in India Burma and Ceylon* (London, 1938), pp. 361, 376, 389, 392, 393, 400, and 402.

132-133. For the air cargo figures: Maj. Murray C. Woodbury, "Cargo and Transport," *Flying and Popular Aviation* (September, 1941), pp. 124-125. Cf. also an Associated Press dispatch from Washington, D. C., dated December 8, 1943, concerning C-87 army freight planes "regularly" flying the "longest air freight line in the world" (from the United States to India and back). This dispatch indicates that transports capable of carrying four tons are now seeing regular use.

134. Right Honourable Sir Halford J. Mackinder, *Democratic Ideals and Reality, A Study in the Politics of Reconstruction* (1942 Reissue, Henry Holt and Company, New York). Mackinder lumped traditionally known continents of Europe, Africa, and Asia into a "new" geographic unit called the "World-Island;" within the "World-Island" he found a "Heartland" which stretches from Siberia (in the northeast) to Eastern Europe (in the northwest) and Iran (in the southwest). *Ibid.,* especially p. 150. For a brief summary of Axis geopolitics, *vide* (for example) H. W. Wiegert, "German Geopolitics," *Harper's Magazine* (November, 1941), especially pp. 587, 588.

138-139. Sun Yat-sen, *The International Development of China.* Reprinted from the second edition (1928) (The China Publishing Company, Chungking, Hong Kong, 1941), p. xi; cf. "The International Development of China," *Contemporary China (Chinese News Service,* II, No. 17, January 11, 1943), for a helpful summary. *Vide* p. 126 *supra* for evidence that the Chinese Nationalist Government has been attempting to carry out such colonization of Sinkiang in 1943 and 1944.

INDEX

The entries which follow are selective and do not include page citations for the Reference Notes, Glossaries, or Working Bibliography.

190

Caspian Sea, 28, 131
Castagné, M., 53
Cathay, 33
Catties (see chin)
Caucasus, 30
Central Asia, 30, 33, 47, 49, 50, 54, 64, 70, 78, 84, 102, 126, 137, 140
Central News, 118
Ch'a-han-wu-su, 115
Ch'ahar Mongols (see also Mongols), 87
Chai-o-pao, 117
Ch'an Hui (see Wei-wu-erh)
Ch'an-t'ou (see Wei-wu-erh)
Chang Chi-luan, 38
Chang Ch'ien, 49, 145
Chang Pei-yüan, General, 44
Chang Wei-hua, 24
Ch'ang-chi, 31, 111, 114, 115
Changsha, 123
Chanto (see Wei-wu-erh)
Chao Lieh, 59, 106
Chao, Samuel, 108, 109, 110, 112, 115
Charklik, 31, 84, 111
Charter, Six-point (see Six Great Policies)
Chatir Köl, 53
Ch'en Chi-jung, 109, 119, 120, 121
Ch'en Chung, 43
Ch'en Li-fu, 150
Chen-hsi, 31, 42, 68, 110, 111, 115, 116, 118
Cheng Jun-ch'eng, 43
Ch'eng-hua, 31, 53, 65, 111, 119
Ch'eng-pao (or ch'eng-p'u), 96
Ch'eng-tu, 123
Cherchen, 31, 84, 111, 116
Chi-mi chou (see chün-fu)
Chi-mu-nai, 31, 111
Ch'i-chio-ching, 31, 42, 44, 111, 119
Ch'i-erh Shan, 114
Ch'i-t'ai, 31, 44, 51, 111, 116, 118, 126, 143
Ch'ia-pa Shan, 116
Ch'ia-tzu Wan, 113
Chiang Chün-chang, 55-57, 71, 83, 107
Chiang Kai-shek, Generalissimo, 17, 30, 39, 41, 125, 126, 128; Madame, 125, 126
Ch'iao-li-k'o River, 116
Ch'ieh-mo (see Cherchen)
Chien-kuo (see K'ang-chan Chien-kuo)

Ch'ien Kou, 116
Ch'ien Lung, 50, 84, 112, 142
Ch'ien Ti Tsung Chih-hui (see Commander-in-Chief at the Front)
Ch'ien-fang (see Front, War; see also K'ang-chan Chien-kuo)
Chin (catties), 109
Chin Shu-hsin, 43
Chin Shu-jen, 38, 40, 41, 42, 43, 46, 55, 67, 68, 69, 70, 82, 97, 106, 141
China (see also Northwest China; Chungking government) 124, 127-128, 129, 130, 132, 137, 138, 144, 146; Central China, 65-66; Central Government of, 18; China Proper, 12, 127, 131, 136; Japan's blockade of, 128; National Political Council of, 122; Nationalist China, 28, 30, 60, 65, 124, 125; Northeast China, 102, 138, 141; Republic of, 136
Chinese (see also Han; Turkestan); Central Asia, 11, 126; Communists, 18, 65, 75; Eastern Railway, 40; Far West, 24, 28, 127; frontier activity initiated in Central Asia, 49-50; historical concern for Sinkiang, 9-11; history in Central Asia, 49; imperialism, 49-50; migration to Sinkiang, 121, 126-127; National Government, 44, 76, 99, 100, 124, 139; Northwest, development projects for, 125, 126; scientists, 10; Turkestan (see Chinese Turkestan)
Ching Setkhiltu League (see also Mongols), 87
Ching-ho, 31, 87, 111
Ch'ing (see Ta Ch'ing or Manchus)
Ch'inghai, 31, 41, 74, 83, 86, 96, 100, 111, 120, 136, 137, 146; Tsaidam wastelands of, 32
Chira, 84
Chou, 95
Christianity, 36, 88
Chu Shao-liang, General, 125
Chuan Ch'eng-tzu, 31, 111
Chuguchak (see T'a Ch'eng)
Chun-ko-erh Pu (Jungars; see Mongols)
Chung Kou, 116
Chung Kuo (see China)
Chungking, 26, 34, 76, 119, 120, 121, 123, 126, 130, 131, 133, 136; Chungking government, 30